The English Gentlewoman

The English Gentlewoman

The jacket illustration for The Provincial Lady by
E.M. Delafield, published by Macmillan & Co. in 1947.
Left: The daughters of Edward Rooks Leeds, painted
by Arthur Devis, c. 1764-8.

FLORA FRASER

GUILD PUBLISHING LONDON

This edition published 1987 by
Book Club Associates by arrangement
with Barrie & Jenkins Ltd

Copyright © Flora Fraser 1987

Printed and bound in Spain by Cayfosa, Barcelona
Dep. Leg. B-27489-1987

Contents

Frontispiece to Richard Brathwait's The English Gentlewoman *(1631). In common with earlier and later counsellors, Brathwait praised qualities in the gentlewoman conducive to others' welfare, not her own. "Her discreet providence makes her family look with cheerful countenance."*

PROLOGUE

The Nobility of Women

JAMES I TOLD HIS NURSE THAT HE WOULD MAKE HER SON A lord, as she wished it, but he never could make him a gentleman. His lowly birth and breeding precluded it. The history of the English gentlewoman, mate to the gentleman, is one of rigorous breeding and training for the taxing position she would assume on marriage; which was "crown to her husband", comptroller of a large household, and worthy matriarch of a distinguished family. For four hundred years, from the late fifteenth century to the late nineteenth century, a succession of women "of birth above the vulgar" were trained unwaveringly for this multiplicity of duties, disguised as a life of leisure. This book explores the ideals which gave birth to this ancillary tradition, the changing perceptions of the gentlewoman and her lot, and the incompatibility of what would now be called a career with a gentlewomanly existence.

The scope of this book is necessarily large, just as the term, "gentle-woman", has historically had a wide application. The word "gentle" derives from the Latin, "*gentilis*", which has the simple meaning of belonging to the same gens or race, or family. The understanding that the family is a good or noble one appears only later in the Romance languages – for instance, in the Italian "*gentiluomo*". From the Italian and the Spanish comes the English family of "gentles" – gentlemen, gentlewomen, gentlefolk. Originally "gentle" and "noble" were synonymous. Later, in heraldry, a gentleman came to be one who was "lawfully entitled to armorial distinction", or to bear arms, but who was not of any degree of nobility. The term "nobility" now denoted persons of title only; within this exalted group, dukedoms, marquessates, earldoms and the lesser ranks expressed degrees of nobility.

Gentlefolk, then, were "of birth, of extraction, though not noble", and occupied a place above the vulgar or commonalty, or "simples", but below that of the nobility. They became known as "the gentry". However, because of the old synonymity between gentle and noble, because of a fellow-feeling between nobility and gentry and because of the distaste both felt for "the vulgar" the two terms "gentleman" and "gentlewoman" were also used of any man or of any woman, however high in degree or rank, who exhibited suitable qualities. In

7

this book, then, princesses and queens, squires' wives and countesses, great ladies and indigent spinsters are all equally candidates for examination as gentlewomen – though some may be unmasked as unfit for the fair name. Steele's apothegm in the *Tatler* of 1710, "the appellation of Gentleman is never to be affixed to a man's circumstances, but to his behaviour in them," holds equally true of the gentlewoman.

When was the first English gentlewoman? Surely before 1485, when this book begins? Certainly, but to discover the roots of the gentlewoman's code, we should follow Boccaccio and look into antiquity. Gentlewomen have existed since Homer created Nausicaa, that grave and maidenly daughter of King Alcinous who was startled, when pausing from washing her bride-clothes to enjoy a game of ball with her attendants, by a naked Odysseus striding up the seashore towards her. Nausicaa's attendants fled, as attendant gentlewomen so often do, but she, a stouter kind of gentlewoman altogether, stood her ground, behaved with modesty and charity, offered food, clothes and hospitality at her father's house to the stranger, heard his story and fell victim to his charm. But Nausicaa was a very model of a gentlewoman, even when the bride-clothes she had washed as a speculation were not needed, and Odysseus sailed away. "A gentlewoman should have no wrath in her, for she ought to have gentle heart, and fair and soft in answer," advised the French Knight de la Tour Landry in his book, translated for the gentlewomen of England in the late fifteenth century. Happily, Nausicaa, as daughter of the King, was much courted, and we must hope that her father approved a steadier suitor than Odysseus.

Nausicaa was submissive to her father, and the later Christian gentlewoman was expected to be submissive and obedient to her father and then to her husband, just as they were obedient to God. The English gentlewoman's obedience to her lord and master had only this limit: if "the husband should command anything contrary to her honour, credit and salvation", what was not "comely in the Lord", then she should refuse to submit. However, women were legally "under the rod" of the head of the house and without rights over their estate, income and children till the First and Second Married Women's Property Acts of 1870 and 1882; conscientious objection was not always feasible and all the weight of Church teaching was against it. With luck, the gentlewoman would find her husband reasonable in his commands; else, she must pray for widowhood when she would assume a measure of independence.

The gentlewoman expressed her submission in tangible form. As all gentlemen of rank equal to hers might conceivably end as her husband – if not this time round, then perhaps the next – so she must "carry herself as inferior" to them all. The modest, downcast gazes, soft voices, self-effacing conversation – all the stuff of etiquette and deportment manuals – were the external evidence of the inward obedience. Decorum, propriety, respectability were the watchwords. With them went chastity, a most necessary virtue for a gentlewoman who wished to be a credit to her husband and display, by her restraint, superior birth and breeding. Of course, some fell from the ideal. Ballads and songs give

us frail models of goodness like Queen Guinevere before she loved Lancelot, and of endurance, like Elaine, Lady of Shalott, after she loved Lancelot. Morgan Le Fay is the darker side of womanhood, as is Robin Hood's cousin, the Prioress of Kirklees, who let the weakened outlaw's blood from his veins with her blood-irons "wrappèd all in silk".

Ladies like these might break the code of the gentlewoman, but they knew it. When we come to the fifteenth century, we find an interesting group of new and aspirant gentlewomen, wives and daughters of prosperous wool merchants and farmers, whose male kin are busy buying lordships of manors to celebrate their new wealth. In Coggeshall in Essex some wool merchants called Paycocke had begun as close to "the vulgar". They advanced in fortune through the fourteenth century to a point where they built a fine large house in the centre of the town. They paid for a chantry, or memorial in the neighbouring church, where prayers were said annually for their family dead in return for a large endowment. The abbess of the local convent, a great gentlewoman, condescended to come and dine. Again, gentle behaviour was necessary for the Paycocke women now. They withdrew from the rougher elements of the wool business where before business and domestic life had been tangled up together.

In a Norfolk village, the family of Paston bought land consistently throughout the fifteenth century. The menfolk became lawyers, judges, Members of Parliament. In 1469 Margery, sister of John Paston, newly created a baronet, outraged her upwardly mobile family. She declared her intention of marrying her brother's bailiff, Calle. Sir John declared that Calle, "should never have my good will to make my sister sell candle and mustard in Framlingham". The marriage took place and Calle, indispensable to the family fortunes, remained as bailiff. But Margery's mother cut her out of her will.

As the class of gentlefolk expanded, nobility and gentry, including those gentlefolk who had newly raised themselves above "the vulgar" by acquiring position and wealth, strove to close gentle ranks against "the vulgar" and to maintain a lofty style of behaviour. The upbringing of young gentlemen and of gentlewomen became a matter of importance. With the invention of printing in the 1470s, a number of books appeared which presented codified systems of training up youth in "gentle" ways, particularly useful for parents who had not themselves been trained in such ways. By the end of the sixteenth century the term, "jonteel", later "genteel", had emerged – from the French *"gentil"* – to describe the style of manners, dress, education, food and dwellings that befitted gentlefolk.

In 1628 "love locks" were castigated by William Prynne as "ungodly fashions" which "transform our light and giddy females of the superior and gentile rank". In 1665 Samuel Pepys ate "the genteelest dinner . . . I have seen many a day." In 1790 Bewick's Quadruped described the dalmation dog as "frequently kept in genteel houses, as an elegant attendant on a carriage". Polite, elegant in behaviour, civil; graceful in mien; elegantly dressed – so Dr Johnson characterised the genteel person in 1785. It was the term in common

9

parlance till the mid-nineteenth century, when it came to be used to ridicule those who dreaded being taken for members of the populace, and so fell into disrepute.

There was another term in common parlance from the mid-eighteenth century which reflects the piteous plight of those excluded from genteel society of the day. This was "shabby-genteel"; the *Connoisseur* of 1754 deprecated this class of persons, who were "the chief support of the clothiers in Monmouth street". "The vulgar" were attempting to become gentry by buying their cast-off clothes. Richer members of "the commonalty" aped the gentry to more effect with smart carriages and costly jewels, but inevitably, as James I feared for his nurse's son, birth and education were inadequate to the demands of Society. In *Emma* (1816) there is a neat illustration of this. Emma Woodhouse arranges in her own mind that her young protégée, Harriet Smith, shall marry an agreeable monied gentleman of the district, Mr Elton. Harriet suffers in worldly terms only from the disability of being a "natural daughter", or illegitimate. Unfortunately, Mr Elton looks higher than Harriet, and tries to propose to Miss Woodhouse of Hartfield herself. "Everybody has their level . . . I need not so totally despair of an equal alliance as to be addressing myself to Miss Smith," is Elton's mortified reply to Emma's remonstrances that he take Harriet as a bride instead. He ends by marrying a Miss Hawkins whose advantages – beyond £10,000 – over Harriet, Miss Woodhouse cannot see. The new Mrs Elton talks only of a brother-in-law's newly acquired "barouche-landau", "doats" on music, and thinks Miss Woodhouse's beloved governess "really quite the gentlewoman". Mrs Elton is, in Emma's heartfelt opinion, "a little upstart, vulgar being. . . self-important, presuming, familiar, ignorant and ill-bred". Failings of birth and breeding are neatly balanced in Harriet Smith and Mrs Elton. The latter wins, with her £10,000.

In 1838, the Reverend Archer Clive paid a series of country visits in the county of Herefordshire. A handsome and cultured bachelor of means, Archer was aware of his own worth. He noted after his first visit that Mrs Case had "three *filles à marier*, but none will I take". After visit number three, to some country Clive cousins, he mused: "If gentlefolks are dull, there is an ease and *savoir vivre* which makes their house pleasant. Good books. Good vittle. Good music. My cousin Henrietta Clive is a proof of what good manners and education can do for a plain person; without these and were she the dowdy daughter of the lawyer or apothecary, she would be absolutely ugly; with them, well dressed and clean, hair well done and clothes well made, very well informed and accomplished, she is pretty enough and will make a very good wife and pleasant companion." Here was a proper gentlewoman, with the credentials of impeccable birth. Natural disadvantages and faults had been bullied out of her, or disguised with copious application of hairdressers, mantua-makers, dancing masters, drawing masters and other useful aids. Thus presented, Henrietta should fulfil her destiny, and win a valuable prize in the marriage mart – though Archer himself did not succumb.

Upon occasion, it was necessary not to look too closely into the pedigree of a gentlewoman, if marriage to her would mean financial security for a noble house. In Trollope's *Is He Popenjoy?*, Lord George Germain, heir to the Marquessate of Brotherton, proposes marriage to Miss Mary Lovelace, daughter of the Dean of Brotherton – but also granddaughter on one side to the keeper of livery stables, and on the other to Mr Tallowax, candlemaker in the Borough. (As a result of this pedigree, she had £30,000.) When Mary became Lady George, all her spinster sisters-in-law at Manor Cross, her new home, set themselves up simultaneously as her tutor. Not till Lady George became an expectant mother was there "a very great difference in Mary's position . . . Mary was very much exalted . . . All their hopes were centred in Mary . . . In early married days she had felt herself to be snubbed as being merely the Dean's daughter. No one snubbed her now." With the birth of her child, Lady George was accepted as a gentlewoman – else how could her son be a gentleman?

If riches could elevate descendants of "the vulgar" into the ranks of gentlefolk, it was also easy, through poverty, to slip downwards in the world. This was a problem particular to gentlewomen who, for one reason or another, had no masculine source of support. In Mrs Gaskell's *Cranford* (1853), "elegant economy" was the device whereby the community of genteel ladies maintained standards. The Misses Jenkyns spread careful paths of paper from drawing-room door to each chair to preserve a new carpet, when they expected guests; Mrs Forrester looked on as her maid got the tea tray out from under the sofa as if it were the most natural place in the world to keep it, and viewed the cakes her maid then brought on it with as critical and detached an eye as if she had never made them herself that morning.

If economy was a disagreeable watchword for gentlewomen in reduced circumstances, there were very real reminders of what the alternative brought. In Rebecca West's *The Fountain Overflows*, young Rose is taken by her mother at the beginning of the twentieth century to visit Cousin Constance and her daughter, Rosamund, in South London. "I realised without emotion," records Rose, the narrator, "that Constance lived among the kind of people which in those days were called 'common' . . . More fortunate children . . . might have called them 'poor', but . . . most of them were no poorer than we were. They were people who live in ugly houses in ugly streets among neighbours who got drunk on Saturday nights, and who did not read books or play music or go to picture galleries, and who were unnecessarily rude to each other . . . as well as not having baths every day . . . We had understood that we had to rely on our own efforts if we were not to find ourselves living on that level, and I was not surprised . . . to find that a relative of mine had sunk to that level . . ."

Cousin Constance and Rosamund were reduced to doing piecework for a shop in Bond Street, embroidering the monograms of more fortunate gentlewomen on bodices and scalloping hems in an attempt to increase the pitiful sum that Cousin Jack allowed them. The picture of them in Rose's garden, bent patiently over the cambric laid over clean cloths on their laps, is a sort of parody

Prologue

of the English gentlewoman, who covered yards of cloth with fine embroidery to show that she had the hours of leisure available to do so.

The qualities demanded of the English gentlewoman do not change dramatically over the centuries. Charity is as desirable in the sixteenth century as in the twentieth, but the gentlewoman's charitable work takes different forms. We trace her charitable journey from the still-room where, in the sixteenth century, she makes up medicines for the household, into the village in the seventeenth century where she dispenses cures for backache and, besides, establishes charity schools and almshouses. In the eighteenth century, she ceases to do much practical nursing in the village, but offers financial assistance to charitable causes in Town. She sponsors children at the Foundling Hospital, visits the Magdalen reformatory for their mothers, and patronises "pet" charities like Sunday Schools. The nineteenth century sees the gentlewoman's charitable endeavours burgeon; individuals like Florence Nightingale, Barbara Bodichon, Rosalind Paget, make a practical commitment to relieving suffering among the sick, the needy and ill-educated, women in childbirth. Columns of lady philanthropists, most famously Baroness Burdett-Coutts, bring up the rear with welcome supplies of money, and less wealthy gentlewomen organise bazaars and clothing clubs. The Committees which administer the funds are generally, however, under masculine control. In the 1870s and 1880s any charitable institution with a pretension to fashion is under the patronage of the royal Duchess of Teck, ebullient, extravagant mother of Queen Mary. This commitment to voluntary work proves of inestimable value in the First World War. Georgina Lady Dudley, for instance, organises the loan of houses and apartments at hotels "in England or abroad" to officers recovering their health – at the expense of herself and her friends. The rise of State assistance, pensions, and the social changes in England following the First World War hamper Lady Bountiful. The English gentlewoman herself in some cases becomes a candidate for charitable aid; the Distressed Gentlefolks' Aid Association recognised the plight of "decayed gentlewomen" as early as 1897.

The gentlewoman's childhood and education vary with the demands of each period. There is no linear development here. Coincidentally with the closure of nunneries and the education they offered, the sixteenth century sees gentlewomen acquiring a sound classical education in numbers not seen again till gentlewomen turn university scholar in the late nineteenth century; the seventeenth century sees the rise of a ladylike education, with "French conversation" and other "extras" peculiar to English girls' education – needlework, handicrafts, and music lessons – featuring strongly. The eighteenth century adds piano lessons and painting to the curriculum; not till the late nineteenth century and the advent of the hundred-strong girls' boarding school are sports days and school uniforms and "team spirit" concocted in imitation of boys' school systems. The victims of the gradual move in favour of sending girls to these "reformed" schools are the needy gentlewomen who till now have wrested a living as governesses in the home or in "select seminaries". The fact

that they have neither qualifications to teach nor useful information to impart only matters now that the "reformed" schools seek teachers with degrees from such august sources as the Cambridge Local Examination Board. Flocks of English "misses", or governesses emigrate to the Continent, even to Russia, where there are no such unreasonable demands made of them.

The English gentlewoman first steps abroad during the seventeenth century, excepting rare examples in the sixteenth century like Jane Dormer who married a Spanish Ambassador and went to live as Duchess of Feria in Estramaduira, taking her gentlewoman, Damasyn Stradling, as company. We see the gentlewoman's response to life abroad, and the response abroad to her. The building of the Englishwoman abroad's twin reputation as daring adventurer and needy pensionnaire is traced – from Calais to Kandy, and from Lady Mary Wortley Montagu to Mary Kingsley.

At home, the traditional pursuits and pastimes of the gentlewoman are not forgotten. We see how gardening ladies like Miss Jekyll and Vita Sackville-West have no long root in the history of English horticulture. Francis Bacon declared in the seventeenth century that gentlewomen would do themselves only good to kneel upon a cushion and do some weeding. Few took him seriously, till the mid-nineteenth century. The eighteenth-century ladies of Llangollen boldly planted pinks and "a great quantity of Primroses", and had gardeners do the rest. Collecting dried flowers, and painting plant specimens – and, of course, arranging flowers sent in to the house by the gardeners – represented the very limits of most gentlewomen's enthusiasm for things horticultural till the mid-nineteenth century. As a practical hobby for ladies, gardening owes its popularity to a husband and wife, Mr and Mrs Loudon, who wrote brisk and informative manuals on the subject in the 1840s.

Gentlewomen then took to gardening in droves, once reassured that it was an occupation which would set off their feminine graces charmingly. This was always the caveat with activities; archery as a sport revived at the end of the eighteenth century and enjoyed a century's popularity because it showed off the figure to advantage. Equestrianism and hunting were at different periods felt to be womanly, unwomanly, dangerous, delightful, woefully "fast" and very healthy exercise. Croquet was *much* liked as a sport when it appeared in the mid-nineteenth century, because, in addition to the grace it bestowed on the fair player, no separate sporting costume need be donned to participate. Bicycling, or rather, tricycling, only became a popular recreation for ladies, however, once a respectable "touring costume" had been devised, which was similar in colour and cut to the dress worn by clerical wives and wives of doctors.

The homes which the English gentlewomen administered necessarily changed dramatically over four centuries. A book published in 1920, *The Servantless House*, could not have been envisaged a century before. Again, the development of the gentlewoman's home is not a steady line of progress towards a nuclear unit of efficiency. Mrs Beeton catered for larger households in her *Book of Household Management* of 1861 than had *A New System of*

Practical Domestic Economy (1824), which counselled purchase of "a dumb-waiter", to replace one single "living servant". The tendency of English gentlefolk to endure, or to revel in, discomfort and cold in the later nineteenth century is traced, in part, to their distaste for facilities available to the middle classes like gas lighting and heating.

The gentlewoman's attitude to her children, her own experience of childhood, varies wildly with the centuries. From tight swaddling bands and wet-nurse to adult dress to "placing out" at the age of seven a young gentlewoman of the sixteenth century would progress, and, on being "placed out" with a family of rank, she might not return home till marriage. If this was barbaric, the experiences of young gentlewomen in the homes of the 1890s are no less the stuff of nightmare. A nurse terrorised Eleanor Farjeon, the second Mrs Compton-Burnett far outdid *The Second Mrs Tanqueray* in mischief towards her step-daughter Olive.

For three centuries after the closure of the convents in the 1530s, gentlewomen had little escape from their home life, be they daughters or wives. Then came a change. The foundation of Anglican and Catholic convents, the increase in missionary posts abroad, the establishment of universities, medical schools, and training colleges for women in the latter half of the nineteenth century gave gentlewomen an alternative to marriage. There was known to be a preponderance of women in England long before the First World War; why sit at home, and wait for a marriage which might not transpire? The 1880s and 1890s saw women, "by birth above the vulgar", flying in the face of the hallowed code of their kind. "The Odd Women", as George Gissing christened them in 1894, refused to regard the life of the home as paramount; they went triumphantly, typewriter ribbons waving, out to work with women *not of their own sort*. Families were horrified but what could they do? The divide between this New Woman and her peers who stayed at home, performing traditional ancillary work, did not narrow. As the New Woman sought the vote and political recognition of women's existence, gentlewomen who stayed at home began to make much of their work in the homes. Those artistic gentlewomen, The Souls, who had leaders of the Arts and Crafts movement like William Morris to paper their walls in the 1880s, and ladies like Mrs F.S. Carey who wrote *A Profession for Gentlewomen* in 1916, praising housekeeping, were on the same side.

The First World War brought all disputes to an end, and the traditional skills and virtues of the gentlewoman – nursing, kindliness, endurance, forbearance – were as much in demand as typewriting skills. Endurance and forbearance were also needed by gentlewomen after the War, when many of them found themselves widowed and fatherless and brotherless. Casualty figures for officers and men were in a ratio of three to one; apart from the personal losses, the death duties exacted when owner and, say, four heirs of an estate died within years of each other were crippling. Titles became extinct; estates were sold; England in 1919 was a very altered place, and not necessarily conducive to a gentlewomanly existence.

The Nobility of Women

Reserving consideration of life after 1919 for the Epilogue, let us now return to a time when England had just come to the end of another war, the Wars of the Roses, a time when the English gentlewoman had yet to blossom.

SOVVENT ME SOVVIENT

CHAPTER ONE

Ancient Tongues and Modern Dances

1485-1600

IN 1484 WILLIAM CAXTON TRANSLATED AND PUBLISHED *The Book of the Knight of the Tour Landry*, written in France a hundred odd years earlier. The Knight wrote his book for his daughters, to teach them the "qualities in pure and perfect womanhood". If they demonstrated these, then they would secure a rich knight in marriage. Good manners, humility, piety and modesty were wanted. Once married, subservience and affection should be uppermost. If one adds to these the practical virtues of economy and efficiency in running a household, the sum of the medieval lady's parts is made up. The fourteenth and fifteenth century in England present us with few ladies who soar beyond the private world of their home and marriage. Thousands of them, anonymous, consulted daily with stewards and directed servants that their lord's home – and estates, in the absence of the master – might run smoothly. We know little about them, although much about their fighting lords. Few of them could read or write, but then their education was chiefly in housewifely skills.

In 1485, the Wars of the Roses end and an astonishing transformation begins. During the next hundred years a stream of gentlewomen tumble over themselves to attract our attention. They read – not only English and French, but Latin and Hebrew, and they can converse in Greek, or Italian, or Spanish. They display their linguistic skills by translating, or "englishing", foreign literature. They learn from distinguished tutors, besides, an astonishing range of academic subjects – astronomy, philosophy, history, geography, mathematics, botany. They write books and treatises arising from their studies; they correspond with scholars on the Continent. Queens, princesses, noblewomen and ladies of town and country gentry all dazzle with their learning. Margaret Roper, Lady Jane Grey, Queen Elizabeth – the names are legendary. There are English gentlewomen who come to the fore in the sixteenth century in other fields too. Henry VIII's six wives are famous for their number. Bess of Hardwick and Lady Anne Clifford dominated Derbyshire and Westmorland with their building programmes. Amy Robsart, Countess of Leicester, became a tragic heroine of romance with her death at Kenilworth. Some gentlewomen were still esteemed for quieter virtues, like skill in physic or exquisite needle-

Opposite: Lady Margaret Beaufort (1443-1509), Countess of Richmond and mother of Henry VII, by an unknown artist. Energetic matriarch of the Tudor dynasty, she foreshadows later erudite gentlewomen in her patronage of universities, printers and booksellers.

17

work. Others were praised for knowing the art of confectionery and for their skill in gilding marchpane, or for playing the virginals or the lute or singing sweetly, or dancing well. Italian and French influence brought refinement to these accomplishments in the sixteenth century, but they had their roots in the outward graces which the fourteenth-century Knight of the Tour Landry had urged on his daughters as marks of inward virtue. Where the Tudor gentlewoman differed from her grandmother of the fifteenth century was in her interior graces. She thought, she read, she wrote. By 1559 she elicited the paeon, *The Nobility of Women* where the author William Bercher, or Barker, translating from the Italian, added a list of learned English gentlewomen.

The movement from illiteracy and cursory education for women of the upper classes to formidable scholarship began with Lady Margaret Beaufort, mother of Henry VII and forerunner of all the cultured ladies of the sixteenth century. She was born into the feudal troubles of the fifteenth century. She was the only child of the Duke of Somerset, and inherited his vast estates in the North. On grounds of her descent from John of Gaunt, her son claimed and won the English throne at Bosworth in 1485. However she was not content to live merely as royal dowager or territorial magnate. She used the income from her estates to endow university colleges at Cambridge and to commission books from Caxton's and Wynkyn de Worde's printing presses. Lady Margaret has been called "more man of the Renaissance than any in England". Certainly she exemplifies that impressive ability to diversify which so characterises the Renaissance abroad. She advised her son throughout his reign, and was possibly made Lord President of the Council of the North in 1503; the honour and responsibility would be fitting to Henry VII's conception of her abilities. She was renowned, also, as every gentlewoman should be, for her modesty, her chastity and her piety – and she was no mean needlewoman.

Lady Margaret's redoubtable qualities were widely recognised wherever she turned her attention. A variety of Cambridge colleges received her patronage. Then, in 1505, she decided to found two new ones, Christ's College and St John's. Building began at St John's only after her death; but she spent happy months, in the last years of her life, at Christ's. A chamber was appointed for her special use in the Warden's Lodgings, an exceptional honour. Here her coat of arms, with spotted deer, the Tudor rose and portcullis crowned, was painted on a background of daisies and forget-me-nots, recalling her motto, *souvent me souvient*. These arms still decorate the chamber oriel, and perhaps from this window she "saw the dean call a faulty scholar to correction". She rebuked him: "*Lente, Lente*, [or Gently, gently] Mr Dean," ... accounting it better to mitigate his punishment than procure his pardon.

The Latin is a reminder that this language, rather than English, was employed in daily college life. Lady Margaret's disinterestedness in founding these exclusively male provinces is the more remarkable that, like most educated women of her age, she knew only snippets of Latin. "Full often she complained that in her youth she had not given her to the understanding of Latin,

wherein she had a little perceiving," Bishop Fisher reveals. (Lady Margaret had Latin enough, he stressed, to understand "the Rubric of the Ordinall for the saying of her service".) She could make little contribution to college life other than a financial one.

Lady Margaret's interest in higher education at the universities was of no direct benefit to other gentlewomen. However, her encouragement of the English printers prompted gentlewomen who could read to read more widely – and perhaps prompted those who could not read to learn to do so. There had been little enough reading matter to tempt gentlewomen who knew only English and French before this. Most books were written in Latin. Young ladies

From The Mirror of Gold for the Sinful Soul, *translated into English by Lady Margaret Beaufort from the French. When little original literature existed in English, she encouraged translations from the French and also from Latin, of which she was ignorant.*

in nunneries might own a *Life* of St Catherine of Siena, martyred in 1347. English ladies in the secular world had owned French romances, in the original and in translation, since the mid-fourteenth century. They read of Tristram and Lancelot and Troilus. With inherited books of hours, psalters, breviaries and primers beautifully bound, a literate gentlewoman's library in the 1470s might comprise some four or five volumes.

With Caxton's and de Worde's presses, twenty copies of one work could be printed more cheaply and easily than one manuscript could be hand-copied. Lady Margaret Beaufort, conscious of her deficiency in Latin, asked for a stream of Latin – and French – compositions to be "englished" and printed at her expense. Many of these were religious works. Wynkyn de Worde printed Walter Hylton's *Scala Perfectionis* in English for her in 1494. Lady Margaret

herself translated *The Mirror of Gold for the Sinful Soul* from the French in 1506, and one book, also from French, for a complete English edition of the *Imitation of Christ*. Lady Margaret did not show unusual piety in this; the bulk of literature printed throughout the sixteenth century was religious. Nor would other gentlewomen have been reluctant to read such books. Of fifty-eight compositions written by women between 1524 and 1640, thirty-six were original religious compositions and sixteen were translations of religious works.

A page from the fourth book of The Following of Christ *(1503), giving all honour to "the full excellent Pryncesse", Lady Margaret Beaufort, who commissioned the translation. Devotional literature constituted the bulk of the gentlewoman's library throughout the sixteenth century.*

However, Lady Margaret did not disdain secular literature. On a lighter note, Henry Watson translated *The Great Ship of Fools of this World* for Wynkyn de Worde, "through the enticement and exhortation of the Princess Margaret". She owned a copy of Chaucer's *The Canterbury Tales* and in 1489 she requested Caxton to translate and print *The History of King Blanchardine and Queen Eglantine*. Caxton stressed that the History would prove "honest and joyfull to all virtuous young noble gentlemen and women for to read there-

in as for their pastime". Prejudice existed – and grew – in Tudor times against French romances, just as it did against French novels in Georgian England, on the grounds that the amatory nature of these works might arouse unchaste impulses in the feminine reader's breast. (When women began to learn Latin, there were similar worries that certain classical authors like Ovid would influence them to lewd behaviour. Cicero and Plutarch – and, curiously, Propertius – were approved.) It was undoubtedly a boon to the gentlewoman with a taste for light literature that holy Lady Margaret sanctioned romantic literature. The variety of books available in English continued to increase. As well as translations, original works in English began to make an appearance. Works on etiquette, household management, child nurture and medicine were calculated to appeal to the gentlewoman now acquiring books for the first time.

For ladies keen to improve the standard of food served in their homes and the etiquette surrounding its serving, there appeared in 1500 a *Noble Boke of Feasts Royal and Cookery*, and, in 1508, *The Boke of Kervynge*, or carving. *A Book of Courtesy, or Little John*, published in 1492, together with *A Little Treatise for to learn English and French,*' of 1497, offered polish for adults; children, too, had their etiquette manual in Legrand's *Book of Good Manners* (1487). "When thy better speaks to thee, Do off they cap and bow they knee," was one part of its sage advice. In 1532 *A Little Book of Good Manners for Children*, translated from Erasmus' Latin original, became very popular – among parents. Possibly, children would have preferred to read a *Book of Merry Riddles*, published in 1530. "A good book of medicines", printed in 1539, supplemented their mother's recipes for the still-room, and from 1559 she had Gesner's *Treasures of Euonymus* or "The new jewel of health . . . with approved remedies, . . . and distillations of waters" as the Bible of distillery.

The English gentlewoman had formed the habit of reading for her "passe-tyme" by 1509, the year in which both Lady Margaret and her son, Henry VII died. Education now had point, where earlier female literacy had seemed to serve no useful purpose. Social conditions were now favourable to reading, too. The family no longer sat in the great hall of an evening but in an upper chamber or parlour. The introduction of wall chimneys, of glass windows, of mold candles, all helped to minimise smoke and maximise light. Later in the century, the Long Gallery would provide a warm, draught-free haven for cosy grouping of chairs, and "my lady's closet", an early sort of study, became a retreat where the lady of the house could spend hours with her books.

From about 1520 onwards parents spent substantial sums on tutors for their daughters, not for those daughters to gratify some intellectual bent in private, but to display their marvellous learning in public. Erudite Catherine of Aragon continued Lady Margaret's royal patronage of printing; she commissioned from the Spanish scholar, Juan Luis Vives, *de Institutione Feminae Christianae*. He finished this manual for the instruction of a Christian woman in 1523 – it was translated into English in 1529 – and Catherine asked him to come to England and draw up a plan of study for her seven-year-old daughter,

21

the Princess Mary. Vives' *De Ratione Studii Puerilis* is duly dated, "Oxford, the Nones of October, 1523". The plan was pioneering: Catherine wanted her daughter to learn Latin. In place of grammars and oral recitation of verbs and declensions, the ordinary English tools, Vives suggested the use of "Paper Books", or notebooks, where the student, informed with the rudiments of grammar, should build up a knowledge of accidence and syntax from the ancient texts themselves. He also suggested that the student should better acquaint herself with the foreign language, by double translation – from English to Latin, then back again.

Vives' system of thorough drilling was copied by other educationalists,

Portraits of erudite Lady Jane Grey, c. 1545 (left), and of her cousin, Princess Elizabeth, c. 1546 (right). Learning was generally "so very modish" among gentlewomen at this time, that "Plato and Aristotle untranslated were frequent ornaments of their closets."

including Roger Ascham when he came to teach Mary's step-sister, the Princess Elizabeth. Vives himself owed much to correspondence with educationalists like Thomas More and Thomas Linacre (who wrote a grammar specially for the use of the Princess Mary). While Vives condemned modern epics of love and war and certain ancient authors as unsuitable for maidens, he provided leaven in Princess Mary's curriculum with time appointed for nature study, a subject quite new to the English gentlewoman. Mary remained interested in botany and dialling, the study of shadow and time, all her life. As we have seen, attention paid to the education of gentlewomen in England had until now been scant. For Lady Margaret and her contemporaries sufficient Latin to con their prayer books and adequate French had been the chief academic jewels in the medieval woman's crown. Mary's thorough knowledge of Latin, French and Spanish became the wonder of the Court. Her mother Catherine, after all, was a

foreigner; no English princess had been educated to the Princess Mary's standard ever before. Courtiers hastened to provide tutors in Latin for their daughters in emulation of the accomplished princess, and overnight learning became a necessity for the well-bred gentlewoman.

Other royal ladies, Elizabeth I and Lady Jane Grey, learnt more languages than Mary and were more serious scholars. Mary, for all the care lavished on her education, loved above all to pet her spaniels and discuss details of fashion with the silliest of her ladies. But she was the first English scholar princess; her learning provoked lesser mortals like Edward Seymour, "Protector" Duke of Somerset, Henry Fitzalan, Earl of Arundel, and Henry Howard, Earl of Surrey, into giving their daughters a sound classical education. The three Seymour sisters used their education to compose a hundred couplets in Latin honouring Margaret of Navarre at her death in 1549. Jane and Mary Fitzalan influenced their father to stock his library at Nonsuch Castle with books on music and much classical literature. Both made translations from Greek into Latin. Mary, who married the Duke of Norfolk, died aged sixteen; Jane married Lord Lumley, but agreed to live permanently with her husband at her father's home. The addition of her books and manuscripts to her father's collection led to his library being called the Lumley Library, so she may stand as England's first lady librarian. The Howard daughters shared John Foxe, the martyrologist, as tutor with their brothers, and Jane Howard in particular benefited. "Few men may compare with her," wrote William Barker in *The Nobility of Women*.

These women were scholars, encouraged by scholarly parents. Catherine's motives in having Mary taught Latin had been to give Mary a greater understanding of the Catholic faith. Other ambitious parents understood only that learning was now a fashionable accomplishment that might gain their daughter a better husband. Henry and Frances, Marquess and Marchioness of Dorset, took this to extreme lengths when they provided for their daughter, Lady Jane Grey, a most superior and gruelling syllabus of education – in the hopes that her learning would attract her scholarly cousin, Edward VI, into marriage. The Dorsets saw no reason to show any interest themselves in academe. While Lady Jane was reading the *Phaedo* in the original Greek – and conversing in that language – with her scholarly tutor, Dr Aylmer, her parents continued to hunt the stag in the park every day with undiminishing rigour.

One parent who did interest himself closely in his daughters' education without thought of worldly gain was Sir Thomas More. By 1500, before his first marriage, he had published a popular Latin grammar which children could use, *Lac puerorum, or Milk for Babes*. With the birth of three daughters, and then a son, his interest in education became more personal and he took the view that education for boys and girls should be the same. "They both have the name of human being whose nature reason differentiates from beasts; both, I say, are equally suited for the knowledge of learning by which reason is cultivated."

More set up a household school in his Chelsea home beside the river in the second decade of the sixteenth century. Here he taught, besides his daughters

23

The Lady Barkley.

Holbein's studies of Elizabeth Dauncey (left) and Cecily Heron (right), daughters of Thomas More, Henry VIII's Lord Chancellor. Of City stock, they married sons of other Court officials of intellect rather than pedigree. The "middling class" was emerging.

and son, another five girls and one boy. More himself was of sound City stock; his father became Judge of the King's Bench, and was knighted. Thomas More's first wife came from Essex; Dame Alice, step-mother to his children, was widow of a London mercer. The pupils who joined his children in the school and learnt Latin, Greek, logic, philosophy, theology, mathematics and astronomy, were all from professional, mercantile families. The erudition being acquired in Chelsea might thus have gone unknown to the nobility but for More's position at Court. From 1517 he was a member of the Council and, from 1529 to 1532, he was Lord Chancellor. His fellow councillors at Court were curious to see the practical results of his advocacy of liberal education for girls as well as boys. In about 1529 his daughters "disputed in philosophy" before the King, and the reputation of More's household school, long a legend in academic circles, spread. More's daughters all married coming young men of the professions who acquired positions – even knighthoods – at Court. Cultured nobles like Arundel and Surrey and Somerset were encouraged to consider educating their own daughters more thoroughly.

More had his own reasons for wishing his daughters to be conversant with Latin and Greek. He was in the forefront of humanism, or the New Learning. This curious phrase is misleading, for a large part of the New Learning consisted in mastering ancient Greek. This language was unknown in England till the 1490s, and then for two decades remained the province of a very few scholars like John Colet, Linacre, or More himself. The aim of the New Learning was to read and follow the dictates of Old and New Testaments in the original Hebrew

and in Greek. Around the Latin or Vulgate translation of the Bible a whole weight of medieval mysticism and symbolism had accrued. Humanists, disciples of the New Learning, felt as a result that much of the Catholic dogma of their time rested on faulty foundations.

Colet, Erasmus and More went back to the teachings of the Early Christian Fathers, and examined the Testaments in the original. In 1516 Erasmus edited the first printed Greek New Testament. They wanted others, who did not know Greek, to read the Bible translated from the original Greek into English, not the corrupt Vulgate edition. In 1526 Tyndale printed the New Testament in English, translated from Erasmus's Greek text. In all this work, education in Greek and in Latin was no accomplishment but an absolute necessity. All hands – male and female – were welcome at the wheel, for there were hundreds of documents in Greek and Latin which required study and translation. More's daughters were diligent in this work. In about 1526 More's best-beloved and eldest daughter, Margaret Roper, translated Erasmus's *Precatio dominica* as *Treatise on the Pater Noster*, and Richard Hyrde, a tutor in More's school, wrote an introduction, defending her unusual learning. In 1523 Erasmus

Sir Thomas More and family, by Rowland Lockey (1530). In the Great House at Chelsea, handsomely equipped with library, books, gallery, garden and orchard, More's daughters learnt Latin, Greek, Logic, Philosophy, Theology, Mathematics and Astronomy.

Margaret Roper (right) and
Margaret Clement (left),
daughter and foster-
daughter of Sir Thomas
More. Both showed
themselves true Christian
gentlewomen when Henry
VIII imprisoned More and
his other critics. Margaret
Clement fed Carthusian
monks "tied and not able to
stir" and took from them
"their natural filth".

dedicated his *Commentary on the Christmas Hymn of Prudentius* to her,
accepted an emendation in the text of Saint Cyprian, which he edited, from her,
and sent a kiss when her first child was born. Margaret married, at the age of fifteen, young William Roper, a lawyer's son and pupil of More. They continued
to frequent the Chelsea house after their marriage, for More could not have
done without his "Meg" – secretary, scholar, quiet absorber of his wisdom.

When More was executed, "protesting that he died the King's good servant but God's first", William Roper was consigned to the Tower. Margaret
was found, "not puling and lamenting, but full busily teaching her children"
just as her father had once taught her. One of those children, Mary Bassett, went
on to render into English the part of the *Treatise on the Passion* which her
grandfather had written in Latin while a prisoner in the Tower.

Of course not all parents bowed to the fashion for learning "Ancient
Tongues". There was, after all, the example of Lord Pembroke, the great soldier
who built Wilton, to encourage those gentlemen and ladies of the sixteenth
century who sneered at the advantages of education. Lord Pembroke had his
place in Queen Elizabeth's Council, for all that he was quite unable to read or
write. An illiterate nobleman would not relish a learned wife. But Lord Pembroke was exceptional in his achievements and in his ignorance. As the sixteenth
century progressed, illiterate ladies and noblemen became scarce, except in
remote country districts where boorish squires and rustic wives lingered on. A
nodding acquaintance with the literature of the day, religious and secular,
became necessary for anyone who wished to cut a dash at Whitehall. William

Harrison observed the Elizabethan Court: "Our ancient ladies of the court do shun and avoid idleness," he wrote in his *Description of England*, . . . some in continual reading either of the Holy Scriptures, or histories of our own or foreign nations about us." Other ladies at this studious Court wrote books or translated "other men's into our English and Latin tongue". Correspondingly, the leading courtiers of Elizabeth's Court in the 1570s could have sprung straight from the pages of Castiglione's *The Courtier*. The ideal courtier combined the soldierly and chivalrous qualities of the medieval knight with the administrative and executive abilities of the medieval clerk. Verse, dancing, the lute, the hunting field – and the council chamber, audiences with foreign envoys in a variety of languages, transactions at the treasury – should be equally within his powers. William Cecil, Lord Burghley, Sir Nicholas Bacon, Robert Devereux, Earl of Essex, were all capable of this merriment or gravity by turn.

It was not surprising that these men sought educated women as their wives. The duties of these wives went far beyond administering a household, and bearing children. Queen Elizabeth herself paid tribute to the conduct in Paris of Elizabeth, wife and widow of Sir Thomas Hoby, the ambassador who translated Castiglione's *The Courtier* in 1561. "We think it. . .a commendation of our Country, that such a Gentlewoman hath given so manifest a testimony of virtue in such hard times of adversity." Elizabeth Hoby, later Lady Russell, was known as "the English Sappho" for her poetic gifts – she wrote a quantity of epitaphs in Latin and Greek. Her sister, Mildred, married William "Secretary" Cecil, Lord Burghley, and was a most effective political hostess. Her fluent Latin was a boon to her in this, for Latin was the diplomatic *lingua franca*. She took a part in Edward VI's education besides recommending Sir John Cheke, the scholar, as his principal tutor. Another sister, Catherine, was married to Henry Killigrew, long-serving diplomat, so her proficiency in Latin, Greek and Hebrew was again of use. The last of the sisters, Anne, married Sir Nicholas Bacon, Keeper of the Great Seal. Understandably, as mother of Sir Francis Bacon, she was the most gifted of all the sisters – and the most religious. All her many translations – of sermons from Italian in 1548 and again in 1551, of Bishop Jewel's *Apology in Defence of the Church of England* from Latin – she thought of as furthering the glory of God. Archbishop Parker ordained that a copy of her translation of Jewel be placed in every church in England.

The father of these splendid daughters was Sir Anthony Cooke of Gidea Hall in Essex. He educated them all himself, with the pleasant results detailed. Exceptionally for a man of his rank – Thomas More was, after all, of the merchant class – he held that "sexes as well as souls are equal in capacity." He taught his daughters, however, to regard all study as recreation; their real business was with "the needle in the closet, and housewifery in kitchen and hall". A certain degree of filial disobedience crept in here. At least, we never hear of the English Sappho's or her sisters' love of embroidery. Elizabeth Lady Russell, for one, was much too busy protesting against "one Burbage" converting rooms in Blackfriars, where she lived, to "a common playhouse". His drums and trum-

pets drowned divine service, she told the Privy Council, and it brought "vagrant and lewd" persons into the neighbourhood, to her "great annoyance". The sisters probably conceived their chief duty as being to advance the cause of Protestantism. Anne Bacon corresponded with Theodore Beza, Calvin's successor in Geneva. She invited Puritan preachers to live at Gorhambury, her home at St Albans; Mildred helped Puritan divines at Court to secure appointments, and the other sisters were active too, Catherine standing a staunch friend to Edward Dering, the nonconformist preacher.

Together with higher educational standards for women, More, Vives and Cooke all advocated sparing the rod and enthusing pupils by praise and gentle handling. Lady Jane Grey told the scholar Roger Ascham in 1550 that her lessons with Dr Aylmer provided her with her only escape from the cruelly unhappy home life at Bradgate Manor in Leicestershire. Within the roseate brick mansion with white facings and eighty-foot Great Hall, all was pomp and luxurious ceremony – but her mother beat her, periodically both parents taunted and threatened and pinched her for the most minor of faults. "I think myself in Hell," said Lady Jane, till the time came for her lesson with Dr Aylmer. He employed "such fair allurements to learning that I think all the time nothing while I am with him. Whatsoever I do else but learning is full of grief, trouble, fear and whole misliking unto me."

At the age of nine in 1547, Jane had been sent off for two years to the household of Queen Catherine Parr, who continued to live at Chelsea Palace following her husband's death and her step-son Edward VI's accession. Catherine was a fervent Protestant who went much further than her late husband in rejecting Catholic dogma. In 1547 she published *The Lamentation of a Sinner*, which gives a clear picture of Protestant tenets at this date. Most important was the concept of direct, non-mystical contact with God. Purgatory and the terror of damnation were alike rejected, and heaven was conceived in concrete terms, as described in *Isaiah* and in St John the Divine's *Revelations*. Young Jane was, like her cousin Edward, greatly attracted to this radical theology to which all Catherine's circle – including Coverdale, translator of the Bible, Archbishop Cranmer, and Nicholas Udall, translator of the Gospels – adhered. With Edward's accession, this serious Protestantism, based like More's Catholic humanism, on reading texts in the original, came into its own. Frances Dorset had not dreamed that Lady Jane's classical education would lead her to adopt the extreme religious position which was Protestantism in the late 1540s. Lady Dorset was, however, nothing if not pragmatic; if Protestantism made Lady Jane closer to the King, why then, let her be as ardent as she wished.

Under the popular system of "placing out" in the sixteenth century, both girls and boys were sent between seven and nine years old to live, as Jane did with Catherine Parr, with a family of equal or superior status to their own – or they might be sent to "board" in a convent. Foreigners disapproved of this, but they thought that the English nobility showed very little affection to their children at the best of times. One Italian observer thought that "placing out"

Opposite: Mildred Cooke Cecil, Lady Burghley (1536-89), by Hans Eworth. Daughter of educationalist Sir Anthony Çooke, she was praised by Roger Ascham as equal in quality to her politician husband. Appreciative Burghley kept her portrait in each of his three residences.

stemmed from the English vice of gluttony. When others' children were of the household they could be fed cheaply on ale and bread. When children of the house were at home, the lord and lady of the manor could not reserve all the delicacies for themselves. But his argument was faulty. In "placing out" their children, parents had to pay board wages and provide a suitable wardrobe.

The whole question of whether the medieval and Tudor parents cared for their children as we do is vexed. At birth the infants were considered "pulli", or dirty and polluted. Baptism occurred hastily, within two or three days. Salt was put on the child's mouth, and oil on its forehead, to cleanse it of its sin. An important part of the baptism was the choice of sponsors, or godparents. Those

Woman and children in church, by Holbein. Enlightened mothers sometimes released their infants' arms from swaddling bands after a few months. Not till the age of two were all the bands removed and the child put in miniature adult dress.

honoured might later receive their godchild for "placing out"; meanwhile, the acceptance of the honour by a person of consequence would swell the parents' standing. When Bess of Hardwick, wife of Sir William Cavendish, had her first child, she chose old friends as godparents; two years later, in 1550, for the christening of her first son, she chose William Paulet, the Lord Treasurer, as a sponsor. Her politicking had begun. Following baptism, the gentlewoman's child was generally put out to be breast-fed by a wet-nurse, or woman paid to divert her breast milk from her own child to her noble charge. In this age of high infant mortality, the wet-nurse's child whose birth initiated the flow of milk might well have died. The tiny gentlewomen and gentlemen placed in her care might equally do so. There was a high incidence of infants dying when their nurses, sleeping in the same bed, "overlay" or smothered them. In 1516 Sir Thomas More prescribed that every mother in Utopia should feed her baby herself, unless prevented by illness or death. Erasmus in his colloquy, *The New*

Mother (1526) stressed that nursing her infant was every mother's duty. In 1573 Thomas Tusser would again urge that every good wife offered her breast to her child. Regardless of this masculine concern, gentlewomen continued to entrust the little swaddled bundles which were their infants to wet-nurses.

The tight swaddling bands in which infants up to the age of a year at least were confined, did not help the rate of infant deaths. It was thought that constriction of the spine and limbs would prevent crooked growth, and, only on the infrequent occasions when the bands were changed, were the baby's limbs allowed to kick freely. The rest of the time, with a piece of coral resting as an amulet on its chest, later, a teething ring stuffed in its mouth, the junior Tudor lay unattended. It might even be hung up by one of its bands on a peg on the wall. Just because gentlewomen did not nurse their babies themselves, however, one cannot assume they felt no love for them. A Huguenot refugee who taught French in London in the 1560s wrote a dialogue where a mother addresses her infant's nurse: "Unswathe him, undoe his swadling bands . . . wash him before me . . . Pull off his shirt. Now swaddle hime again but first put on his biggin [or nightcap]. Where is his little petticoat? . . . God send thee sound rest my little boykin," she concluded.

We know little of the childhood at home which followed till the age of seven or so, when "placing out" occurred. From swaddling bands the child went direct into a full-dress version of its mother's or father's clothes. At the age of three, the Princess Elizabeth's wardrobe was neglected, following her mother's disgrace. Lady Bryan, appointed her governess, complained that the child had "neither gown, nor kirtle, nor petticoat, nor no manner of linen, nor fore-smocks, nor kerchefs . . . nor body stitchets [or stays]." The only concession to childhood ways were a "muckinder", or long handkerchief, which trailed from the child's waist and was used as a general cleaning rag, and a "pudding". This was a padded, sausage-shaped band, which was fixed round the child's head as a bumper against tumbles.

Plague, smallpox, any manner of illness might strike a child at any age. It was neither wise, nor was it customary, to pay much attention to children, until they were first to be "placed out", and then, till girls reached the interesting age of twelve, and boys, fourteen, and could legally marry. Children often regarded the family with whom they were placed out as their own, and sometimes returned only briefly to their parental home before marriage.

Thus, when Lady Jane returned home to Bradgate on Catherine Parr's death, her allegiance was still to Catherine's circle – and to Admiral Thomas Seymour, handsome brother of Protector Somerset and widowed husband of Catherine. Jane was besotted by the Admiral – who had, apart from trying to seduce her, with Catherine shown her genuine kindness, which she did not receive at home. The Admiral attempted to marry Jane on his wife's death, but Frances Dorset was still scheming for her daughter's future as Edward's wife. Part of the resentment which Lady Jane felt and openly declared for her mother was born of Frances's rejection of the Admiral's suit. Frances Dorset has more

in common with Lady Macbeth than any other woman of the sixteenth century. She stopped up her flow of mother's milk without compunction in pursuit of her own aims.

In the ten days during 1554 when Lady Jane was Queen of England, her parents – and Frances in particular – treated their daughter without a whit of natural affection. Her marriage to the Duke of Northumberland's son, Lord Guilford Dudley, was concluded "by blows from the mother and curses from the father". Her parents had orchestrated her coronation as Queen; when Mary Tudor had won the day, and Jane's father told her to "put off your royal robes," she replied, "I much more willingly put them off than I put them on. Out of obedience to you and my mother, I have grievously sinned. May I not go home?" Lady Jane could not, of course, go home. Astonishingly her father and mother – instigators of her short reign – not only both turned coat on the instant, and declared themselves loyal to Mary, but left their sixteen-year-old daughter to assuage Mary's vengeance as best she might. Dorset, Duke of Suffolk since 1551, in fact, did not escape, although he declared himself a Catholic. He was executed. His daughter's reaction to his conversion and death was noted by a gentleman who found Lady Jane at dinner in her jailer's apartments in the Tower of London. What had prompted her father's conversion, mused the stern Protestant. The hope of pardon, someone suggested.

"Pardon! woe worth him," responded Lady Jane. "He hath brought me and our stock at most miserable calamity . . . Who was judge that he could hope for pardon, whose life was odious to all men? But what will ye more? Like as his life was wicked and full of dissimulations, so was his end hereafter."

Interestingly, as the sixteenth century drew to a close, the enthusiasm for a liberal education for females slackened. Influential educational writers, like Bruto in 1598, argued that exposure to classical literature would expose young gentlewomen also to lewd and amorous stories popular in antiquity and should be avoided. She should read accounts of women who loved their husbands. Women had no part to play in the law or government or diplomacy. Then why learn Latin? As the religious troubles of the mid-century became resolved, and Anglicans, Puritans and Catholics hardened their positions, there seemed less burning need to con texts in the original Greek and Latin. In the Anglican Church in 1547, under Edward VI, books of twelve sermons in English had been issued to every parish to be read in church in rotation by "parsons, vicars, curates, and all others having spiritual care". Elizabeth reissued Edward's Sermons in 1562, and added twenty-one more to be read on specific occasions. The eighteenth homily, for instance, was entitled, "Of the state of matrimony".

Great attention was paid to these sermons in English by the common people and by the gentry. The eighteenth homily taught that marriage was "constituted of God to the intent that men and women should live lawfully in a perpetual friendship, to bring forth fruit, and to avoid fornication". Women should obey their husbands. The cap on their heads was an outward sign of their subservience. As they were "lighter and more vain in their phantasies and

opinions", their husbands should be the leaders and authors of their lives. Spiritual authority for the lesser importance of women was thus dinned into the Anglican congregation's ears, and did not encourage parents to educate their daughters.

In 1574 it was noted: "The Court has great plenty of ladies to hear sermons." Elizabethan England saw a taste develop among ladies for listening to sermons, and a series of fashionable preachers arose. These preachers were often Puritan, one well-known one being Stephen Egerton, minister of St Anne's, Blackfriars, from 1590. His "little church or chapel up stairs" was crowded with "a great congregation, specially of women". Devout Lady Hoby indulged in a riot of sermon attendances when she visited London from Yorkshire in 1601.

A rubbing from a 1550 memorial brass to Mary Fitzwilliam in a Sussex church showing mother and eight daughters. Children who predeceased their mother are customarily depicted alongside the surviving children as constituting the sum of her labours and her chief glory.

She heard Mr Grant preach at Westminster Church, and went "to the minister" to hear "one Mr Smith preach, where I heard, to my knowledge, nothing worth the noting". Egerton was undoubtedly her favourite preacher. Lady Hoby always had notes to write after one of his sermons. As her mother-in-law, Elizabeth Lady Russell, lived conveniently in Blackfriars, Lady Hoby could hear the divine preach, then have dinner at Lady Russell's, return to St Anne's "to his exercise", and finish the day by writing "some of his notes" in her Testament.

Other country ladies journeyed to London to acquire a knowledge of the new fashions in dress, knowledge they would then disseminate back at home. Lady Hoby came agog for religious revelation and for any new "physic" the capital could offer. As lady of Hackness Manor, she was responsible for the religious health of four waiting women, all widows, besides a changing series of

33

young relations and gentlewomen who were "placed out" with her. Lady Hoby faithfully "examined" and "catechised" these dependants, and taught those who could not read to make out the Ten Commandments at least. (Bible reading was considered most important by Puritans, and as a result they took pains to encourage literacy at every level.)

Thoughts fresh from the fashionable pulpits of London could only enliven the taxing hours Lady Hoby and her Yorkshire household spent in religious devotion. In the matter of "physic", the health of the Hackness estate workers

A young Englishwoman by Holbein. This charming study of hastening womanhood recalls the busy manor ladies of Grosynhill's Mulierum Pean (1540): "Estates commonly where I go/Trust their wives to overlook,/Baker, brewer, butler and cook."

depended upon the manor still-room. Here Lady Hoby concocted remedies for backache, sore eyes and all the ailments common to an agricultural worker. Her enthusiastic visits to doctors in York and in London were, one hopes, of use in providing new cordials and ointments for use of her own household and of the parish. From Lady Hoby's diary, however, – the first English woman's diary extant – one has the impression that London preachers and physicians supplied an emotional excitement which her life of dutiful housekeeping did not offer. Gentlewomen of later centuries, similarly confined and restricted, would lavish similar attention on "dear vicar" or "dear doctor".

34

Woodcuts of the herb centaury and a woman baking from The Grete Herbal, *translated from French in 1526. Herbals were an invaluable source of "physic", household hints, recipes – for manufacture of toothpaste and ink – and even of designs for embroidery.*

What were the duties, what the expectations of a sixteenth-century gentle-woman, from which a book of sermons – or, indeed, a pack of cards – might offer relief? Her first duty was to marry and, to this end, she must acquire as a girl a prescribed row of skills. Dancing, music instrumental and choral, fine needlework and good manners – including the etiquette of eating pie and sneezing – must all be mastered by the time she came of marriageable age. These accomplishments constituted the "better manners" which parents hoped their children would learn on being "placed out".

In the fifty years between 1525 and 1575 when it was fashionable for girls to learn the "Ancient Tongues", mothers did not cease to worry about their daughters' progress in these more practical lures to marriage. Lady Lisle, wife of the Governor of the garrison in Calais, "placed out" her daughter, Anne Basset, with a French family in 1536. She made her expectations clear when she heard that Anne had lost a pair of shoes at gaming to her sewing maid: "I would she would ply her work, the lute and virginals." Anne was destined to be a Maid of Honour at the English Court, the best marriage mart of all. Her sister Katherine learned to play the lute, the virginals, and the spinet at another French family. They did not teach her to write her name, which possibly told against her when she too sought to become a Maid of Honour. In spite of Lady Lisle's judicious gifts of quail and other delicacies to Queen Jane Seymour in 1537, this less handsome sister had to be content in the service of the Countess of Rutland. One guardian, Sir John Parrott, refused to pay fees to a couple called Stephynton, with whom he "placed out" two young relatives, Dorothy and Jane Parrott. He discovered that the girls were used "as servants to do all the vilest business in their house". The Stephyntons retorted that the girls were "brought up ... as young gentlewomen and maids of their ages are accustomed". This consisted of learning "writing,

Lady Grace Talbot in 1591. Music was a solace to this child-bride who bore her husband, Henry Cavendish, no children. His fertility elsewhere brought him the admiring title of "the common bull of Derbyshire and Staffordshire".

reading, sewing, both white work and black work, and playing of the lute and virginals".

The ladies whose "service" young girls entered to acquire these skills regarded them as a pleasant charge, until they proved otherwise. Catherine Countess of Huntingdon brought up Margaret Dakins, later Lady Hoby, among other girls. Daughterless herself, she felt proud of her education of the girls entrusted to her. "I think there will none make question," she said, "but I know how to breed and govern gentlewomen." Though she taught Lady Hoby to be a fervent Puritan, and Puritan writers inveighed against ladies learning music, theory parted company with practice. At Hackness Manor, as a married

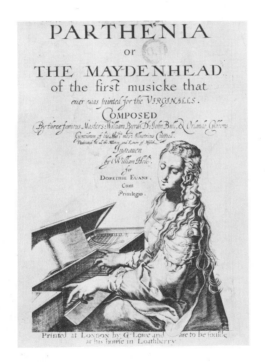

The title-page of Parthenia *(1611), one of the numerous music manuals published between 1560 and 1640. Skill on the virginals was an accomplishment approved in gentlewomen. The lute, with its corpus of love-songs, was thought to be less suitable.*

lady, it was Lady Hoby's pleasure to play the "alphorion" or orpharion and sing, for pleasure, as well as in the service of God. From 1570, with publication of Tye's *Acts of the Apostles*, songs for amateur singers, and, in 1571, Whythorne's *Book of Madrigals*, there was a stream of song books printed and books of music for the virginals, lute, orpharion, bandore, cittern and the viols, besides books where the principles of music and instruction for playing the various instruments were set out. These were of help to the tutors whom the ladies like the Countess of Huntingdon employed – at some cost – to teach their "maidens" music and singing. The "Golden Age" of English music was reflected in the greater attention paid by gentlewomen to their instruments.

*A couple – traditionally
Elizabeth I and Robert
Dudley, Earl of Leicester –
dancing* La Volta *.
Extravagant dances were
popular at the late
Elizabethan Court – and
dangerous. "Some have
broke their legs with
skipping, leaping, turning
and vaulting," warned one
spectator.*

William Harrison noted that the younger ladies at Court gave all the attention, which their elders gave to books, to the lute and to "prick-song".

The most popular instruments were the virginals and the lute. The "virginalls" or "pair of virginalls" was properly a rectangular key instrument – with single or double keyboard – and a plucking mechanism. Henry VIII and Elizabeth were both accomplished performers. The term was used loosely throughout the sixteenth and seventeenth century, however, to refer to the other plucked keyboard instruments, the harpsichord and the five- or six-sided spinet. The music of William Byrd, of Orlando Gibbons, composed for "the virginals", could be played on any of these instruments. The lute was frowned on by some educationalists as unsuitable for ladies, largely because there were a good many love songs written for its accompaniment. This disapproval did not deter ladies from learning the instrument and the songs. Some moral preceptors were best ignored – like W. Averell, who thought that letter writing and playing the lute, singing sonnets, fixing hair, and dancing, were all "lewde and unseemly pastimes". Thomas Morley's *A Plaine and Easie Introduction to Practicall Musicke* (1597) purports to be lessons given to a gentleman who is socially disgraced when he admits to being unable to sing from a part-book after supper.

Dancing steps, the ladies or their waiting women could teach themselves to the girls in their care. There was a good deal of prejudice expressed throughout the century against the "light, lewde and lascivious" form which modern

dance had taken. John Northbrooke issued "A Treatise wherein Dicing, Dancing, Vain Plays . . . are reproved by the Authority of the word of God" in 1577. The saraband and other dances where men and women danced together were described as "serving as the bellows to inflame lust" by John Downame. Earlier Vives had abused: "this new fashion of dancing of ours, full of . . . uncleanly handlings, gropinges, and kissings . . . what good doth all this dancing of young women, holden up on mine arms, that they may hop the higher?" But no invective could prevent dancing from being the most popular pastime. A painting exists of a dancing couple – probably Elizabeth dancing with Leicester. She has indeed hopped the higher. Her twinkling feet are a foot off the ground.

Responsible ladies would probably teach their young gentlewomen the stately "low" dances like the pavane or almain, danced with the heel firm on the floor. These would impart the grace of bearing which was the true purpose of a gentlewoman learning to dance. Devout ladies might not teach their girls any dancing steps, but only the equally important degrees of courtesy with which to greet differing groups of people. How to stand, when to rise, when to make a courtesy and how deep, how to hold a fan – hours were spent at this drill. In 1499 Erasmus had written to a friend in Paris how wherever you went in England, "you were received with kisses from everybody; when you leave you are dismissed with kisses . . . people arrive: kisses; they depart: kisses . . . in fact, whatever way you turn, everything is full of kisses." Sadly, in the course of the sixteenth century this wanton bestowal of kisses was replaced by a rigorous etiquette of salutation and withdrawal – all of which must be painstakingly learned.

What benefit did the ladies who took in pupil gentlewomen derive from their charity? They had the affection and loyalty of these girls generally – though Lady Anne Clifford, Countess of Dorset, "fell out with" one Kate Burton at her mansion, Knole, and swore she would not keep her. If the young girl was an heiress, then her benefactress might secure her in marriage for a son or a kinsman. The young gentlewoman's parents were generally agreeable, for they had placed their daughter out with a family outranking theirs, in the hope of just such an event. If no kinsman needed a bride, then the chief benefit a lady had from the girls committed to her was in the companionship they offered her, in 'huswiffry" which they learned from her, and in the "work" at which she kept them busy when household duties were done.

"The practice and study of housewifery . . . is the most commodious and honourable science and occupation of a woman – this is her special mistress-quality": thus Lennard's translation of Pierre Charron's *Of Wisdom Three Books* summed up the current thought in 1606. When a gentlewoman married, she might still find that all her learning was beside the point. Katherine Howard, erudite daughter of the Earl of Surrey, married a profligate Lord Berkeley in 1554 when she was sixteen. Her studies in astronomy and Latin and Greek went by the board, and she administered Berkeley Castle in extravagant feudal style. She and her husband, Lord Henry, went hunting daily with a "tail" of a

hundred and fifty retainers in "tawny cloth coats in summer, with the badge of the white Lyon rampant" embroidered on their sleeves. In winter, the retainers wore "coats of white frieze lined with crimsen taffeta". After the morning's work, lord and lady sat down daily with the servants to a banquet in the Great Hall – and then, to further swell the household expenses and Lady Katherine's duties, baskets of food were distributed to the neighbouring poor three times a week. Lady Berkeley could use a knowledge of casting accounts more readily than the rudiments of philosophy under these conditions. Responsible ladies regularly taught this skill to the girls in their charge.

The master of the house supplied the cash, the lady had the keys of the cellar, the still-room, the laundry room at her girdle. A man was dubbed a "cotquean" if he interfered with his wife's household management. Though in theory he supervised the male servants, in practice the lady of the house, through conference with the steward, had their direction. The master's chief duties within the home were to bring the family to church, to entertain guests and preachers, and to appoint tutors for his sons. Business took him abroad if he were a responsible landowner, visiting outlying estates, or he might be out hunting and hawking all day. Litigation might occupy him in Town – or he might like Court life, and play the gallant there, like Sir Anthony Mildmay, while his wife occupied herself at home. The purse hung at his girdle, he could do as he liked. Whether the home was well ordered or not was his lady's decision.

Elinor Fettiplace, lady of a Berkshire manor, kept a Receipt Book at the turn of the seventeenth century, which shows how the country gentlewoman was busy through the summer and autumn, preserving and laying in provisions – winter cabbages, pickled cucumbers – to last through the winter. In the winter fell the three great banqueting festivals – Michaelmas, Christmas and Twelfth Night. Enormous numbers of guests were regularly accommodated in the outlying country districts for the banquets, and they consumed appropriate quantities of food. Sixteen raised pies, fifteen joints of veal, three geese and a whole sheep were among the delights offered at Sir William Petre's Essex manor at dinner on Twelfth Night, 1552, for instance. Breakfast was a simple affair. The main meal was dinner, which consisted of two or three courses of twenty odd dishes each, and was served at midday. Supper was a less lavish version of dinner, and eaten in the late afternoon. In the earlier sixteenth century, family and retainers ate together in the Great Hall; by Lady Fettiplace's day the family tended to eat in the privacy of a withdrawing chamber. With smaller dining-groups, showpieces – pastry castles, or ships in full sail, or wild boar encased in gold leaf – were less in evidence; flavour and delicacy were paid greater attention. Musk, ambergris, sheet gold and seed pearls are decorative ingredients in Lady Fettiplace's menus. Recipes for French confectionery and creams and custards all show a lightness of touch and simplicity lacking in the pottages and syrupy meat dishes which were the staple diet of the earlier Tudor Great Hall. Though there were cooks to prepare these meals, the mistress of the house

would sometimes dress the meat herself, or make a dish from a new recipe herself. Naturally, she taught the girls in her care all the kitchen lore she knew – skill in confectionery was often praised in gentlewomen.

Ladies also had to brew, or supervise the brewing, of the ale and beer which accompanied the daily dinners and suppers. This was done in the still-room, where the lady also made her medicines. In the country, doctors were scarce, and the mother of Robert Burton, author of *Anatomy of Melancholy*, was famous in Leicestershire, he tells us, for her skill in "chirurgery, sore eyes, aches &c". She wrought "many famous and good cures upon diverse poor folks". Lady Danvers' house was "a Court, in the conversation of the best, and

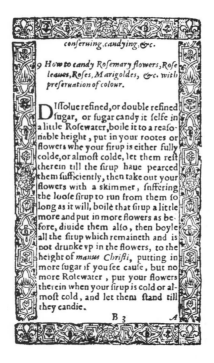

A recipe from Sir Hugh Platt's Delights for Ladies *(1602), for candying flowers. When banquets were ostentatious, edible trickery, like a dinner service made entirely of sugar-plate, or fondant, which Platt describes elsewhere, was much admired.*

an Almshouse, in feeding the poor, . . . an Hospital, in ministering relief to the sick." Charity was part of the Christian gentlewoman's training. In Westmorland, in the late sixteenth century, Margaret, Countess of Cumberland, divided her time between her devotions and the still-room. Her practical daughter, Lady Anne Clifford, founded an almshouse for twelve "sisters", as she called them, who dined in the Painted Room at Appleby Castle with her, as if they were the greatest ladies in the land.

Ingredients for the ladies' recipes and medicines were grown in the garden which furnished vegetables and flowers, too, in season. The summer garden offered a mixture of roses, sage, peonies, lilies and gillyflowers; from the winter garden came onions, fennel and saffron. No gentlewoman was to be seen

41

without a nosegay in summer to smell at. Walking in the garden was a popular pastime, and advocated even by Bruto; the ladies might carry their "work" out there, as the title page of *The Needle's Excellency* shows. In Greene's *Orpharion* (1599) Philomenes finds a charming scene in the privy-garden of the court: "all the ladies sparseled about in sundry borders, some gathering flowers, others in discourses of the excellency of the place, some in prattle with the birds, all busy, none idle".

The time spent on all arts was scant in comparison with the long hours all gentlewomen devoted to their "work" and, when a girl was placed out, her mistress reaped the benefit. She kept the "work" done by all in her household. What was this "work" at which gentlewomen, old and young, were constantly busy? It was fine needlework, or embroidery with silks and gold and silver yarn on silk and satin and cambric ground. The gentlewoman did not sew or embroider clothes for herself and the family, she patronised professional dressmakers. In her household she had one or more sewing women, who mended bed linen, and made shirts for the gentlemen. A great lady like Mary Stuart might employ a *tapissier* permanently, to embroider "bed furniture", as sets of bed coverlets, curtains and valances were called, and "carpets", or wool covers, for tables and seats. Lesser ladies bought their bed furniture and carpets from professionals or sometimes combined to work them themselves.

The title-page from The Needle's Excellency, *one of the printed pattern books which provided ladies with novel stitches and designs for their embroidery. The seated needlewoman is appropriately labelled, "Industry", for gentlewomen called their embroidery their "work".*

*Two slips from a set of
eleven, embroidered with
flower and fruit designs.
Ladies sewed motifs culled
from herbals, bestiaries and
florilegia, on conveniently
small pieces of material or
"slips". The slips were then
appliquéd as ornaments to
cushions and bed-hangings.*

Their clothes and their linen and their hangings and carpets were all pro-
fessionally worked; what then was there left for gentlewomen to embroider?
The answer is, they embroidered "slips" or small panels, sometimes cruciform,
sometimes octagonal, with animal and floral motifs and heraldic emblems
culled from bestiaries and florilegia and herbals and books of heraldry. These
"slips" were infinitely useful; they would make a pretty border when sewn to
bed hangings, or a charming pattern on a dress, or on a cushion cover. The sewing women of the household did the drudgery, embroidering the background of
a hanging spread awkwardly over a large table; the ladies "supervised" the
sewing women's work, and stitched at their small panels in the comfort of the
parlour; a tapissier then married the work of drudge and lady together.
Lady Bridget Vere wrote from the home of her aunt, Katharine Countess of
Northumberland: "As for the working of slips it is some part of our daily exercise, and the drawing of them." Lady Northumberland was famed for her
collection of cushions worked with flowers and pomegranates. Bridget and
other young girls whom she "bred up" were useful in increasing the store.

   In 1537 Emmanuel Lucar, merchant tailor's epitaph to his wife Elizabeth
who had died, aged twenty-seven, praised her skill in embroidering: "Pictures
artificial . . . Beast, Birds or Flowers, even as things natural." In 1569 Bess of
Hardwick found common cause with her husband's prisoner, Mary Queen of
Scots, in their interest in embroidery. "Mary daily resorts to my wife's chamber, where . . . she sits devising works," commented the Earl of Shrewsbury.
These works were "slips", which, mounted later on green velvet curtains, now
hang at Oxburgh Hall. Mary had with her Mattioli's *Herbal* and Gesner's
Icones Animalium. From the woodcuts in these books, the ladies culled designs
for their slips – a stinking iris, a cat, knotted serpents, a pruning hook – and

43

surrounded the emblems with Latin tags taken from Erasmus's *Adages*. Up and down the country, throughout the century, ladies illustrious and insignificant plied their needles. As we shall see, the finest work was done in the nunneries, and the destruction or disappearance of these convent embroideries, these repositories of stitch and design, were a great loss to English embroidery. Professional sempstresses and ladies began to make their own records of designs and stitches, which they did on strips of canvas called "samplers". They kept them rolled up in a drawer, for consultation.

The dissolution of the religious houses of England between 1535 and 1540 was a bitter blow to gentlewomen who sought an agreeable alternative to matri-

Geometric designs from Johann Sibmacher's book of needlework patterns, Schön Neues Modelbuck *(1597). With the dispersal of the exquisite English needlework in the convents, pattern books from the Continent provided a source of new stitches and designs.*

mony, as it was to the art of English needlework. The composition of the nunneries was reassuringly upper-class, and the pattern of life correspondingly aristocratic. The Abbess of St Mary's, Winchester, in 1535 had her own house and staff including waiting woman, cook, and laundress. The Abbess of Barking generally dined in state in her parlour, joining the nuns in the frater only five times a year. She sallied out, enveloped in furs, to pay visits to neighbouring grandees – like any contemporary lady of the manor. The nuns had pet dogs which they sometimes even brought into the choir, to their bishop's fury. Again, this reflected the custom of the secular nobility. Ladies were accustomed to caress dogs on their laps in church, while their husbands carried – in medieval times – a hawk on their wrists.

Larks and sparrows, rabbits and monkeys were other creatures on which

the nuns lavished attention which should have been directed to God – and again roused the bishop's ire. The bishops paid visitations every three years to each of the convents in their diocese to question the nuns on their conduct. In the records of these visitations are preserved the bishop's findings, his discovery of *corruptelae* or abuses, and his commands for reform. Gay clothes were a constant source of complaint: at Elstow in 1531 head dresses of "lay fashion" with "cornered crests", and the habit of exposing the forehead "more like lay people than religious", gowns "depe voyded at the breste," and "red stomachers" were all condemned. Silver and gilt pins and slashed shoes were constantly inveighed against. In 1532 at Carrow some of the nuns wore silk girdles – and commended their use. The nuns, in short, shared all the foibles of their lay sisters. The bishops' repeated – and fruitless – injunctions to the nuns against gossiping and expensive clothes and making frivolous visits outside the convent find their parallel in secular husbands' complaints about their wives' behaviour. As the craftier nuns saw, once the bishop had made his visitation and recorded his displeasure, it was three years before he would return to see if the reforms he recommended had been effected. Husbands were more pressing.

The convent could be a fine place for romance. As the nuns were officially supposed to observe the rule of enclosure, a steward was generally appointed to live in the convent gatehouse and administer the business of the outlying convent estates. He was an obvious suspect when visitations periodically uncovered the birth of a child in the nunnery. Anne Boleyn attempted to help a relation by marriage, Dame Eleanor Carey, become Abbess of Wilton in 1528. Unfortunately, Henry VIII wrote to Anne, "she hath confessed herself to have had two children by two sundry priests." At Littlemore Priory in 1517 the Prioress, Katherine Wells, ordered her nuns to say, *"Omnia bene"*, or "All's well", to the bishop when he inquired at his visitation what complaints they had. Nevertheless, he discovered that she had had an illegitimate child, a daughter – and had sold "pannes, pottes, candilsticks", the convent's treasures, to provide a dowry for the child. In 1490 the Prioress of St Mary Delapré was alleged to be a married woman who had left her husband for lover, and lover for convent. In these cases, and others like them, one might expect the abbess or prioress to beg forgiveness, promise reform and plead to be allowed to remain within the convent. Generally, they promised reform, but otherwise the ladies were quite unabashed by the discovery of their sins, and sulked and complained bitterly of injustice if they were relieved of their position as head of the house as a result. Quite often, they continued as abbess, on promise of good behaviour – a promise they quite often and quite soon blithely broke.

In the thirteenth and fourteenth centuries there had been reason for the abbesses' pride. The nunneries had been immensely wealthy – with the entry of each nun they received a substantial dowry – and crowded. The Black Death spread like wildfire through the convent communities, and the numbers never recovered. When Henry VIII's Commissioners made their great survey of the property owned by the Church, the *Valor Ecclesiasticus*, in 1535, there were

only four out of a hundred and eleven nunneries with over thirty inhabitants. Sixty-three convents had fewer than ten nuns. In all, there were only about fifteen hundred nuns. The incomes of the various nunneries were similarly scanty. Seventy-three houses had under £100, and only seven houses had over £450 a year. Many of the abuses to which bishops objected were measures to counter severe financial distress. The nuns at Esholt kept an alehouse in 1528, and the custom of taking in "boarders" – both children and matrons – was widespread.

Boys and girls of gentle birth were taken as boarders – at sixpence a week. In the visitation records we read of bishops vainly trying to stop nuns from romping with the little boys, and allowing them to sleep in the cloister. The boys left when they were nine or ten, and of an age to be educated; they seem to have been taken in as playthings for the nuns more than for any purpose. Girls came to the convents as boarders at all ages. A spell in a convent was a traditional alternative for young ladies to "placing out". A novitiate did not necessarily follow. Lord Lisle's daughter, Bridget Plantagenet, was one of the young ladies who "boarded" with the nuns at St Mary's, Winchester, in 1535.

The only problem was that the education available in nunneries by then was abysmal. Few abbesses could even sign their names to Visitation Records. The Latin offices were taught by rote and sung from memory, not from psalters. Henry VIII's Commissioners found few books, and those of little value – mostly service books – in the nunnery libraries. The limitations of the convent education were those of the education available in most secular homes of the day. Certainly, no young lady left a convent better informed than when she entered it – except in gossip and subterfuge. As for religion, there was precious little of it in the convents to be absorbed, though long hours were spent in chapel and at devotion. Most of the nuns could give only the haziest account of the foundations of their belief. The Rule of St Benedict was translated into English by the Bishop of Winchester in 1517, precisely so that "none of them" (the nuns professed under the Rule), "shall now afterward probably say that she wist not what she professed, as . . . some of them have said in time past. . ."

Where the convent-educated girl shone was in her skill in needlework. Where the monks had copied and illuminated manuscripts for centuries past, the nuns "wove histories with their needles". Needlework and fine embroidery were traditional occupations for gentlewomen; with a will, the nuns covered copes, dorsals and altar cloths for the monasteries and churches and for the convent chapel, with an exquisite variety of silk stitches. They also embroidered caps and coifs, and silk purses – and even "blood-bands", used after blood-letting – for customers in the world to supplement convent incomes. Enough variety of embroidery remained in the convents to afford study and imitation by generations of nuns, and they taught the young ladies in their care stitches and designs culled from items such as existed at Langley in 1485: "a coverlet of green and yellow with lilies and swans; a coverlet of blue and white wool knots . . . four fronteys (altar frontals) of green damask powdered with swans and eagles . . . great cloth of red powdered with harts heads and butterflies . . ."

With the suppression of the convents, these delicate items were destroyed for
lust of the gold and silver thread they contained, or were taken abroad by
fugitive nuns, or passed into private ownership, where daily wear and tear reduced them to rags. Medieval English embroidery was a chief casualty of the
Dissolution of the religious houses.

The nuns fenced with Henry's Commissioners, as they had fenced with
their bishops, to stave off closure in the late 1530s. On payment of a fine the
closure could be deferred; again and again the nunneries stumped up – some of
the poorest and smallest houses surviving till the end. But the end to the agreeable, principally self-regulatory life "under the rod" of no man – except the

*Portrait c. 1545, probably of
Anne Bodenham, a Dorset
nun pensioned off at the
Dissolution. The
blackwork, or black silk
embroidery on her collar
was fashionable – and
useful for disguising grime
and stains on visible parts of
the chemise.*

despised bishop – came. Pensions were distributed – at Elstow in 1539 the
Abbess was awarded £50 a year, the Prioress £4. John Skelton, Henry VIII's old
tutor, mourned the early closures in *Colin Clout*:

> Dame Dorothe and lady Besse,
> Dame Sare our pryoresse,
> Out of theyr cloyster and quere
> With an hevy chere,
> Must cast up theyr black vayles.

It was not only spinster women who were reluctant to leave the monastic life.
Several of the nuns were widowed ladies of rank who had decided in favour of a

life of contemplation, following years of child-bearing and administration of a large home. (Katherine Ingham and Eleanor, Lady Scrope both joined the Minoresses without Aldgate in London on widowhood. They were both made Abbess, and a life of contemplation denied them till the hereafter.) Widows, virgins, dowered and portionless, there was henceforth no sanctuary for them. They must live "under the rod" of father or brother or a husband from now on. If dowerless ladies, despite their gentle birth, were unable to attract a husband, then they might become a companion, or abigail, to a gentlewoman, and be known as her gentlewoman. Alternatively, they could become a governess. Either career would bring upon them brands of serfdom and mortification unknown in the independent nunnery.

Grace Sherrington, Lady Mildmay, recalled in her diary her childhood in the 1550s at Lacock Abbey, the nunnery in Wiltshire which her father, Sir Henry, bought following its dissolution in the 1530s. Mistress Hamblyn, an impoverished niece of her father's, was Grace's governess, and Grace loved her dearly. Mistress Hamblyn was "very wise, religious and chaste" – she could "set her mind down in writing, as well as most men could have done", she knew "physick and surgerie", and, besides, "her mirth was very savoury and full of wit." When Grace, aged sixteen, married Anthony Mildmay, Mistress Hamblyn "sent (her) furnished into the world" with plentiful advice on seemly conduct – and Grace remembered it all, and found it good. Indeed, she took some of the advice about not seeking bad company so seriously that she did not accompany gallant Anthony to Court. She stayed in the country quietly reading her Bible, and practising the psalms which her governess had taught her to sing, and ministering to the sick with the help of the Herball Mistress Hamblyn had given her. "Also every day I spend some time in works of mine own invention, without sample or pattern before me for carpet or cushion work, and to draw flowers, and fruit to their life with my plume upon paper." This was unusual. Gentlewomen at this date generally employed a pin to prick out the outline of a design they wished to use. They shook soot on to the page, over the material, and particles fell through to form the required pattern.

Mistress Hamblyn evidently had a proper respect for books, in teaching Grace to use her imagination. The pupil was happy with her occupations – but what happened to Mistress Hamblyn and her kind, when their properly accomplished pupils left them for marriage? Or outgrew their governess's educational skills, as Lady Anne Clifford did those of Mistress Anne Taylour? Lady Anne graduated in 1598 to the care of Samuel Daniel, the poet, but she did not forget Mistress Anne. In the Great Picture at Appleby, which shows Lady Anne Clifford with her dependants, Mistress Anne's portrait is on the wall, described beneath as of "a Religious and good Woman". She was the daughter of a Mr Cholmley of London, and a widow when she came to her noble charge.

Mistress Anne Taylour and Mistress Hamblyn were fortunate in their pupils. Kat Ashley, too, was a governess who was lucky. The Princess Elizabeth on her accession, made Kat chief gentlewoman of the Privy Chamber, and

*Ancient Tongues
and Modern Dances*

allowed her a freedom of speech she denied all her ladies. (When Kat died in 1565, Elizabeth showed a regard for childhood ties again, in choosing Blanche Parry, who had been her nurse, to succeed her.)

The situation for most governesses was less happy. The fact was, if a woman could marry, then marry she should, as it would protect her from the mortifications associated with spinsterhood. There were, of course, special trials associated with marriage. A wife or widow was held responsible for her husband's debts, as Bess of Hardwick found when her husband, Sir William Cavendish, was found guilty of embezzling the Treasury in 1557 – and then died. Besides the lavish building programme at Chatsworth, the expenses of the

Bess of Hardwick, highly independent widow, following three marriages "for richer". Bess knew the value of lavish outlay. She impressed all with the splendour of her personal trappings, long before she built Hardwick Hall anew.

Cavendishes' town house near St Paul's with the parlour decked with flowers, the substantial meals of salmon and eels served on silver by servants in blue livery, had far outrun their legal income. Conspicuous extravagance had been the rule in their marriage, from the litter in which Bess went visiting – lined with quilted silk – to the marriage bed with its coverlet of black velvet embroidered with silver and pearls. Bess had to make a further good marriage before she paid off the £5,000 to the Treasury which Sir William had embezzled. Her daughters' dowries depended on clearing the debt.

There were other hazards for the gentlewoman in marriage in the sixteenth century. In fact, in the reign of Queen Elizabeth, the very fact of their marriage

49

put some gentlewomen in great peril. "Gloriana", the Virgin Queen, chose not to marry; still, she insisted on a bevy of gallants paying court to her, until the day she died, as though their one object was to marry her. When she was seventy, and the favourite of the month, Robert, Earl of Essex, was aged twenty, this would have seemed ludicrous – but for Elizabeth's timeless power to dazzle. "When she smiled," wrote her godson, Sir John Harington, "it was pure sunshine that everyone did choose to bask in if they could." "Blessed are they that can be away and live contented," wrote another observer of the Court.

Increasingly through Elizabeth's reign, the Court and London became the focal point of the kingdom; the county magnates found that their territorial

Lady Anne Clifford, when Countess of Dorset. Despite the splendour of her dress and surroundings, Lady Anne was unhappy in this and in her second marriage. "The marble pillars of Knole in Kent and Wilton in Wiltshire were to me but the gay arbours of anguish," she wrote.

power was the less, as favours and privileges and even judgment against them could be obtained up in Town. By the end of the century, appalling debt had reduced both household and estates of improvident landlords like the Berkeleys. Others reduced their establishments in the country in order to cut a fine figure necessary at Court. Costly jewellery was much used in adornment of clothes, for instance. In 1517 four hundred and fifty ounces of gold, and eight hundred and fifty pearls were taken from the robes of Henry VIII for re-use. The liking for jewelled clothes did not abate; in 1617 Lady Anne Clifford sent to the Queen "the skirts of a white satin gown all pearled and embroidered with colours which cost me fourscore pounds without the satin."

The Middle Ages had not seen much variation in female costume. The lady's gown with trailing ends and long sleeves tucked up to encumber her hands, her hood or wimple, were serviceable year in, year out. Tudor England suffered from a surfeit of fashion. Ladies abandoned coifs, and took all morning to "fix" their hair. Well and truly fixed it was when they had finished. The Elizabethan lady dyed her hair blonde with rhubarb steeped in white wine; next she "curled frisled and crisped". Pomades and perfumes were applied and then she underpinned the structure with "forks, wires, & I can not tell what". Finally, wreaths of gold and silver, baubles and rings were hung about the edges of her "crisped snaky golden locks". To save time, she might instead wear a wig.

Hair dressing evidently took the most time, out of the gentlewoman's day. "Fixing the hair" is the chief complaint made of her both by husbands and playwrights. Beauty "purchas'd by the weight", or cosmetics, were also a source of discontent. The fashion was for red and white, and *ceruse* or white lead, and *fucus*, or rouge, dealt with the complexion. Eyebrows were kohl-blackened, plucked and pencilled, while belladonna enlarged the eyes. As for teeth, the best advice to a Tudor lady was to keep her mouth firmly closed.

The greatest innovation in clothing was the farthingale, or hoop, or "bumrole". This supported the lady's skirts, and at last left her hands free, where for centuries she had been picking up her train. (She swiftly filled her hands with nosegays.) Some of the fashions the Elizabethan court saw were surprising. In the 1590s the import of a French starch known as "Devil's liquor" made the introduction of the huge stiff lace ruffs of that period possible. The starch and stiffening used in Elizabethan bodices and stomachers, the unwieldy farthingales, led one observer to remark that the wearer looked like a trussed-up chicken on top of a big church bell. Elizabeth and some ladies of the Court made it the fashion to wear bodices which exposed the whole of their bosom. One cannot help thinking that the gentlewomen like Lady Mildmay who remained away from the lures of Court life and could wear that comfortable garment, the nightgown, all day, had an easier time.

To complement her array of handsome gallants at Court, Elizabeth kept a large selection of gentlewomen who would dance in the masque, and attend her out hunting, "all mounted on hackneys", and on her Progresses – and generally look attractive, but not too attractive. (Elizabeth had her ladies dress in white and silver, while she wore brilliant peacock colours.) Inevitably, some of the gay gallants let their eye wander for a moment from their monarch to her ladies. And she reacted with all the bitter jealousy of a rejected lover every time.

To Mary Shelton, Elizabeth "dealt liberal both with blows and evil words", and even broke Mary's finger in 1576, when the maid of honour asked permission to marry James Scudamore. Subsequently, the Queen forgave Mary her sin; she was not always so clement. Her maid of honour, Anne Vasavour, was known as something of a "drab", or tart. In 1581, Anne daringly gave birth to a son in the maidens' chamber, and the young Earl of Oxford, the father,

accepted paternity. The Queen heard of it, and committed Anne next day to the Tower. Oxford she pardoned after only a brief imprisonment.

As her reign progressed, the Queen found all her favourites lacking, except Christopher Hatton – or rather, only Hatton lacked a wife. None of the chief favourites dared admit to having married. Robert Dudley, Earl of Leicester, became a royal favourite after his teenage marriage to Amy Robsart. Amy came to Court once only – in the reign of Mary Tudor, never when Elizabeth succeeded, and made Leicester her Master of Horse. Amy's death at Kenilworth was not Dudley's doing – she probably died of a form of cancer – but it was regarded as such. When Leicester, as he became, married Lettice Knollys in 1578, he continued to pose as a forlorn widower adoring only his Queen. Her rage when she discovered the truth in 1579 was terrible. Lettice was not allowed to appear at Court. Furthermore, after Leicester's death in 1588, the Queen insisted that his goods be auctioned to meet his debts to the Crown, of £25,000 – and to ruin Lettice.

In the 1590s Elizabeth was again betrayed – this time by Sir Walter Raleigh. Some time in 1591, he seduced Bess Throckmorton, a lady of the Privy Chamber of no special beauty and of no fortune. She became pregnant and they married secretly. Bess remained at Court till February 1592, the month before she gave birth to a son, then put the child out to nurse and returned to her duties at Court. By now rumours were flying about, and in May the Queen discovered the truth. Into the Tower went the clandestine husband and wife. Sir Walter was released after five weeks: his lady wife remained in custody till the end of the year. The Raleighs then retired tactfully for ten years to Dorset.

The Queen was unable to stomach marriage outside as well as inside the precinct of her Court. Matthew Parker, her Archbishop of Canterbury, had met, while Chaplain to Henry VIII, a learned young gentlewoman, Margaret Harlestone. In 1540 he told her he loved her, but they "abstained from wedlock". Henry's Act of the Six Articles of 1537 had reaffirmed the celibacy of the clergy, and Margaret and Parker would not transgress the Act. Other clergy had wives who lived abroad, as Thomas Cranmer's wife did in Germany, or they married in defiance of the Act. Seven years later, under the reforming Edward VI, the Act of Permission for Clerical Marriage was passed, and Cranmer brought his wife home from Germany. Margaret became Mrs Parker. Two sons were born, and for a time the Parker family lived contentedly.

Then came Mary Tudor, the Catholic, in 1553, and the order that priests must "put away" their wives, or be deprived of their living. Parker wrote *The Defence of the Marriage of Priests* this same year, to no avail. Two-thirds of the clergy in England who were deprived, suffered because they were married. Parker was among them, and he, Margaret and the children went into separate hiding. With Elizabeth's accession, Parker reappeared and was chosen as Archbishop of Canterbury in 1559. He worked with Cecil and Bacon to make the Elizabethan Settlement, whereby the Anglican Church was put on a firm basis. However, Parker was unable to persuade the Queen to restore her brother's

Opposite: Lettice Knollys. Very low-necked bodices became fashionable at Court in the late sixteenth century. Astonishingly, it seems that some ladies followed prostitutes of the day and displayed fully exposed breasts.

statute of permission for the clergy to marry. As her father had ignored Cranmer's marriage, she ignored Parker's, and Margaret and the children had perforce to live in Cambridge.

Eventually Parker, miserable without his wife, brought her to Lambeth Palace, and established her there as 'Her Grace'. Margaret assumed the reins of the housekeeping, and her favourite injunction to her household was, "Keep it sweet and clean." Margaret appeared at all State occasions at the Palace; but she could not attend at Court, and, indeed, Parker had to struggle to have their children legitimised following Mary's annulment of the Edwardian Permission. Margaret, though styled "Her Grace", was still officially "Margaret Parker *alias* Harlestone".

The Queen's curiosity led her to visit Lambeth Palace at last, to see the improvements Parker had made. He had laid shingles in the Great Hall, made sewers, repaired the aquaducts and laid out the gardens. The Queen stayed to dine – and to see Margaret, of course. The occasion being concluded, Elizabeth thanked the Archbishop, then turned to the woman whose domestic happiness she had delighted to blight: "And you, Madam, I may not call you, and Mistress I am ashamed to call you, so I know not what to call you, but yet I do thank you." Thus Elizabeth began the tradition whereby patron ladies of the district delighted in snubbing their clerics' ladies. Lady Catherine de Burgh delivered no more masterly insult to Elizabeth Bennett than this.

Elizabeth Tudor was not a woman who liked other women to shine in her element, and Margaret Harlestone was a scholar of Latin and Greek, as Elizabeth was. Elizabeth liked the ladies of her realm to be busy embroidering hangings, which she would admire when she came to stay for a few days' hunting. The hunting field and her expertise in bringing down with her bow three or four driven stag thrilled Elizabeth. It is noteworthy that her lasting passion was for Leicester, her Master of the Horse and of the Royal Buckhounds.

Perhaps Elizabeth inherited her taste for archery from her mother. In 1530 Sir Harris Nicolas' Privy Purse expenses show a payment to the royal bowyer for three bows, shafts, belt, braces and shooting glove for "the Lady Anna Boleyn". Elizabeth's tutor, Ascham, was a keen advocate of archery as a noble and chivalrous skill. Elizabeth may have been enthused by his *Toxophilus*, printed in 1544, four years before he was appointed her reader. Other ladies of the sixteenth century are known to have enjoyed archery – both at the butts, and on the hunting field. Katherine, Lady Berkeley, delighted in her cross-bow and in hawking. A member of her household describes her, "keeping commonly a cast of two of merlins, which sometimes she mewed in her own chamber". Her gowns and kirtles were apparently sometimes unbecomingly spotted, as a result. By the time John Smyth of Nibley author of the *Lives of the Berkeleys . . . from 1066 to 1618* joined her service, Lady Berkeley was old and had abandoned her sporting life, but he saw her "bowes, arrowes, gloves, bracer, scarfe, and other ladylike accommodations". He heard from all that she "was in those days, among her servants, so good an archer at the butts, that her side by her was not

54

the weaker." When ladies were out in the hunting field with Elizabeth, they did well to sham ineptitude, however adept archers they might really be. Lady Desmond at Cowdray Park let many a "high-palmed hart" go by within range of her cross-bow, when the Queen was by her side.

Most gentlewomen rode out to the hunt, like Elizabeth's ladies on their hackneys, but then sheltered behind a palisade, and took no active part in the sport. As a result, the ladies who did hunt and bring down beasts acquired a certain glamour – and some followed Elizabeth in finding that the hunting field had a sexual thrill all its own. Lady Jane Grey's mother, Frances Suffolk, that keen huntswoman, married her groom, Adrian Stokes, after the execution of her first

Queen Elizabeth and her falconers flying their hawks at herons, in an illustration from Turberville's Book of Falconnerie *(1576). The Queen was an energetic sportswoman who enjoyed hunting with bow and arrows as well as with her hawks.*

husband The Queen expressed her shock, "What! Marry a horse-keeper?" Cecil answered slyly, "Yea, Madam, and she says you would like to do the same with yours." Hunting was ever a solace to Elizabeth. "Her daily music is the sweet cry of the hounds," was still the report in 1600, when she was over seventy. The hunt represented life and youth to her. When she died in 1603, it was at Richmond, "warm winter-box to shelter her old age", her favourite hunting-ground from childhood.

Diana Kirke
Cſs. of Oxford.

Content to Serve?

1600-1700

Opposite: Diana Kirke, later Countess of Oxford, by Sir Peter Lely (1618-80). Made Principal Painter in 1661 by Charles II, Lely depicted the chief ladies of the Restoration Court – characteristically with rumpled gown revealing an alluring expanse of bosom.

T HE PORCUPINE LOOK OF THE LATE TUDOR GENTLEWOMAN, with her barbaric ruff-points and stomacher stiff with jewels, dominates at the onset of the seventeenth century. From about 1625 onwards the outline softens with the Stuart fashion for billowing sleeves and skirts in unadorned softest silk. Farthingale, bodice and kirtle give way to basqued bodice, lace collar and cuffs, and a loosely gathered skirt; on top would be a gown of the same material. Ribbon knots are more common as decoration for clothes now than jewels, and hair descends from Tudor heights to frame the face with frizzed fringe andd side curls. The Puritan modes are not very different from those adopted by their more worldly sisters, black replaced Tudor "goose-turd" greens and "popinjay" blues as the fashionable colour throughout the early period and the Commonwealth. Sober woollen materials and avoidance of frivolous accoutrements, a display of

The family of Arthur, Lord Capel, (c. 1639), showing the Little Hadham gardens. Elizabeth, Lady Capel, was a knowledgeable horticulturalist, unusually for a gentlewoman of the period. Most ladies confined their gardening to sowing seed for essential vegetables and herbs.

modesty with tuckers, pinners and coifs, marked the dress of the devout Commonwealth lady, rather than any extreme plainness of style. The Restoration brought in French styles, heavy damasks and rich velvets. From 1680 the gown became the principal garment, open over an embroidered or quilted underskirt. The mantua, a loose wrapping gown, developed from the earlier nightgown to become a most sumptuous affair of drapery in silk (from Mantua in Italy which gave it its name), or in brocade or crêpe. By the end of the seventeenth century, embroidery and pattern had run riot; coloured stockings were fastened with jewelled garters, and a quantity of lace ruffles above silk elbow gloves were matched on the head by an edifice of lace tiers, called a *fontange*, which towered above curls piled high above the forehead. Fashion had come full circle, and a lady of fashion in 1690 had to spend all the hours her great-grandmother had a century before, dressing her empty head at her mirror.

The century had wrought one important change in the lady's lot. In 1690 her children might well be gathered round her mirror. "Placing out" was a custom which disappears in the seventeenth century. We see the gentlewoman experiencing intimate pleasures and pains of motherhood as her ancestresses had not. Domestic content was the ideal which gentlewomen – of whatever religious and political persuasion – strove to realise against the troubles of the century. Ladies no longer "bristled" with intelligence; their concerns now were all domestic. Before the Civil Wars they aimed to be virtuous, and a "crown to their husband"; during the Civil Wars and under the Commonwealth they tried

The Saltonstall Family, attributed to David des Granges, showing the lying-in of Sir Richard Saltonstall's wife, Elizabeth. Lyings-in became fashionable events in the seventeenth century, and sumptuous bed-hangings and apparel were often specially prepared.

to preserve their homes; after the Restoration, a certain holiday atmosphere prevailed, and, with it, they bestowed liberties and kindnesses on their children not generally their lot before.

Certain aspects of child nurture remained unchanged. Midwifery was still a hit-or-miss affair. Between 126 and 158 of every thousand children born in the first half of the seventeenth century died as infants; it was no very great advance that, in the second half, between 118 and 147 of every thousand perished. No figures are available for the deaths of mothers in childbirth, but harrowing accounts are preserved of ladies' labour – among them that of Mrs Frances Drax in the 1660s who had a dead child within her for several days. On a Saturday she went into labour, though her midwife did not recognise it as such. A doctor was called to supplement the midwife's endeavours, when it was understood that "the Child came wrong". He tried unsuccessfully to induce delivery of the dead child. "She growing faint and light-headed, begged of the Doctor for Christ's sake, to let her die at rest . . . we got her to bed, where she continued all that night without any rest, her spirits being spent by the flood of those, that came from her . . . the child dead within made her never lie still one moment." Mrs Drax was told death was inevitable – "she was very willing to die, and hoped God would receive her." When an autopsy was performed after her death, it was discovered that "her back bone was so bowed" as to make passage of "so much as . . .a limb of the Child" impossible.

If the baby survived, it was swaddled and put out to nurse as it had been in the preceding century. Hallowed by tradition, swaddling was questioned for the first time in the late seventeenth century. John Locke attacked the custom on health grounds in *Thoughts Concerning Education* (1693). He remarked that Spartan nurses had brought up their charges "admirably" without encasing them in bands. Far into the eighteenth century, mothers continued to swaddle their newborn infants, but an amount of baby clothes dating from the seventeenth century argue that they began to release them from their bands within the first year of existence. However, babies in effigy on church monuments of the late seventeenth century are evidently padded with bands beneath their cambric and lace chemise and mantle. In 1671 the celebrated midwife, Jane Sharp, advised a mixture of constriction and liberty which was probably general: "After four months let loose the arms but still roll [or swaddle] the breast and belly and feet to keep out cold air for a year." Was the infant of gentle birth, once swaddled, always put out to be fed by a wet-nurse? As in the previous century, physicians, writers of child nurture manuals, educationalists and busybodies exhorted the mother to feed her baby herself. The character of the wet-nurse was believed to affect the child she nursed – by some mysterious osmotic transference. Thomas Phaer, author of the first compilation of childhood diseases, thought that, in addition to "bad conditions and inclinations", a wet-nurse "of vile complexion and worse manners" might also communicate some "imperfections of her body" to her charge. "Would I let my child . . . suck the milk of a servant, and mingle the royal blood with the blood of a servant?" asked James I's wife, Queen Anne.

The old fear of "overlaying" continued. The Countess of Lincoln exhorted her daughter-in-law to nurse her own children in *The Countess of Lincolnes Nurserie* (1622). She regretted now that she had nursed none of her own eighteen infants, and commented: "I fear the death of one or two of my little babes came by the default of their nurses." But Lady Lincoln reveals other factors which decided mothers of the upper classes not to feed their babies themselves. Milk stained their dresses, feeding interfered with their social duties like "going to the play". (There was the additional factor that a nursing mother with a baby in the bed supposedly felt less eager to resume sexual relations with her husband.) In *Ten Pleasures of Marriage* (1685), the playwright, Aphra Behn, comments on putting a baby out to nurse: ". . . both you and your wife are freed from tossing and tumbling with it in the night." Lady Lincoln protested that it was "the express ordinance of God that mothers should nurse their own children", and she cited the case of Elizabeth who had despite her advanced age, given her breast to John the Baptist to suck – and there was milk.

Gentlewomen of Puritan belief took the duty of nursing their children themselves seriously. For others, it was a question of fashion, or of personal preference. *The Queen's Closet Opened*, being "true copies of her Majesty's [Henrietta Maria's] own receipt books", was published in 1655. It contains one treatment: "To make a woman have a nipple that hath none, and would give suck", and another: "To dry up milk in a woman's breast". The choice, to nurse or to put out to nurse, with the various moral, social and religious connotations, was in the seventeenth century a dilemma only the mother of upper social strata confronted. It has its echo in the general debate about breast or bottle feeding today. Frances, Lady Hatton said it all in 1678. She longed: "to suck my poor child myself but my sore nipples would not give me leave . . . I am resolved if ever I should have another I must try again. Everybody is against it."

The country became much favoured as a healthy home for the child put out to nurse, as families spent more time in Town, and London enlarged. Fear of the plague which attacked London in 1603 and in 1665 with severity, as well as in other years, also fostered a belief in the innocent virtues of the countryside. Once back in the bosom of the family the baby was, indiscriminately of sex, dressed in "long clothes", rather than bands, then "short coats", or a frock to the feet, and then skirt and doublet with leading reins, "pudding and muckinder". At the age of seven came the great divide. Boys were "breeched", or put into long trunks, or breeches, according to the fashion of the time,

The boy-child's discarding of his skirts was something of an event. It marked the curtailment of his life in the domestic, female orbit, and of his mother's responsibility for him. Her pride in him increased. In 1641 little Thomas Slingsby was breeched early because Lady Slingsby "had a desire to see him in them how proper a man he would be." The little gentlewoman had no ceremony to mark her emergence into public life, nor did she so emerge or go to school – if she went at all – till some time after her brother had begun his Latin and rhetoric at his grammar school. Interest in female education of an academic

kind continued in the doldrums where it had begun the century. There are payments for paper and quills for the Ladies Diana and Margaret Russell's lessons at Woburn Abbey from 1646 to 1651. It was an economy, while their brothers were at home, to share their lessons and tutor. The boys, and not the girls, however, learnt Latin from Comenius' *Orbis Pictus*. "Yes, but can she spin?" King James had asked, weary of being told of some paragon's fluency in languages and literary abilities. Latin only made women "more cunning", he asserted, though his own daughter, Elizabeth of Bohemia, was carefully educated in it, as well as in French and Italian. As we have seen, Elizabeth I had done little to encourage learning in other women; the Court was swift to follow

Lady Anne Clifford, a panel of The Great Picture *from Appleby Castle, celebrating her succession in 1646 to her father's Northern estates. The portraits on the closet wall courteously recall her earlier marriages in the South, which she thereafter visited with distaste.*

King James's lead, and bolster the prejudice against higher education for females not of royal blood which had developed during the late Elizabethan period. Lady Anne Clifford had a voracious appetite for reading all her life, but it must be in translation if it were a book in Latin or French; her father had expressly forbidden her to learn foreign languages, as useless to a woman.

Once the boys went off to Westminster School, the Russell ladies' tutorial expenses are for dancing masters and music teachers. French was taught to them, admittedly, as it was not to Lady Anne. Queen Henrietta Maria had done much to bring the language and manners of her native land to prominence on

her arrival in England in 1625. Till that date, and from about 1580, things Italian were all the rage. The Queen, aged fifteen on her arrival, was almost completely illiterate, and hopelessly ignorant of the English language. Conversation was her retreat, and she chattered away night and day in French to the attendants who came with her from home to ease her homesickness – when she was not dancing. The personal preferences of the frivolous young Queen were widely copied. The most stolid courtiers mouthed French phrases if they could not converse in the language at length. Dancing masters and French tutors – best of all, French dancing masters – became prized members of society, and French romances were read in the original with great enthusiasm. Mlle de Scudéry's *Le Grand Cyrus*, published in ten volumes between 1649 and 1653, was probably the most widely read and enjoyed of all the romances from across the Channel. "I would willingly have the French book you write me word of," wrote Brilliana, Lady Harley, to her son at Oxford. "I had rather read anything in that tongue than in English."

Though Charles I complained that his wife would never learn any English if she confined her circle to French speakers, the passion for "French conversation" which she instituted was of some benefit to the ordinary gentlewoman of the seventeenth century. As "placing out" faded, girls might remain at home till of an age suitable for marriage. There was no onus on them, as there had been "in service", to be a credit to their "mistress", and to dress brilliantly, or to display musical or choric talents, *or* to converse amiably and amusingly. Living at home they might enjoy the benefits of a warm relationship with their parents. Dorothy Sidney's mother treasured her daughter, she told her husband, next to him and above all else in the world. In 1685 John Evelyn mourned the death of his graceful daughter, Mary: "nothing affected but natural and easy as well in her deportment as in her discourse". He had observed her closely. She had sung and played the harpsichord charmingly, and her dancing and talent for recitation, though known only in the home, were equally pleasing. Daughters of young widows often testify to the close care they lavished on their children. Following her husband's execution after the Rye House Plot of 1683, Rachel Lady Russell was left with two daughters aged nine and seven and a son of three. Cried up as a pattern of widowhood, by 1703 she had succeeded in making her son a very wealthy Duke and her two daughters Duchesses. Equally, estranged wives might prove excellent mothers. Lady Anne Clifford's mother, Margaret, Countess of Cumberland, was a tiger in defence of her daughter's Northern inheritance, and promoted her welfare, spiritual and domestic, all their joint lives. When the Countess died in 1654, her daughter erected the "Countess' Pillar" on a desolate Westmorland road, to mark the spot where they had embraced and parted for the last time.

Amiable and maternal relationships might flourish where girls sheltered at home till marriage. Their education, however, could be sketchy or consist almost entirely of very worthy instruction in household management. Needlework and music were the only skills which, it was taken for granted, must be

Content to Serve?

taught – how else would a lady pass a winter evening, except at her needle or at her lute or viol? It became noticeable, when young gentlewomen finally emerged from their childhood country homes, that they were wholly unfitted for social intercourse. Hannah Woolley, the wife of a school teacher in Newport and author of *A Gentlewoman's Companion, or a Guide to the Female Sex* (1675) commented on this awkwardness: "many Country Gentlewomen stand like to many Mutes or Statues when they have hapned into the company of the ingenious; their quaint expressions have seem'd to them Arabian sentences and have stared like so many distracted persons in that they should hear the sound of English and yet understand but here and there a word of their own language."

An illustration from an English song book, one of the many collections of words and music which were published for domestic use in the later seventeenth century. Musical accomplishments were only acquired by ladies with leisure – and were thus proof of gentility.

Lessons from a French schoolmaster might tinge the "natural and easy" deportment and discourse which Evelyn had approved in his Mary. Still, if the fashionable French master succeeded in persuading his mute pupil to understand the art of conversation, this must be an improvement.

Perhaps fortunately for their future husbands and families, not all gentlewomen remained at home till marriage. The seventeenth century saw an explosion of boarding schools for young ladies which replaced, in some measure, both nunneries and the system of "placing out" as establishments where a measure of education could be won. Boarding schools were particularly popular with City merchants; these parents recognised their own and their daughters' social deficiencies where country gentlefolk did not. In Hackney, Islington and other salubrious villages north of the City of London, girls' schools burgeoned. Here the French master and the dancing and deportment master ruled supreme, with needlework and music sometimes reaching surprising levels of competence. In Hackney Mrs Perwick started a school in 1643 which became celebrated for the musical education it offered. Simon Ives, contributor to song

books like *Playford's Collections*, and Lay Vicar of St Paul's, taught singing; Albert Bryne, composer and organist at St Paul's, taught the harpsichord. The best advertisement for the various visiting masters' attentions was Mrs Perwick's own daughter, Susanna. She gave highly acclaimed performances on the violin, played the lute and harpsichord besides, and led other girls of the school in a chamber music orchestra. Musicians like Henry Lawes and John Jenkins came to the school to hear her perform, and her fame made the school popular with the nobility and gentry from all over England. Over a hundred girls at a time – each with their maid – boarded together at Mrs Perwick's. They danced country and French dances which Susanna and the dancing master, Mr Hazard,

Mirror frame (c. 1665), with silver thread, pearl, chenille and silks, framed in tortoise-shell. Seventeenth-century ladies forswore precise, geometric designs for their needlework, and decorated treasured objects with a hotch-potch of brilliant insects, animals and biblical scenes.

devised; they learnt how to walk and how to hold the head, perform deep and more perfunctory curtsies, they studied the *Book of Demeanour* (1619) and, later, the *Rules of Civility*, translated in 1671. They laboured at the samplers or at the "stumpwork" which were now both popular work for the needle.

Drawing and painting appear, surprisingly, on school curricula from 1600 and before. These lessons taught girls to copy freehand designs for their needlework. Earlier, they had traced these with pinpricks and charcoal powder from books. Few gentlewomen learnt to paint or draw for its own sake. Anne Heather, a ward of the Court of Aldermen, was placed at Mrs Friend's school in Stepney in 1628, to be instructed in "learning at her needle, writing, musick and

Content to Serve?

other qualities" in return for £21 a year. Beyond these staples, the proprietors of the schools did not attempt to go, nor were they expected to provide any sounder education.

Needlework was the chief expression permitted of an artistic talent, and gentlewomen in the seventeenth century composed some striking needlework pictures. Biblical scenes like the Annunciation or the Sacrifice of Abraham were popular and might be woven in silk thread on to canvas and then treated as a picture and framed and hung. Ounces of gold and silver thread feature in the accounts for girls' education; these might equally be used for needlework pictures, or in the "stumpwork" with which gentlewomen covered Bibles, boxes, caskets, mirror backs and all mannor of trinkets. "Stump work", or "raised work", began in the normal way by stitching in silk designs drawn on fabric, usually canvas. The designs for "stump work" were again often biblical. It is a feature of much needlework of the seventeenth century that birds walk as tall as kings, and ladies dwarf trees, but in turn are miniature beside the cats at their side. Drawing masters do not seem to have noticed this quarrel with the laws of perspective, or have attempted to introduce a sense of proportion into their pupils' work till late in the century. Blithely, the ladies continued to copy exactly, size and all unaltered, from their design books to their canvas. Once the canvas had been drawn upon, it was then glued to the object it was to cover, and beneath certain prominent features of the design – like the men and women or the birds and animals – wool or wood blocks were placed to "raise" the design. The effect of the embroidered padding, of lively design and bright with colour, with which our gentlewomen decked their personal treasures is at once amateur and delightful.

Samplers were now a wearisome task prescribed by the school authorities. At least, "stumpwork" and needlework pictures were stitched by ladies till their eyesight failed them; only girls of school age among the upper classes worked samplers. They had ceased to be solely repositories of different stitches, as an increasing variety of needlework books, new and foreign, showing stitches were printed. A sampler was proof that a girl knew her alphabet, and her numbers, so that she could mark household linen. She had mastered an assortment of stitches, and she was familiar with blackwork, whitework and other techniques like cut-and-drawn work – a kind of crocheting. The completion of her sampler was equivalent to her young brother's breeching; her education was completed.

Besides needlework, teaching of handicrafts, or "curious inventions" featured in the prospectuses of many superior girls' schools. These "inventions" might be work with straw, wax, or feathers, glass or "bugle beads". This work was designed to encourage dexterity in pupils, and to ward off idle hours, Satan's delight. It was also an opportunity for the lady to give proof of her innate gentility. If her house were covered with straw baskets and beaded bell-pulls, then here was proof of idle hours of the most genteel quality, when others were doing menial household tasks and she was at leisure to fashion such trinkets. (In the 1660s Mrs Pepys spent hours sticking shells on to boxes to give

65

the impression, at least, that she was a lady of leisure.) The fashion for handicrafts or "curious inventions" was rooted in a strange misunderstanding of Bacon's *Advancement of Learning* (1605). This great educationalist urged that nature should be studied by observing the facts of nature, and thereby general principles would be discovered. Comerius, disciple of Bacon, spoke of "sensibles", and suggested that all tangible things should be presented to the touch, visible things the sight and so on. This was the beginning of elementary science teaching. Proprietors of girls' schools, urging on their pupils to experiment with collages of feathers and gummed paper, could not have misunderstood the notions of applied science more completely. The teaching of handicrafts, nevertheless, joined needlework and music and dancing, the staples of the seventeenth century feminine education, as youths like Robert Boyle and John Locke began lessons in science and natural philosophy.

Still, what use would academic subjects and ancient languages be to gentlewomen who were going to lead fashionable lives, and administer large households? The merchants' daughters had no intention of making a career for themselves, any more than their noble sisters. Learning was of little use to them. As City wives they would beat the apprentice, and as City widows perhaps manage the business on their husbands' death. But their mothers managed that without knowledge of history or mathematics. If they achieved their fathers' dearest wish and lured a nobleman into marriage, then all the less need to have an education. Elizabeth Cradock, or 'Widow Bennett", was a mercantile agent's daughter from Staffordshire who pursued an immensely successful marital campaign. Her merchant husband, Richard Bennett, left her a fortune on his death in 1628 and she could then select her next husband from four ardent suitors. She chose Sir Heneage Finch, Recorder of London, of Kensington House; Anne, the daughter she bore to him, became Viscountess Conway. All this Widow Bennett achieved without education – though it must be noted that her daughter Anne became a philosopher admired by Leibnitz. We might think, what would Widow Bennett herself have been, if educated?

For all the social and conversational opportunities which boarding schools offered, bookish girls probably did best to remain at home and, behind "mute" faces, develop their minds by reading, not conversing. It was fortunate for Elizabeth Tanfield, Lady Falkland, that few boarding schools existed when she was growing up. Born in 1585, she taught herself Latin and Hebrew at home. On marriage, she enraged her mother-in-law by refusing to humour her conceit. Lady Cary then locked Elizabeth in her chamber: "which . . . she little cared for but entertained herself with reading." Enraged, Lady Carey "took away all her books, with command to have no more brought to her." Even this punishment was vain. Elizabeth "set herself to make verses". Lady Falkland would have been quite unsuited to the frivolous life of a boarding school.

Other perils besides a frivolous atmosphere might dissuade the conscientious parent from sending a daughter to a fashionable school. The pursuit of heiresses was not an uncommon sport in the seventeenth century, and the

boarding schools in Hackney were a favourite haunt of fortune-hunters. They considered, often rightly, that cooped up together, the pupils would be bored and ripe for coquetry and blandishing words. The rural quiet made assignations easy – and the kidnapping, too, if the girl would not consent to run away.

Sara Cox was a rich orphan, and ward "of the City of London", who suffered for her inheritance. In 1637, aged fourteen, she attended Mrs Winch's boarding school in Hackney where she struck up a friendship with a Miss Fulwood. Katherine Fulwood's brother, Roger, was struck by Sara's prospects and had his sister propose marriage on his behalf. Sara would have none of it – whereupon Roger engaged "an array of horsemen with drawn swords" to seize her. He bundled her into a coach, and carried her off – to the Bishop of Winchester's house in Southwark. In these respectable surroundings, with Roger's mother Lady Fulwood presiding, Sara's fears were lulled – but, next morning, on the pretext of being shown over the house, she was lured into the chapel. A minister waited and she was forcibly married to Roger, then hurried up to a bedchamber, stripped naked, and placed in bed with her new husband. Fortunately for Sara, help was at hand, officers of the law arrived, and Roger was arraigned for his life, for the offence of abducting a woman for "the lucre of their substance". He was pardoned, but released only when he had in turn released Sara from her unwanted marriage by agreeing to a suit of nullity.

Stumpwork picture of David and Bathsheba (1656). Stumpwork was a seventeenth-century phenomenon. Motifs in an embroidered, often biblical scene, were raised with wool or wood underneath, and then framed as a picture, or used to cover a precious Bible.

As the century proceeded, a few protested against the "pride and wantonness" which characterised many of the girls' schools. D'Urfey's comedy, *Love for Money, or the Boarding School* (c.1690) satirises the short commons on which the avaricious proprietresses kept their pupils. "Cut a hundred and fifty pieces of bread and butter round the loaf", the cook-maid is ordered; the greedy pupils take bites at this, while endeavouring to practise a trill at the same time. Hardly an example of elegant refinement.

In the 1640s, Lettice Lady Falkland was an early critic of the schooling available to girls. She was, admittedly, unusually bookish, like her mother-in-law, Elizabeth. This, as well as her beauty, may have attracted her husband Lucius Cary, later Viscount Falkland, who was a chief ornament of Charles I's Court. The outrage when he married in 1630 a Miss Lettice Morison, of no importance and bringing no dowry, was commensurate with his popularity. The oddest reasons – she looked like her brother, whom he had loved – were put forward to account for the love-match. Lucius felt the fault he committed against his father in bringing no fortune into the family, and offered to resign his estate. Nevertheless, he insisted on marrying his Lettice. Thirteen years later, at the age of thirty-three, he was killed at the first battle of Newbury and the love-match was over.

Lettice became very devout in the brief widowhood which followed. She died, aged only thirty-five and from no apparent cause except grief, six years

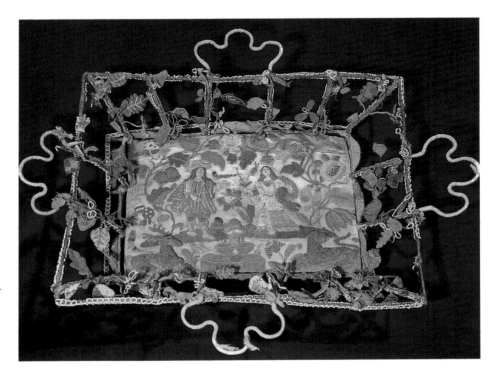

Open-wire basket, with satin base (c. 1670). Beadwork or "buglework" came next top after "needlework of very different sorts" in the list of accomplishments on which Mrs Hannah Woolley, author of The Gentlewoman's Companion *(1675) prided herself.*

Content to Serve?

Portraits of Charles II and Catherine of Braganza, in rolled gilt and coloured paper (1660). An example of the predilection among aspirant gentlewomen for "curious inventions". To emphasise the leisure at their disposal, they exhausted themselves tricking out household items with fancywork.

after her husband in 1649. In the interim she proposed a plan to found "places for the education of young Gentlewomen and for retirement of Widows (as Colleges and the Inns of Court and Chancery are for men) in several parts of the Kingdom". These colleges would be secular sanctuaries of learning and repose, she affirmed, but the comfort the nunneries had once afforded widows wishing retirement from the world is clearly in her mind. A century had passed since the convents had closed; the shoddy education they had provided had been forgotten. There was, however, no reason why educated women should not be the teachers in the new colleges Lettice envisaged. Her idea foundered in the uncertainties of the period; in 1697 Mary Astell reintroduced the idea of the collegiate school, "a Seminary to stock the Kingdom with pious and prudent Ladies, and . . . to expel that cloud of Ignorance which Custom has involv'd us in." Unfortunately, Mary Astell's *Serious Proposal to the Ladies for the Advancement of their True and Greatest Interest* defined the school of her dreams as "A Monastery or Religious Retirement". The project foundered, and the heiresses who were to be "kept secure from the rude attempts of designing suitors" and the "daughters of decayed gentlemen", who were to have been accepted as incumbents and teachers, if the revenues of the house could support such charity, had to look elsewhere for their education and livelihood.

A governess or schoolmistress of the quality of Elizabeth Elstob, "the

Saxon Maid" who had pioneered Anglo-Saxon studies while living at Oxford with her brother, was not appreciated. After his death, Elizabeth tried to find pupils for a dame school, but was nervous that she could not offer spinning or knitting. If only Mary Astell had opened her "college". Miss Elstob was sadly out of place out of a university setting, and could be of little use in such establishments as the school Hannah Woolley boasted of having started, where "Setting out of Banquets" and "All manner of Cookery" featured, together with buglework, or sewing of beads on to reticules. But then the pupils who attended such a school would not find Anglo-Saxon much use, either.

There was one group of English gentlewomen who did have the opportunity in the Civil War period, and before, to acquire a proper education. These were the daughters of Catholic noblemen and gentlemen. From about 1610 onwards, it became safer for English Catholics to send their sons to be educated in the Catholic faith at St Omer, and then the English College at Rome. Their daughters travelled, sometimes under arduous or dangerous conditions, to convents in Holland, or Italy. Education on Catholic lines in England was an extremely hazardous affair. Gentlewomen in traditional Catholic or recusant strongholds like Yorkshire and Derbyshire ran secret schools which prepared pupils for later despatch to seminaries abroad. One such was run by Lord Vaux's daughter, Anne, in her old age in Derbyshire in the 1620s; she taught both boys and girls Latin so that they could follow the Mass. (Puritan teachers encouraged literacy among boys and girls equally for similar reasons. Reading the Bible was an important part of Puritan worship.)

Another gentlewoman who courted danger in efforts to provide a fitting education for her fellow Catholics was Mary Ward from York. She took the veil as a Poor Clare at St Omer. Between 1608 and 1618, however, she led a daring existence in England, "disguised" as a normal lady of fashion in rich silks and taffeta and paying visits round the country to other ladies of equal apparent frivolity. In reality, at the meetings which Mary held in her friends' houses, they said Mass, and she recruited young gentlewomen for the boarding school she founded at St Omer. Government spies were always busy trying to stop her. With Queen Henrietta Maria's arrival from France in 1625, and her patronage, Mary was able to establish some Catholic schools in England in the late 1630s; the royal family's flight from London ended that, and by 1645 Mary, having lived through the siege of York, in her native county, was dead.

The difficulties posed for Catholic parents wishing to educate children in their religion at home were immense. Most chose to send their progeny abroad. On the Continent there were fine scholars and teachers among the nuns; Catholic noblewomen such as Lady Frances Paulet or Lady Catherine Talbot emerged, enhanced by their convent education, in the 1640s, and acted as patrons to the group of English Catholic poets and literary men, including the poets Richard Crashaw and Edward Thimelby, who formed a clique in exile in Rome. There exists a collection of verses written by these Catholic poets in the mid-seventeenth century, called *Tixall Poetry*; the titles call to mind the joys

and trials of the Catholic gentlewomen who settled and brought up families abroad. "On the Death of the Lady Catherine White, in Childbirth at Rome" was written by Lady Catherine's brother-in-law, the poet Thomas White (or Blacklo) in 1645. There is a monumental inscription to match the poem in the church of the English College at Rome, telling of the husband and five children who survived this esteemed daughter of the Duke of Portland. A more cheering work was dedicated to the Lady Anne Brudenell by the Catholic priest, Richard Lassels. *The Way How to Heare Masse* was composed in 1644 in Paris, where Lady Anne was living with her husband, Richard, later Earl of Cardigan, and her children. It is a most amusing condemnation of the slack attendance and observance of the Mass by English Catholics which Lassels had noted in Paris and elsewhere. Do not miss Mass because it is cold, or the streets are wet, he urged – it is not the play you are going to. Let children, if they are brought to church, kneel before their parents, and not be left to wander and chatter at will. (This may have been meant with particular reference for Lady Anne and her progeny.) We receive an exact impression of the fashionable English Catholic exile loth to do her religious duty, half-occupied with the colour of the ribbons on her gown, hushing quarrelsome children – and of the priest, Lassels, striving to confine her attention to the Word of the Lord.

Though Richard Brudenell was a Catholic, it was not to escape the swingeing fines for non-attendance at the Anglican service that he and his family had left home. Theirs was a time-honoured reason for living abroad –

Two paintings from a series commemorating the life of Mary Ward, a Yorkshire Catholic gentlewoman who travelled abroad to become a Poor Clare at St Omer. Against opposition, she founded convents and Catholic schools all over the Continent.

Richard was heavily in debt. Lady Anne's mother, the Countess Rivers, supported them, providing an annuity of £400. In 1642 the Countess's home in England was sacked and she probably joined the Brudnells abroad. Her other daughter, Elizabeth, had married another Catholic in exile, Sir John Thimelby, great-nephew of Anne Vaux in Derbyshire. The trauma of the loss of her home, her close acquaintance with these cultured exiles, brought the Countess to convert to Catholicism before her death in 1650. We find in *Tixall Poetry* lines by Edward Thimelby, poet brother of Sir John, "On the death of the Countess of Rivers"; a poem surviving in *Tixall Poetry* of five years later shows that the Catholic community continued to be close-knit abroad during the Commonwealth years. Mrs Henry Thimelby expressed the community's anxious hopes for her sister-in-law, in "To the Lady Elizabeth Thimelby on New Years Day 1655 Looking daily for her son from travail".

In the Civil Wars and afterwards, during the Commonwealth, there were several Anglican gentlewomen who, like the Countess Rivers, found respite from their sufferings in the Catholic faith. As England discovered to its cost in the early 1670s, James Duke of York, later James II, had become a Catholic. Of less constitutional importance but of equal interest is the conversion of Su, Countess of Denbigh. Su Denbigh was wholly committed to the King's cause. As lady-in-waiting to Queen Henrietta Maria, she accompanied her royal mistress to Holland in an effort to raise money and troops. Her husband, the Earl of Denbigh, was equally committed and fought in 1642, aged sixty, at Edgehill, the first battle of the Civil Wars. On the Parliamentary side at that battle was Basil, Lord Feilding, son and heir of the Denbighs. "I shall suffer more for the ways you take than ever I did to bring you into this world," his mother wrote to him. In 1743 the Earl was fatally wounded at Birmingham; Basil, hastening to visit him under a flag of truce, found him already dead. His adherence to the Parliamentary side was now "hideous and monstrous", his mother told him. Betty Bourchier, daughter of the Earl of Bath and Basil's third wife, was more supportive. She expressed her joy at being two years married to him in practical terms – ate three cherry pies, drank his health with his niece Su, and dispatched to him cake and candied borage and marigolds. Her mother-in-law went abroad to Paris, and was soon friend and patron to the Catholic poet, Richard Crashaw. "What Heaven-entreated heart is this/ Stands trembling at the gate of bliss?" he wrote to her. His suasions and the piety of the English gentlewomen who ran a convent in Paris had their effect. In 1650 she converted to the Catholic faith.

What of the women who refused to leave their homes and castles? While our Catholic ladies were performing Grand Tours of Italy – a century before this cultural experience was widely available to English women – and devout Anglicans in Paris were endeavouring to develop a taste for "potage" and "legumes", the majority of gentlewomen considered their duty was to preserve their house or castle against all comers. The Countess of Derby was staunch in defence of Lathom House near Warrington, when Sir Thomas Fairfax and the Parliamentarians besieged it in 1643. Her husband, the Earl, was away on the

Queen's business, and Charlotte, Lady Derby, was left with two daughters, the Ladies Mary and Katherine Stanley, to combat Fairfax with what wits she possessed. Lady Derby took advantage of her status as chief lady of the North; she refused to exit from her fortress to "treat" with Fairfax, "conceiving it more knightly that Sir Thomas Fairfax should wait upon her, than she upon him". Nor would she accept the safe conduct repeatedly offered to her by her besiegers, who were highly embarrassed by their opponent's sex and noble birth. Fairfax's great mortar pounded the wall, but the Countess stayed firm and, as for her daughters, "the little ladies had stomach to digest cannon" a diarist of the siege assures us. The Countess had, as her military chief within Lathom House, one Captain Farmer, and he successfully led a party to capture the besiegers' main weapon, the mortar. Later in the year, Prince Rupert of the Rhine arrived to relieve the besieged company. Still, the commanding officer of the enemy, Colonel Rigby, knew whom he had to thank for his humiliation – he was "sick of Shame and dishonour, to be routed by a lady and a handful of men".

The Countess of Derby was a haughty autocrat, who showed her mettle on other occasions. Some gentlewomen, however, emerged from obscurity during the Civil Wars to show lion-hearted courage in defence of their homes, and, after the Wars, sank thankfully into obscurity once more. This passionate love of house and home, overriding affection for husband and children, was an intrinsic feature of the English gentlewoman's life in every period. In her patient defence of her home against besieging forces in the Civil Wars, lies the most impressive testament to this quiet passion. Lady Bankes of Corfe Castle in Dorset was one heroine who, unlike the Lady Derby or the Marchioness of Winchester, had caused no stir before the Civil Wars. Her husband Sir John was a lawyer who bought Corfe Castle about 1634; the couple lived quietly there in great comfort with white dimity hangings in "my lady's bedroom", a silk quilted carpet for the withdrawing-room, and crimson velvet throughout.

Lady Bankes was alone here in 1643 when the local Parliamentary Committee at Poole required her to give up the four guns the castle housed. She had a garrison of only five men; the whole town of Poole was against her, and, if she insisted on defending the castle, a siege was inevitable. She played for time, gave up the guns, took advantage of the lull in hostilities to lay in extra provisions. Fifty men came to supplement her garrison, and she had a mass of devoted maidservants to supplement them. When the siege began in June, Lady Bankes herself, with her daughters and her maids, defended the upper section of the castle, and sprayed the besiegers with hot embers to deter them from scaling the walls. "The loyalty and resolution of this honourable Lady" saved the day, and the besiegers fled at last on hearing a report that the King's troops were approaching.

Lady Bankes remained at Corfe free from further attack till December 1645, when Sir Thomas Fairfax came besieging. Lady Bankes' husband had died a year before but she showed no less tenacity in defending Corfe again. It was only after several months and owing to treachery that the Parlimentarians won

the day, and "slighted" Lady Bankes' splendid home, crimson velvet and all. She was allowed to depart in safety, honoured and admired by all sides.

Many devout Protestant families had followed the harassed Catholics abroad in the 1640s, when the Puritan restrictions of the Long Parliament threatened their freedom to worship in High Anglican form. Following the destruction of their property and sequestration of their estates in the late 1640s, more followed, and many newly impoverished members of the English gentry and nobility were to be found living in discomfort on the French seaboard. Mary, Lady Verney, was among these voluntary exiles. Her father-in-law, the Royalist Sir Edmund Verney, fell at Edgehill in 1642. Mary then left for France

Mary, Lady Bankes, one of many châtelaines who emerged from obscurity in the Civil Wars to defend her home with remarkable wit and courage and, having endured, returned to domesticity.

in 1643 with her husband, newly Sir Ralph, and children, Peg and Edmund, aged five and seven. In 1644 Sir Ralph was duly named a delinquent, and his estates sequestered. Far from seeking consolation in religion for this rebuff, Lady Varney's one aim was to recover the estates at Claydon for her husband. It was generally felt that, in petitioning the Government for return of estates and reversal of attainders, the women of the family stood most chance of success. "I am confident if you were here, you would . . . instruct your wife, and leave it to her to act it with Committees," wrote a friend to Ralph in 1646. Supplication was, after all, a role traditional to women since antiquity; tears might soften hard hearts, where reasoned arguments never would.

Content to Serve?

So Lady Verney crossed to London in late 1646, incidentally knowing she was pregnant, with just her faithful gentlewoman, Luce, for company. "I never had so sad a time in all my life," she wrote to Ralph. First she must obtain a certificate of sequestration from the Buckinghamshire Committee which had imposed the measure; this Committee proved "very malicious and extremely insolent", and only granted her the certificate in April. Her baby, a boy, was born on 3 June in London, and she immediately went with him down to Claydon to visit her four-year-old Jack, whom she had left with her husband's disagreeable spinster sisters. In the general sequestration of estates and destruction of property, many gentlewomen found themselves without any portion at all, and this was the fate of Su, Pen, Peg, Molly and Betty Verney. They sat at Claydon, growing steadily more discontented – more disagreeable to any suitors who might offer. At last, because they were bred and trained for nothing else, they married – beneath their station – and had the satisfaction of seeing their husbands turn out most unsatisfactory.

Claydon, once Lady Verney's polished pride, was in a miserable condition. Worse was to come. Baby Ralph died of convulsions, leaving his mother delirious from grief for forty-eight hours. Poor Lady Verney had yet to learn that in France at the same time six-year-old Peg had died too. And still she had the ticklish business of presenting the prized certificate of sequestration together with her petition to the House of Commons. Only in January 1648 did the Committees at Westminster lift the order, and Mary could return to her "dearest Rogue", Ralph, in France. Triumphing over poverty and privation, she had achieved her end. The year and a half of responsibility and suffering in England had taken its toll, however, and Mary was to live only another two years. In the spring of 1650 she fell ill with consumption and gallant Mary, Sir Ralph's "deare dear" died, aged thirty-four.

The woes of English gentlewomen during the Civil Wars and under the Commonwealth, were considerable. Their very attachment to their property made them susceptible to anxieties and griefs, which brought premature death on many of them. We have noted the difficulties newly dowerless daughters faced. There were also problems at law for their newly widowed mothers; whether or not their husbands had been branded "delinquent", they should still be entitled to their jointure, their widows' pension. But this jointure was often sequestrated with the "delinquent's" estate, and had to be begged back from one of the unfriendly Committees at Westminster. (When Margaret, Duchess of Newcastle, appeared there, she found the members so rude that she turned round and left in disgust.)

Still, under the Commonwealth there was still enjoyment to be gleaned for some. In the late 1650s appeared the first of a series of literary ladies, Katherine Philips or the Matchless Orinda. A product of a Hackney school, she was a cheerful, bourgeois woman who read French and Italian with ease, and translated two Corneille plays, *Pompey* and *Horace*, besides publishing a slim volume of poetry, and one slimmer still of letters. The Matchless Orinda's

works lack interest today, but they pleased her friends, and it pleased her to be an author. Her businessman husband pleased her too, though she was sixteen when they married and he, fifty-four. She revelled in the literary circle she made of her friends by the easy expedient of christening them all with poetic soubriquets. Mary Aubrey was Rosania; Anne Owen, Lucasia. John Aubrey summed Mrs Philips up as "very good natured . . . pretty fat; not tall; red pumpled face".

The Matchless Orinda enjoyed dabbling in authorship, and reading her efforts aloud to her lady friends while they nibbled on pastries. Many other pastimes which the gentlewomen traditionally enjoyed were forbidden or discouraged under the Commonwealth; poetry and confectionery were permitted,

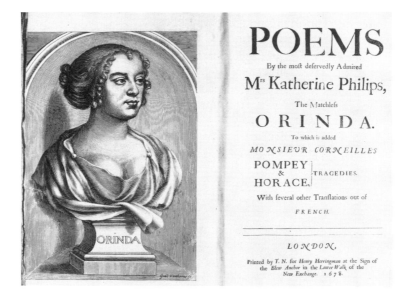

Title-page of Poems, *by the most deservedly Admired Mrs Katherine Philips (1678). Mrs Philips enjoyed whole-heartedly the conceits of a literary life. She bestowed poetical pseudonyms on her friends, read her poems aloud to them and nibbled cakes.*

at least. Joan Cromwell was known to enjoy cookery. The theatres were closed, although playwrights continued to write; card games and gambling of all kinds were forbidden. Oliver Cromwell disposed of the stud at Tutbury, where Henry VIII a century before had established a breeding and training establishment for racehorses. Horse racing, hare coursing, bowls all faded; Sunday sports were strictly forbidden, and gardening and fishing were recommended.

The Commonwealth period has been described as a time of "domestic lethargy". For some it was a time of tranquillity. Anne Finch, daughter of "Widow Bennett" and born in 1631, married in 1651 Edward, Viscount Conway. They lived at Ragley Castle in Herefordshire, and here Anne entertained her circle of philosopher friends, chief among them Henry More. She had the misfortune to suffer from agonising headaches but despite her pain, Anne pursued her philosophical enquiries and ran a comfortable home.

Content to Serve?

The Ladies Companion, or A Table furnished with Sundry Sorts of Pies and Tarts (1653), including Lady Goring's recipe for syllabub, and advice on boiling sparrows and larks, *A Queen's Delight, or The Art of Preserving, Conserving and Candying* (1655) offering methods of preserving pippins and quinces, and conserving borage flowers "in the Italian mode", were useful in these years of hospitality. With the Restoration, Anne's husband spent an increasing amount of time at Court. She had "her library-keeper Mrs Sarah", a gentlewoman attendant, for company down in the country where she dosed her frightful headaches with red and blue powders, opium and tobacco.

The quietude of the Commonwealth appealed to other gentlewomen, particularly those who pursued activities which required tranquillity in the home. Mrs Mary Beale, daughter of the Reverend Craddock of Suffolk, married Charles Beale, a Puritan, in 1650, some years after she had begun to study painting. Her father was an amateur painter and had encouraged her to make headway beyond drawing designs for embroidery. In the mid-1650s the Beales moved to London and made their home in Covent Garden, London's first fashionable suburb. Laid out in 1630, Covent Garden boasted artists' studios, noblemen's mansions, fruit and vegetable markets, – and taverns, brothels and theatres (closed since 1642). Mrs Beale had no interest in such temptations; she worked away in her "painting room" while her small sons played among the canvases at her side and her husband primed her canvases, later becoming a

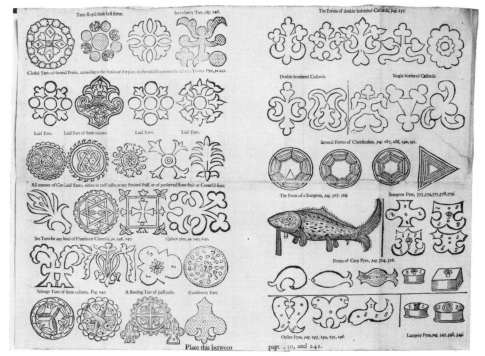

Designs for pies, tarts and custards from Robert May's The Accomplisht Cook *(1685), a favourite cook book of Restoration ladies. It includes recipes for showpieces like "four and twenty blackbirds baked in a pie", as well as more wieldy dishes.*

dealer in paintings. Mary led the most ordinary of lives, tending the family, supervising the marketing and differed only from less distinguished English wives and mothers in her artistic talent.

With the Restoration of Charles II as King of England in 1660 domestic tranquillity gave way to a more boisterous mood. Indeed, the general atmosphere of holiday prompted some criticism. Old Lady Anne Clifford visited the Restoration Court and felt she ought: "to be used as they do ill-sighted or unruly horses, have Spectacles (or Blinkers) put before mine eyes, lest I should see and censure what I cannot completely judge of." Even Pepys was surprised when he visited the Palace of Whitehall one Sunday in 1667, to find the Queen

Self-portrait with her children (c. 1665), by Mary Beale, professional lady painter. Beale set up her studio in Covent Garden and quietly painted the personalities of the Restoration Court while remaining an admirable wife and mother.

with the Duchess of York and other ladies whiling away the Sabbath with a fast and furious game of cards.

The reaction against Puritanism and the resumption of Court life also led to the extravagant fashions that we see in Restoration portraits. Mary Beale now became a portraitist favoured by the nobility and by the King. In 1670 she became a professional painter, charging £10 for a three-quarter-length portrait. Inevitably her success – she admired and studied Lely's work to good effect – changed her life. She took pupils, her sons were roped in to help her in the studio. In the service of Restoration demands for sumptuous display and consumption, Mrs Beale became worker first and wife and mother second.

In the portraits of the 1660s Court, Sir Peter Lely, Mary Beale's mentor, we see a celebration of wantonness, both in dress and in expression, unthinkable under the Commonwealth. The ladies look ready to slip out of their exuberant wrappings of velvet and rich satin at a moment's call; and an unpowdered ringlet or two is pulled dexterously to lie upon a snowy expanse of bosom already exposed. Lely reserved his most riotous painting for royal mistresses. The eyes of Diana Kirke, Countess of Oxford are suitably heavy; she was the most famous courtesan of the period. Mrs Jane Myddleton, another famous beauty, looks ready to bestow a peach from her basket of glistening fruit on anyone who amuses her. With the reopening of the theatres, Charles II introduced from France the novel custom of actresses taking women's parts on the stage. This did nothing for his reputation, nor for that of the actresses like Nell Gwynn, whom Lely also painted.

A double portrait of the Capel sisters, Mary, Duchess of Beaufort and Elizabeth, Countess of Carnarvon, was a more sober commission for Lely. Encouraged by their mother, both ladies were keen botanists; Lady Carnarvon did flower paintings, the Duchess improved the gardens at Badminton. This

Mary, Duchess of Beaufort and Elizabeth, Countess of Carnarvon, daughters of Arthur, 1st Lord Capel, by Lely. Inheriting their mother's enthusiasm for horticulture, Mary was instrumental in laying out the gardens at Badminton House, Elizabeth did careful flower paintings.

horticultural interest was unusual in the gentlewomen of the time, and Lely noted it by placing a garland of flowers in the Duchess's hand, a gouache of her own making in the Countess's. It was difficult to make anything of the Countess's long face – in the Duchess, Lely cannot resist imparting a lingering look to the eyes, a pout to the mouth. Was this wantonness – to be observed also in other Restoration portraits by other artists – a fashion in painting? Or was the seventeenth-century gentlewoman no longer confined and under the rule of her father or husband, as had been the trussed-up Tudor gentlewoman?

There *was* a certain amount of sexual holiday following the Restoration and Lely's portraits reflect this. Dalliance, long absences in London, adultery were overlooked by many husbands, some busy pursuing their own adulterous interests. Others, less tolerant, followed Lord Chesterfield in sending their wives "to the Peak". (The Peak formed part of Lord Chesterfield's estates, whither he dispatched his wife when her conduct in London became intolerable.) Legally, throughout the seventeenth century, the English gentlewoman was as much under the rule of the head of the house, be he father or husband, as she had been in the preceding century. *The Lawes Resolution*, an account of women's position under the law, written at the end of the sixteenth century but published later, was succinct. "All of them are understood either married or to be married," it declared of women, and: "That which the man hath is his own. That which the wife hath is her husband's." If Lady Chesterfield refused to obey her husband's dictate, she would find herself swiftly, fine lady though she was, a pauper. A husband had absolute control of the estates his wife brought him; he could cut off financial supplies to her as he wished.

There was no real redress for the English gentlewoman, should she find her husband a spendthrift, a tyrant, a philanderer – or should she find "Hyde Park and the cherries there . . . very pleasant to me," while her husband preferred to live in the country. Separation of an informal kind was possible; but there was then no guarantee that the husband would provide proper maintenance for his wife. Since his wife's dowry had often made a rich man out of a poor one, the injustice of this was generally her chief complaint. Still, in the lower ranks of the gentry, this informal separation was generally the rule. In the 1650s the heiress Elizabeth Oxinden was deserted by her husband, Tom, who went off to live with a neighbour's wife. In 1668, after a brief career as a highwayman, he died in prison – and his deserted wife could at last remarry, which she did swiftly. With this kind of separation, husband and wife remained tied by the shackles of marriage till death.

An official separation could be obtained in the ecclesiastical courts – *divortium a mensa et thoro,* or divorce from bed and board – but again, neither party was free to remarry. There was a brief interlude, following the Commonwealth Marriage Act of 1653, when the innocent party was permitted to remarry; but this lapsed with the Restoration.

The law, canon or civil, could not prevent desperadoes from remarriage, and many secured a decree of nullity, which established the marriage as void

from the beginning. Non-consummation was the most obvious ground of nullity, but there were others. The *Ladies Dictionary* of 1694 included "Consanguinity and Affinity [of blood] as well as Precontract and Impotency". The last two grounds were not uncommonly invoked. Frances, Countess of Essex, declared her husband was impotent towards her, although not towards the generality of women; she won her decree of nullity, and was free to marry Robert Carr, Earl of Somerset. "Pre-contract" entailed an earlier betrothal or pledge to marry in front of witnesses, or "spousals *de praesenti*". As the age of consent for females was twelve, for males, fourteen, and their parents were often lustful of their children's marriage earlier than this date, a prior betrothal, which had been forgotten, could often be unearthed.

That the present marriage was judged void, did not mean that the wife recovered her dowry. Moreover as the marriage was null, held never to have existed, then there was no reason for the husband to provide maintenance. The thought of destitution, or of living with an aggrieved parent, deterred women from seeking decrees of nullity without secure prospect of immediate re-marriage. Any husband was better than poverty alone; besides, knowledge that her dowry would remain with her husband, should she leave or stay, prompted her to stay, however indignant, and share the benefit of it.

Once a marriage had taken place, then husband and wife were permitted to show a degree of affection to each other which ran close to love. Arranged marriages did not preclude unhappiness but nor did they marital joy. Their expectations of bliss were less exalted than those of their few contemporaries who married for love; they often achieved a more equilibrious union, as a result.

"A virtuous woman is a crown to her husband," was a proverb Puritan ladies were fond of. The Puritan concept of husband and wife as "meet helps to one another" in their endeavours spiritual, had its concomitant in things domestic: wives like Elizabeth Walker were given a share in the financial management of the household denied to their less devout sisters. Mrs Walker was allowed £19 worth of rents to handle by her husband each year; she spent some of this income on carefully chosen charities among the poor. She was "clerk of her little kitchen", as her husband fondly wrote; the pastries and cream cheeses she made there, the salves and medicines she made in her still-room, were for distribution among the needy as well as among her family. The most significant time for the minister's wife, however, were the hours before dawn when she meditated alone in her closet, and read her Bible.

It was axiomatic that romantic love could have no part in the scheme of marriages among the upper classes. The flames of love would be quenched within a few years; then what tie was there between husband and wife but passion spent? Money was, if a shackle, at least a much more suitable basis for marriage. Few were not swayed by this argument. Dorothy Osborne, poet, met William Temple, diplomat, during the Civil Wars, on the Isle of Wight, and the consequence was they wished to marry. But Temple's father was a Cromwellian, in the Long Parliament, and Sir Peter Osborne, father of Dorothy, held

81

Guernsey for the King. The match was deemed impossible, and the two families' opposition grew no less implacable with the end of the wars. Dorothy and William were as obdurate, however. Dorothy rejected suitors by the score – including Oliver Cromwell's son, Henry; she lost her beauty when she contracted smallpox abroad, but William remained faithful. He wandered on the Continent, while Dorothy remained at Chicksands, her father's house, and their love affair was conducted by correspondence. At last in 1655 they married, and lived, as Dorothy had hoped they would, ever after together. A romantic tale, indeed, but Dorothy would have none of it. "Passion" was the enemy of man, and puts "everything else out of order before it can find a place for itself", was her view. The imperious Margaret, Duchess of Newcastle wrote frankly that she felt no "amorous love" for her husband when young. "It is a disease, or passion, I know only by relation." Admittedly, William, Duke of Newcastle was over fifty and she just twenty when he wooed her, but she would have distrusted the ardency he showed in a man of any age: "If you are so passionate as you say . . . yet it may be feared it cannot last long, for no extreme is permanent." This Aristotelian view of passion as one extreme, coldness the other, and affection as the golden mean was the norm.

What of the few who did decide that not all husbands were alike, but that only one would satisfy them? Who fell in love? In 1663 eighteen-year-old Mary Boyle, daughter of the Earl of Cork, married a Mr Charles Rich. The fact that he became, against all odds, Earl of Warwick, could not assuage her father's grief at her folly. "Unruly Mary," he chastised her. When she came to write an account of her life, she held it still as a grave sin that she had gone against her father's wishes – and become a very wealthy Countess, as a result.

Mary, Countess of Warwick, "converted" to her husband's Puritan faith. She spent hours in her closet, meditating. (One cannot but feel that this required solitude was a relief to many ladies – we have countless references to gentlewomen of every faith being found in their closet at all hours of the day.) Her household at Leigh Priory was naturally on a large scale; still, her daily round – making medicine for sick servants, visiting the village girls' school, catechising her maids and teaching them to read the Bible – was not so different from Mrs Walker's. Mary's autobiography, an account of her conversion and a chart of spiritual progress, again has much in common with the diary which Lady Margaret Hoby had kept at the beginning of the century.

The majority of the gentlewomen of the seventeenth century had, despite the restrictions of the Commonwealth, managed to pursue most of the activities which the traveller, Edmund Van Meteren, had noted as beloved of English women in 1614. They employed their time, he said, "in walking and riding – playing cards or otherwise, in visiting their friends and keeping company, conversing with their equals and their neighbours, and making merry with them at child-births, christenings and funerals; all this with the permission and knowledge of their husbands." In other words, while remaining under the rod of their husbands, ladies slipped from under it a good deal.

82

Content to Serve?

The title-page from Country Contentments, or The English Housewife, *a 1623 edition of Gervase Markham's popular manual. The lady in Wenceslas Hollar's etching of Spring putting away her winter furs might consult Markham for cheerful menus following Lenten fare.*

William Barker, chaplain to the botanist Elizabeth, Lady Capel, condemned such ladies in his sermon at his mistress's funeral in 1661. Lady Capel had been "a zealous abhorrer and hater of idleness, a vice grown of late years the common fashion, of too many of her rank and quality; who, because the plenty and abundance of their estates do advance them above the necessity of working for a lifelihood, do therefore look upon themselves as privileged and marked out unto a life of idleness." These wicked women's closets were, he declared, "an exchange only of curious pictures, and of rare and costly jewels". Lady Capel's was a "private Oratory".

The acquisition of jewellery, and of lace and ribbons and less costly trinkets, became a favourite hobby of gentlewomen following the Restoration. Mrs Pepys was always trying to persuade Samuel to buy her expensive lace. He haggled over the price of hers at the Exchange – and then spent a fortune at a superior lace merchant in Cheapside on lace for himself. Still, he had an official position and was required to be handsomely dressed. His wife's wish for finery was whim, not need. Cheapside, traditionally the street of the goldsmiths and silk mercers, in the seventeenth century absorbed a few very superior lace makers and linen drapers. Before the Great Fire of 1666, however, Paternoster Row was where the coaches of the nobility and gentry most often resorted to deposit their eager customers at mercer, silkman and laceman. The Royal Exchange, built in 1567 as a centre for mercantile business, had in its upper arcades more than a hundred dark little shops, selling luxury goods. The walls of Westminster Hall, curiously, were lined with stalls selling clothes of one kind and another, as well as law books and stationery for the Law

Courts next door. The New Exchange, built in 1608 south of the Strand on the outskirts of the City, had other tempting goods – and served as an assignation place for beaux and belles, asserted Ned Ward in his magazine, *London Spy*.

In 1666, beginning in a baker's shop in Pudding Lane, the Fire of London swept from the Tower of London to Temple Bar. Pepys saw the householders of the City carrying their possessions down the water-steps which lined the river, and committing the contents of their homes to barges. Almost every barge so stacked, noticed the diarist, had a pair of virginals atop the load and the quantity of fine furniture bobbing about was surprising. The craze for consumption had affected all. When the Fire burnt itself out, neither shopkeepers nor householders returned to the City. The poor moved east, the rich moved west, and the East End and the West End had their beginnings. Shopkeepers, not surprisingly, followed the rich, and settled in Covent Garden, in St James's, near the burgeoning residential quarters of St James's Square, Berkeley Street and, later, Bond Street and in Holborn, near Bloomsbury Square.

The Fire had no chastening effect on the spirits of Restoration Londoners. Public lotteries enjoyed a craze. In 1683, after the death of Prince Rupert of the Rhine, his collection of jewels was disposed of in a lottery, with tickets selling at £5 each. The collection was valued at £20,000 with the biggest prize, a pearl necklace, valued at £8,000. The drawing of tickets for the prizes was done in the presence of the King in the Banqueting House at Whitehall. By 1694 the craze for lotteries obsessed all social classes. "Married ladies, Virgin Madams, Jilts . . . all relishing the pleasing expectancy of getting Six hundred a Year for a Crown" netted the Government over a million pounds. In 1699, however, William III had an attack of conscience and suppressed lotteries as "common and public nuisances". Queen Anne restored them in 1710 and not till 1826 did State gambling finally expire "after a series of tedious complaints".

William and Mary's reign saw other attempts of a spasmodic kind to restore a degree of sobriety to the feverish card-crazed, horse-crazed, fashion-crazed kingdom they had agreed to rule in 1688. Queen Mary found the frivolity of the English Court shocking – although she herself, as a young princess in England, had spent all her time playing cards. She took to knotting, a form of needlework where silk thread is first knotted at intervals along its length with the aid of a shuttle, then the thread is "couched", or sewn to canvas in floral swirls. Queen Mary persuaded as many of her Ladies as she could to follow her in this unexceptionable pursuit, and to listen to an improving book as they worked. In the sporting field, William did little to encourage the horse-racing which Charles II had made so popular with his financing of meetings at Newmarket Racecourse. But William did plant the first Dutch bulbs in England at the palace in Newmarket that Charles had renovated.

It remained for Mary's younger sister, Queen Anne and her husband, Prince George of Denmark, to restore racing to the popularity it had enjoyed under her uncle Charles. Anne had been a fervent horsewoman since her child-

Sarah Churchill, Queen Anne's confidante, playing cards with Lady Fitzharding, painted by Kneller. Card-playing, with horse-racing, lotteries and other affairs of chance, enjoyed a great vogue during Queen Anne's reign. She established Ascot as a fashionable race-course.

hood in Richmond. Even when she was over forty and in pain from gout, she did not abandon her hunting. Jonathan Swift wrote in 1711: "The Queen was abroad today in order to hunt . . . she hunts in a chaise with one horse, which she drives herself, and drives furiously, like Jehu, and is a mighty hunter." We are informed that she sometimes covered fifty miles a day in her chaise. Anne was the first English royal lady to take a passionate interest in hunting since James I's wife, Anne of Denmark. That earlier Anne had encouraged her husband when he imported French "*valets de chiens*", and fast hounds, and even French jargon like "*Tally-ho*" and "*Loolooloo*", still cried respectively at sighting and at the death of the fox. (They are Provençale corruptions of Arabian falconry terminology.) Anne of Denmark did have one uneasy moment when she killed her husband's dog, Jewel, by mistake while she was out hunting.

Seventeenth-century English playing cards, showing scenes from a courtship. Games of chance were frowned on in the Commonwealth; the Restoration Court played cards on Sundays. Queen Mary wanted her ladies to do knotting instead. Her sister, Anne, revived the vogue.

James stormed but, on discovering she was the culprit, charmingly gave her a large diamond as a legacy from his dead dog.

Her great-grand-daughter, Queen Anne, did much to embellish Newmarket, laying out £1,000 on paving for the town and providing several plates or silver cups worth anything up to £100 each. Admittedly, she paid for this out of "secret service money" but race-going ladies and gentlemen could not know this. Her chief adviser at Newmarket was Tregonwell Frampton, Keeper of the Running Horses to a succession of monarchs and forerunner, all in one man, of the Jockey Club. Anne did not mind a gambler, which Frampton undoubtedly was; her other racing adviser was her Lord Treasurer, Sidney Godolphin.

Queen Anne's enthusiasm for racing survived clashes with both her advisers. In 1711 she had the great pleasure of instituting the first race meeting on "the new heath" at Ascot. She paid fo "Her Majesty's plate of a 100 guineas", for which there were three heats, and for another race worth 50 guineas. Swift was there to inform Stella of the establishment of Royal Ascot. As is appropriate in view of the tradition for chic dress and millinery at Ascot, Swift's information had some sartorial content. He encountered a Miss Forester, one of the Queen's ladies-in-waiting, "on her palfrey taking the air". "She is a silly true maid of honour, and I did not like her, although she be a toast and was dressed like a man." Another observer confirms Swift's rather surprising remark. Miss Forester had made sure of being the focus of all eyes not trained on the runners

Content to Serve?

by wearing a long white riding coat, with a full-flapped waistcoat and court hat with a band of gold lace over a periwig. Queen Anne herself was not allowed to wear such finery by her Mistress of the Robes, Sarah, Duchess of Marlborough. It was noted that the Queen dressed more plainly than was appropriate for her dignity. Sarah, who made a fortune of £90,000 from kick-backs from the Queen's costumiers, was quite satisfied with her royal mistress's apparel. "It would have been ridiculous with her person," she said bluntly of the dumpy Anne, "and at her age to have been otherwise dressed."

Another of Sarah's outspoken comments to her Queen was: "Your Majesty has had the misfortune to be misinformed in general things even from twelve years old." This was, unfortunately, still the lot of many English gentlewomen in the seventeenth century. Small wonder that sports and satins and sugared fruits were their pleasures, when at leisure, and not matters of greater weight.

The Linley larks, celebrated sister singers, painted by Gainsborough in 1772. Elizabeth and Maria Linley were star attractions at their father's Attic Entertainments, or musical concerts, in Bath in the early 1770s. Nobility, gentry and professional musicians mingled at these events.

CHAPTER THREE

Fair Tea-makers

1700-1815

T HERE IS A CERTAIN MIXTURE OF PRIDE IN THE MOST AMIABLE kind of reserve for which the men, and still more the women of this country are distinguished," confided the author of *Brief Remarks on English Manners* to a friend abroad in 1816. This pride was characterised by "a dry, cold, sometimes haughty and repulsive manner towards persons who are . . . of no sort of consequence . . . a gracious affable demeanour towards those of higher rank." Foreigners marvelled at the "democratic" nature of English society, continued this thoughtful critic, where nobility and country squires and merchants mingled at one and the same public function. In fact, "the painful constraint of our manners" sprang directly from the perceived need to maintain a moral distinction of ranks, where the separation of classes was less apparent. This English reserve of "constraint" was most painful, judged the author, in two areas. First, ladies and gentlemen treated their dependants disgracefully. Ladies chose as governesses for their daughters: "those who have had the best education . . . whose manners are pleasing, and therefore worthy of emulation." Then they treated them "with cold reserve", kept them "at nearly the same distance" as their menials. In consequence their daughters neither respected nor attempted to emulate their preceptresses. Worse, "girls . . . who have almost all the early part of their lives in the society of their governesses, contract . . . an early habit of behaving . . . with an unpleasant reserve . . ."

The other area where the English reserve, not to say superciliousness, was shocking was in the habit of constructing closed pews in the churches, "receptacles for the rich to the exclusion of the poor". One family pew for the lord of the manor had been acceptable; but now all the gentry and the professional men of the country towns – even the farmers – built their own pews till the churches looked like stockyards filled with cattle pens.

Respect for rank and consequence was not dispelled, then, even though the eighteenth century saw the nobility and the gentry milling together in large numbers, and in public places such as pleasure gardens – Ranelagh, Vauxhall – and the Assembly-rooms, or at subscription concerts, as never before. The limitation of the monarchy's powers in 1688 caused the focus of business to shift

from Court to the House of Commons and the Lords, to the Bank of England, to the multifarious Government departments which administered the British colonies in America (till 1776) and interests in India. The nobility and gentry became associates and colleagues, together they formed the Establishment, as it developed, and they began to meet socially. Gradation of rank became a very "nice" thing.

Merchants who traded abroad and carried on "foreign correspondence" also formed part of the Establishment, as distinct from tradesmen who were concerned solely with the home market. (Still, Daniel Defoe, butcher's son, noted in *The Complete English Tradesman* (1726), tradesmen, "may on occasion keep company with gentlemen as well as other people." However superior

Promenade in the Mall
*(1744), by Marcellus
Laroon. Walking in public
parks and pleasure gardens
like Ranelagh and Vauxhall
was a favourite
entertainment for
fashionable ladies. The
ladies' caps and gowns are
characteristic of the
"informal dress" adopted
for such excursions.*

merchants might be to tradesmen, they did not share in the heritage of the land, common to nobility and gentry. Tacitly, they were excluded from the Polite Society which grew up in this century – they were "cut" – unless they either sold up and became landowners themselves, or became associated by their "posterity" with the nobility. The merchant family of Beckford did just this. Alderman William Beckford inherited a fortune made in Jamaica from sugar and slaves. In about 1736 he bought a vast country mansion and estate at Fonthill in Wiltshire.

Generally, the daughters of the aristocracy were reluctant to marry into trade, though their needy brothers were happy to do so. (The daughters of rich

merchants or tradesmen – the distinction actually became blurred if the fortune was sufficient – who brought fortunes into noble homes were known as "golden dollies".) Alderman William Beckford's immense fortune touched the heart of an earl's granddaughter, and their son, also William, inherited Fonthill at the age of nine, together with capital of one and a half million pounds. "England's wealthiest son" married the *daughter* of an earl. Though he remained plain Mr Beckford all his long life, because of a homosexual scandal in his youth, his younger daughter married in 1810, to the delight of all, the 10th Duke of Hamilton.

In 1740 a Miss Robinson from Yorkshire visited Bath, the fashionable watering-place. All the morning, it was "How d'ye does?", she informed a correspondent, and, all night, "What's Trumps?" The occupants of the Ladies' Coffee House talked only of diseases. Pretty Miss Robinson was to become famous as the blue-stocking Mrs Montagu. At twenty, she was flippant, and she told of a Dowager Duchess, very tall and very haughty, who had bathed and caused havoc when bathing among lesser mortals at Cross Bath. Bathing was a misnomer; the ladies promenaded in the water, with their feet securely on the bottom. Japanned bowls bobbed about on the surface, offering sweetmeats or oils and essences for their pleasure. The Dowager Duchess discovered that she outranked all the other ladies in the bath and imperiously "ordered it to be filled till it reached her chin," reported Miss Robinson. "All those who were below her stature, as well as her rank, were obliged to come out or drown."

Jane Austen's *Persuasion* was published posthumously in 1819. In the opening sentences we hear of a proud baronet, Sir Walter Elliot of Kellynch-hall, in Somersetshire. He "was a man who, for his own amusement, never took up any book but the Baronetage . . . there, if every other leaf were powerless, he could read his own history with an interest which never failed." Sir Walter was matched in his family pride by his eldest daughter. Anne Elliot, the younger daughter, deplored their self-esteem. "The Bath papers . . . announced the arrival of the Dowager Viscountess Dalrymple, and her daughter, the Honourable Miss Carteret; and all the comfort of No – Camden-place, (where the Elliots resided) was swept away for many days; for the Dalrymples (in Anne's opinion, most unfortunately) were cousins of the Elliots; and the agony was, how to introduce themselves properly. Anne had never seen her father and sister before in contact with nobility." She was mortified by their nervous fawning on the undistinguished Dalrymple ladies, and ended by wishing they had more pride. "She had hoped better things from their high ideas of their own situation in life . . ."

The advent of well-sprung, swift carriages and coaches made travelling a pleasure, and as a result the social circles in the country widened. Wives and daughters emerged daily from "the carriage" at the homes of other ladies, two or three villages distant. Young people made expeditions to Wishing Wells, or, as in *Northanger Abbey*, to historic houses in the locality. They also went further afield. In 1700 Celia Fiennes had been an early indefatigable visitor of

English country houses. On payment of a douceur to the housekeeper, most houses or at least the grounds, were generally available for view. But Miss Fiennes had to travel in sore discomfort, on horseback and with one or two servants as escort. As the century progressed mansions and parks like Longleat or Stowe or Stourhead – where the bankers, Hoare, settled – received a stream of visitors. "A tour of the West Country", or of Norfolk became feasible and pleasant in a comfortable, cushioned conveyance. Travel as a social pleasure was discovered.

Assembly-rooms sprang up in small country towns, to accommodate the general increase in sociability. In 1757 at the Chesterfield Assembly-rooms, visitors to the district and local gentry danced with the Duke of Devonshire. Lord Nelson's sister, Mrs Bolton, regularly took lodgings at the local market town of Swaffham in the 1800s so that her daughters could enjoy the series of balls at the fine Assembly-rooms there. After 1798 one ball was held each year in honour of their uncle's victory at the Nile on 1 August. For Jane and Cassandra Austen, in their youth at Steventon, Basingstoke provided the most convenient Assembly-rooms. Miss Robinson of Rokeby Hall in Yorkshire was sophisticated, and thought her father's *mot*, "Living in the country" was "sleeping with one's eyes open", very good. Aged fifteen, she went "in winter" eight miles to dance to the music of a blind fiddler, and returned home at two in the morning. Aged seven-

Panoramic view of Charlton Park by Thomas Robins (1716-70). A fashionable eighteenth-century family portrait, showing the house and features of the "improved" park in proud detail, the family in miniature dispersed about the grounds.

teen, Elizabeth was happy to drive eight miles with her sister, Sarah, and their two brothers to see the play. They joined other friends to have supper in an inn, and only left it at two in the morning to drive home in very disorderly fashion. In an earlier time, this free intermingling of the sexes would have been unthinkable. The parents of Miss Robinson's friends raised no demur. Similarly, the parents of the Misses Betsey and Eugenia Wynne raised no objection to their teenage daughters striking up friendships with handsome young gentlemen everywhere they went on the Continent in the 1790s. Not all admirers pleased the Wynne girls equally. Aged twelve, Eugenia was sorry to be obliged to dance with "the disagreeable and unsupportable Mr Vouchet" at Zurich. In 1794, aged fifteen, Betsey thought young Max de Lerkenfeld at Ratisbon "a handsome man but full of vanity and very impolite". With the increase in acquaintance, young ladies were not expected to marry the first eligible gentleman they encountered.

It is noticeable that the stock of gentlewomen rose perceptibly in men's eyes throughout the century. In the seventeenth century, the Matchless Orinda, Mrs Katherine Philips, had been thought unusual for her friendships with men. Now Alexander Pope was as intimate with the Misses Blount of Windsor as he was with his male friends; Dr Johnson numbered among his close friends for

Nearing Their Destination, by Thomas Rowlandson. The "view" acquired a new importance for persons of sensibility, after they had read Gilpin's 1780 Essay on the Picturesque. They made constant excursions to find, admire and sketch it.

many years Mrs Thrale, Mrs Delany and Mrs Montagu; Horace Walpole cor-responded daily with the young Misses Berry in his old age; when Sir William Hamilton, diplomat, came to England on "leave", he went first to the drawing-room of his niece, Lady Stormont, a well-known hostess, and his chief cor-respondent was another niece, Mary Hamilton. While the eighteenth century, also saw the rise of the gentleman's refuge, the club, a genuine fondness for the company of women developed. The political hostesses of the late nineteenth century are fore-shadowed in Georgiana, Duchess of Devonshire, friend to Fox and the Whigs at Devonshire House in the 1780s, and in Elizabeth, Lady Hol-land, who made Holland House a centre for Whigs a decade later. These ladies,

A Family Being Served With Tea (c. 1740-5), British School. These "conversation pieces" often included servants and pets as well as prized possessions. Here, the family's expensive tea service and harpsichord are features lovingly displayed.

and others like them, were hostesses in their own right; they did not just do the honours of the house for their husbands. How had this come about?

The custom of tea-drinking had done much to consolidate the ladies' role as mistress of entertainment within the home. Pepys had his first cup of tea in 1660; introduced to England in 1610, it was at first drunk in coffee houses. Slowly, the new beverage gained popularity. Coffee houses gave way to tea gar-dens – where gentlemen *and* ladies foregathered. Fashionable ladies began to serve tea after supper in earthenware pots imported from China. The lady of the house would adjourn from the dinner table to brew it herself, taking the other ladies with her. The gentlemen took the opportunity to fill their glasses, to talk political scandal, and rose from the table only when the brew was ready – or long after. By the mid-eighteenth century this separation of the sexes after dinner had become habit to the upper classes. (It was much commented upon, and criticised as barbarous, by visitors from abroad.) Oddly, absence seemed to make the heart grow fonder. Many gentlemen were glad to go through to the

Fair Tea-makers

drawing-room, free of smoke and alcohol fumes, and full of welcoming feminine smiles.

In 1711 Thomas Twining began selling tea in domestic quantities. In 1740 import duties on tea were reduced, and tea established itself as the preferred English beverage – though not the cheapest. A pound of tea in 1750 cost a third of a skilled worker's weekly wage, and the leaves were preserved in locked tea caddies. Ceramic teapots of English manufacture appeared from the 1740s on, to complement the new fashion for drinking tea in the home. Wedgwood's creamware teapots won great popularity; silver teapots were also fashionable, and by the 1760s any lady of genteel pretensions had her tea table set up after supper. To the teapot were added at first matching tea bowls, later tea cups with handles, a sugar bowl, slop basin, and coffee pot, caddy spoon, and so on. The quality of tea service – earthenware, porcelain, Wedgwood, or Dresden – was a sign of its lady owner's status; for this reason, owners of lustrous vessels chose to be painted poised gracefully above their tea table.

Earlier, the saloon had been a reception room common to both sexes. The eighteenth century saw the withdrawing room become the focus of the house, and very much the ladies' preserve. Here they exhibited the fruit of their accomplishments – their "work", or embroidery, and their music, their flower arrangements, and their sketches and watercolours. The gentlemen had no room of their own, unless they were of a scholarly turn and kept the library sacred to themselves. Generally, the library was now the room where ladies and gentlemen met on less studied terms, and mingled casually through out the day. After luncheon they might look together at books of engravings of classical ruins, or of cathedrals, depending on their penchant for the antique or the Gothic. Someone might read aloud a portion of a magazine or newspaper.

Addison, founding editor of the *Spectator*, made it clear from the outset in 1711 that his publication was designed for ladies and gentlemen. His essays, and those of his co-founder, were intended to elevate women's thoughts from "the right adjusting of their Hair". There were also sections designed for female readers in the *Gentleman's Magazine*, first published in 1731, and in the *Athenian Mercury*, which began in the seventeenth century, the editor answered questions from and about women on the first Tuesday of each month. For Tory households there was the *Examiner*; the Whigs, for their part, had their *Whig Examiner*, with Swift to write for it. Pope wrote of the indiscriminate appetite for newsprint at the beginning of the century: they "are as pleased to hear of a piebald horse that is strayed out of a field near Islington, as a whole troop that has been engaged in any foreign adventure . . ." He was complaining of gentle-men readers whom he saw in the coffee houses, exhibiting "voracious appetite, but no taste". This criticism could fairly be levelled at the literate lady reader of the eighteenth century. She devoured – as they became fashionable – poetry and essays, histories, sentimental novels and romances, Gothic novels, plays, social and historical novels by turn. Cowper followed Gray; Fielding's *Tom Jones* and

95

Clarissa Harlowe and his sister, Sarah's *The Governess* were equally beloved; Goldsmith's *History of England* was admired, if not read all at one sitting. Samuel Richardson's *Pamela*, *Sir Charles Grandison*, Miss Burney's books ceded place to the outpourings of the Minerva Press. After Lady Caroline Lamb fascinated Society with her *Glenarvon*, or *roman à clef* on the doings at Holland House, Mrs Edgeworth and Jane Austen introduced a note of rationality, while Scott's and Byron's wild harps thrilled the sensible heart. Whatever was spoken of, the gentlewoman read, and then spoke of herself.

Similarly, from its establishment in 1769, she visited the fashionable Summer Exhibition at the Royal Academy religiously, and also patronised the studios of the portrait painters, Romney, Reynolds, Lawrence, who exhibited there. Public exhibitions of contemporary painters' work began only in 1760 in England; by 1779 Horace Walpole was writing: "sometimes one cannot pass through the streets where they are . . . it is incredible what sums are raised by mere exhibition of anything . . ." She attended subscription concerts, and heard the first performance of Handel's *Messiah* at Sir Thomas Coram's Foundling Hospital, the beautiful Miss Linley sing at Bath, Mr Attwood, the organist, play in St Paul's. And then there was the theatre. To be elegant and a person of taste, it was important to keep abreast of so many of the Arts; for a large part of an eighteenth-century friendship consisted in exchanging similar opinions, and discovering that the most conventional of tastes coincided. It was no wonder

Coloured fashion plates of 1820 and 1811 from Rudolph Ackermann's The Repository of Arts, Literature, Commerce, Manufacture, Fashions and Politics. *This was a quality magazine published monthly from 1809 to 1828, providing an "indispensable guide to fashion" in everything from candelabra to curtain-rods and, indeed, cottage dresses.*

that the gentlewoman's stock soared so in this century. She made such frantic efforts to present an elegant mind, as well as an elegant rig.

It is a matter of some astonishment that the gentlewoman, mid-century, had time to think of anything but her costume. Fashions widened and narrowed her outline, her hairstyles expanded and contracted in concert. Fashion plates appeared from the 1770s on, to bewilder a hesitant aspirant *à la mode* with choice. From 1806 John Bell produced a monthly magazine, *La Belle Assemblée*, the *Vogue* or *Harpers & Queen* of the day, being largely devoted to beautifully reproduced fashion plates. From 1809 ladies had their *Homes & Gardens* in Ackerman's *Repository of Arts*, also published monthly. If the lady wished not only to gaze at magazines but to acquire the goods they advertised, then to London she must go. The work of a country dressmaker, of a provincial cabinet-maker, could not compare with the wealth of goods to be bought in the Mecca of shopping. There were mantua-makers in Covent Garden and in the New Exchange across the Strand,where finicky gentlemen, far better acquainted with the niceties of the latest mode than their customers, danced attendance. New tea-sets could be purchased at Josiah Wedgwood's impressive showrooms in Soho, later moved to St James's Square. In 1797 John Hatchard opened a bookshop in Piccadilly, which he described as a small London suburb. Covent Garden and Paternoster Row were still then the traditional sites for bookshops; ladies did little shopping in St James's, except for household

"Evening Dress" and "Walking Dress", from Ackermann's Repository *of April, 1820, and December, 1819. The Misses Bennett or Misses Dashwood of Jane Austen's* Pride and Prejudice *and* Sense and Sensibility *would have appeared to advantage in such elegant rig.*

97

Pompoms of lace and ribbons, aigrettes to pin them to gauze caps, pearls to edge the caps – in 1761 milliners stocked all these essentials of headgear. Fans a lady could acquire, unexpectedly, at Dorothy Mercier's print shop.

provisions at Fortnum and Mason's. Hatchard's bookshop and Mrs Humphries' print shop in St James's St, where Gillray's satirical prints of personalities of the moment were exhibited, with Wedgwood's showrooms, enticed ladies into favouring shopping in the West End. The laying out of Regent Street, the first street designed as a shopping mall, and the establishment of the Pantheon bazaar in Oxford Street dealt further blows to hallowed shopping centres in the City of London further east.

Of course the hurly-burly of shopping and socialising in London did not suit all ladies. Henrietta Howard, later Duchess of Suffolk, retired from her irksome position as George II's mistress in 1724, and built a charming villa at Twickenham, called Marble Hill. She spent happy hours designing the house and its riverside gardens with Lord Herbert, designer of the Palladian bridge at Wilton, and Lord Bathurst as her advisers. The gleaming stuccoed walls and pediments of Marble Hill, surmounted by a golden globe and shaded by dark oaks and grassy terraces running down to the river, pleased all who visited Mrs Howard in her enviable seclusion. There was a housekeeper on the ground floor to supervise the smooth running of the house, and she entertained her few guests in a splendid Great Room – white and gold, with green and yellow damask chairs and copies of Van Dyck portraits set in the panelling. This, together with her bedroom and dressing room was elegantly situated at the top of a fine mahogany staircase. Here Mrs Howard could forget her lover, George, "who seemed to look upon a mistress rather as a necessary appurtenance to his grandeur as a prince than as an addition to his pleasures as a man."

Richmond and Twickenham were agreeable retreats for ladies who had

suffered in the world. Lovely Lady Diana Spencer, daughter of the 3rd Duke of Marlborough, chose a drunkard, Lord Bolingbroke, as her husband in 1757, from among a bevy of suitors. When she left him and went to live at a villa in Richmond with her children, Society decided that she had erred in leaving Bolingbroke, while he had not, in abusing her when drunk. Lady Diana took to painting in her riverside retreat, and her work was much admired by connoisseurs. Happily, she found love with a Mr Topham Beauclerk.

A contemporary and sometime neighbour at Twickenham, the Honourable Mrs Damer, was less forceful in her ways, but considered equally independent-minded. Daughter of Field Marshal Conway and of Lady Ailesbury,

Mrs Anne Damer, 1785, by Richard Cosway. Mrs Damer made a distinguished career as a sculptor, following her husband's suicide, and modelled both Nelson and Bonaparte. Horace Walpole bequeathed her his Gothic mansion, Strawberry Hill, distressingly full of spiders.

Anne Damer embraced sculpting as a career, after her husband shot himself at three in the morning in 1776, in a Covent Garden tavern, after suffering frightful gaming losses. She began by modelling in wax after a conversation with the philosopher, David Hume, in which it is alleged he admired some plaster figurines that an Italian was selling in the street. She decried his taste; he replied that no woman could carve anything of half such quality. Her rejoiner was to make his portrait bust in wax. Mrs Damer went on to study anatomy with Cruikshanks, and marble carving with Baron. Beginning with wax, she progressed to carving in marble and in bronze. Portrait sculpture was her speciality, at a time when ladies were expected to dabble only in watercolour.

99

Dr Johnson thought "portrait painting an improper employment for a woman. Public practice of any art and staring in men's faces is very indelicate in a female." And this she must do, if she took his likeness. Mrs Damer ignored such criticism, and carved a full-size marble portrait of George III. An adept hunter of "lions" of the moment, she hastened to visit Lord Nelson on his return to England in 1800, following the Battle of the Nile: her bust of him, unassuming in contemporary naval uniform, among a sea of politicians bewigged and betogaed, at the Royal Academy Exhibition of 1804, hit the popular fancy. This success did not prevent her from accepting several commissions from Napoleon – and it is said that she sent him a message of support before the Battle of Waterloo.

What income Mrs Damer derived from her sculptures we do not know, as she commanded that her correspondence and papers be burnt at her death in 1828. Also at her direction, her modelling tools and her working apron were placed in her coffin with her. She was often to be found at Park Place, her parents' home near Henley where her mother obsessively did worsted work. (Incidentally, Anne sculpted the masks of the river gods, Thamesis and Isis, which adorn keystones of the bridge in Henley, built in 1786.) Horace Walpole bequeathed to her his Gothic mansion at Strawberry Hill, and here she duly lived from 1797 till 1811. Walpole left her £2,000 a year for the upkeep of the house, which argues that Mrs Damer was not rich herself. One of her first acts was to dust the house free of the spiders which Walpole had allowed to accumulate on the grounds that they were Gothic creatures. Mrs Damer's amateur theatricals at Strawberry Hill became celebrated, though her own acting was judged to be uneven – as was her application of the startling rouge she favoured.

Anne Damer was not a sculptor of great merit, but she was the only English lady sculptor of her day. The interest of her story is that she secured a place in the ranks of professional artists, won commissions, and exhibited at the Royal Academy. The aristocracy and gentry were not expected to wish to excel in fields where professionals existed; the odd watercolour exhibited at the Annual Exhibition of the Royal Academy ought to satisfy all cravings for recognition. The Royal Academy was ambivalent in its attitude to woman painters, even established professionals. The German painter, Angelica Kauffman and Miss Mary Moser were both elected Founder Members in 1768, but in Zoffany's Group Portrait of the members, gathered round a nude male model, the ladies are missing. The keen observer will detect their shadowy presence in two vague portraits hung on a wall of the room. Ladies did not study the nude from life. Let them be content to learn anatomical detail from ancient statues and Renaissance drawings. The rule against female attendance at Life Classes remained in force at the Royal Academy till the 1890s. For this reason, ladies were encouraged to make the natural world their study, and let mankind go hang. Mary Moser, daughter of the Swiss-born Keeper of the Royal Academy, was so short-sighted that it is doubtful if she could have seen any useful anatomical

detail in a life model feet away on a podium. She did paint some portraits, but she specialised in flower painting, and a contemporary affirmed: her nose, when she was painting, was within an inch of her canvas. Near-sighted or not, Mary won a formidable reputation, and became a pet of Queen Charlotte and of the artistic Princess Elizabeth. They often visited her studio, and at last commissioned her to paint, for £900, an entire room with her flowers at Frogmore. It was known as "Miss Moser's Room". On marriage, like so many creative women, Mary Lloyd, as she became, abandoned her professional career and, for the rest of her life, painted only for her private pleasure.

Watercolour painting was the perfect amateur pastime. Oil painting remained throughout the eighteenth century a dirty, messy affair while clay and marble modelling was not exactly suitable for ladies, being demanding, dirty and fatiguing. Small wax figurines were occasionally made by gentlewomen with an active interest in sculpture. Japanning, shellwork, silhouette portraits were artistic projects popular in the first half of the eighteenth century, which were suitable for rainy mornings in the drawing-room and would not mess up a lady's dress. Books offering instruction to ladies in these arcane arts and suggesting designs were very popular. There were no instruction manuals for portrait painting – an art, like cabinet-making, best left to the professional. From the mid-eighteenth century on, ladies' interest in decorative arts palled beside the excitement of drawing classes. "Landskip painting" had come into vogue. The countryside of Britain was for the first time in its history thought a worthy subject for artists, and topography overtook physiognomy as the British artists' favoured subject matter. The aristocracy and gentry continued to

Furniture for an Artist's, or Amateur's Apartment.

Furniture for an Artist's or Amateur's Apartment, from Ackermann's Repository, July 1815. Sumptuous testimony to the enjoyment ladies and gentlemen derived from their drawing masters' lessons. Neat bricks of watercolour, replacing messy powder, increased the pleasure.

be painted, but now they were painted in "conversation pieces". Family groups romped and sported – in their best clothes, naturally – on an eminence before their country seat, tiny figures against a splendid show of bricks and mortar and landscaped parkland.

The Evangelical interest in the natural world, and the poetry of Cowper, did much to foster the new interest in landscape painting. Engraved views of nobleman's seats, executed with complete faithfulness, found a market among the gentry who, as we have seen, were beginning to journey around Britain for pleasure. From the mid-century, poets like Thomson created a "horrid", or lyrical atmosphere with topographical descriptions. Horace Walpole wrote *The*

Watercolour of Lawrence Sterne's Maria (1808), by Cassandra Austen, one of the many proficient lady watercolourists. In her teens, Cassandra illustrated her younger sister, Jane's caustic History of England. *Her later watercolours record her family and friends in characteristic, elegant occupation.*

Castle of Otranto, "the first Gothic novel", in 1764, and the floodgates were open for rich descriptions of atmospheric landscape.

With the stimulus of poetry and prose, landscape artists abandoned strict topographical precision and oil for watercolour. They made of their impressionistic preliminary pen sketches a final product. Overlaid with blocks of colour, the pen lines became sketchier, the effect more picturesque. The artist William Gilpin's *Essay on the Picturesque* of 1780 gave clear guidelines to artists in the matter. The ink vanished in the cause of romantic grandeur and colour alone was left, echoing "purple passages" of Mrs Radcliffe's *Mysteries of Udolpho*, a book wildly popular for thirty years after publication in 1794.

Fair Tea-makers

The importance of watercolour as a medium and landscape as a subject was that together they afforded the amateur a golden opportunity to "dabble", or to study, depending on talent and temperament. Ladies would have recoiled from the messy and cumbersome apparatus of oil-painting; after Reeves began to manufacture dry blocks of watercolour in the mid-eighteenth century, only the addition of a little gum and, of course, water, was needed. Elegant watercolour boxes resembling tea caddies, with neat drawers for phials and brushes and a grid for "squaring up", became an indispensable part of a lady's equipment when she travelled. In 1818 Miss Diana Sperling, a keen amateur artist, had the conventional reaction on a visit to Netley Abbey, a medieval structure near Southampton: "It is a spot where I should like to pass many hours with my pencil and drawing book, Charley [her brother] by my side playing his flute and a book of reflections on the encroachment of time . . . this beautiful ruin has inspired me with romantic ideas." Diana had profited by twenty lessons a month in music and drawing at a cost of three guineas a lesson.

When the English gentlewoman began her artistic education, there was no dearth of candidates suitable to become her drawing master. Artists of the eminence of Paul Sandby were regularly employed in the military and naval academies to teach young officers to make sketches of fortifications and battle positions. Draughtsmen were employed to etch pictures for engraving by printmakers. Professional artists found it difficult to scratch a living from the sale of their work, and taught other artists; sometimes they gave a few lessons to a young gentleman who was contemplating a Continental tour, and wished to sketch the curiosities he visited. (Occasionally, a rich patron paid for a painter to go and paint a particular locality, like Sicily or the Swiss Alps.)

There was, then, a large number of gentlemen skilled in draughtsmanship and poor of pocket available, when it became all the rage for young ladies to make sketches and watercolour paintings of the countryside. Needy professional artists were not too proud to teach young ladies, either in a school or at home with private lessons. The artists came of the poorer classes; their contact with their pupils' families widened the market for their works. Also, if their pupils' work was a credit to them, more lady pupils would be forthcoming. (The improving hand of the drawing master can often be detected in the sketches and watercolours of amateurs, for this reason.) The artist, James Holworthy, painted a feeling watercolour of *The Drawing Master*, with two fair pupils seated trustfully beside him. Richard Wilson was one of few painters who refused to take pupils. Invited to a gentleman's house, he asked an acquaintance, "Are there any young ladies?" There were. "Do they draw?" They did. "Good morning to you then," returned Wilson, and turned away. By 1780 or so, no young lady of gentle birth was without her portfolio of sketches and paintings. A few ladies excelled, owing to the excellence of their tutors. Amelia Long, Lady Farnborough had the revolutionary colourist, Thomas Girtin, as her master; Frances Tomline was taught by John Glover; Catherine Maria Fanshawe was another superior artist. In half a century, from 1750 to 1800,

general feminine ignorance of the rudiments of draughtsmanship had ceded to a general competence in pen and brushwork.

Ladies' enthusiasm for art led them into some interesting byways. Gainsborough and Alexander Cozens taught drawing to George III's innumerable children. The princesses Mary and Elizabeth became keen artists and developed an interest in engraving – whereupon their mother, Queen Charlotte, set up a printing press at Frogmore House for their plates to be printed. The process of engraving exerted quite a fascination for amateurs in the eighteenth century. Books of some of their efforts exist in the British Museum; among the etchers content to stain their noble fingers are dukes and countesses and other great people of the day. (The same fancy for playing at working led to the "craze" for cobbling or making shoes in 1810, to which George IV's daughter, Princess Charlotte, among others, subscribed.)

Among professional artists, Sir Joshua Reynolds was one of few eighteenth-century portraitists to possess a close female relation who wished to emulate him. His sister Frances was a devoted housekeeper to the Devon-born President of the Royal Academy from 1752 on, but she pursued a career as a miniature painter "in spite of the contemptuous opinion expressed of her attempts by her brother". Pathetically, stealthily, she made copies of her brother's portrait to try and improve her style, as the artist himself would give her no advice. Making copies for their male relations was, of course, the traditional role for the female dependants of professional artists.

Necessarily, when they were busy with the mechanical drudgery of copying, they had no time to further their own talents – but most of them never thought of doing so. In a different field, that of science, Miss Sarah Sophia Banks, sister of Sir Joseph, acted as her brother's secretary, and made a vast collection of ephemera – play bills, trade cards, visiting cards. These she begged from her brother's many friends in England and abroad; the collection is the first of its kind known in England. Did Miss Banks sublimate a scientific bent for taxology in arranging these slips of paper? The novelist, Fanny Burney, had to write her best seller *Evelina*, published in 1778, at night; all her days were taken up with copying out for her father, the musicologist, Dr Charles Burney, his *General History of Music*. She published *Evelina* anonymously, but her father recognised it as her work. On his informing her that his "set" – including Reynolds, Dr Johnson, Mrs Thrale – were all entranced by the book, Fanny gave expression to her joy by dancing round a mulberry tree. Then she settled down to write *Cecilia*, which had even greater success when published in 1782.

The conditions and materials needed for writing are, of course, less demanding than those required by the secret artist or scientist. Still, determination was required in Fanny's case, as in the case of Caroline Herschel, the astronomer's sister who discovered eight comets. In her early twenties, Caroline came from Hanover to join William at Bath in 1772, and did not leave again till his death fifty years later. On his marriage to a county heiress, William could afford to devote himself entirely to his studies of the skies. Famously, in 1781,

Fair Tea-makers

Silhouette (1782), showing two ladies occupying themselves by reading aloud. The work-basket lies ready on the table. Creating these silhouettes, with cut-outs, or by painting shapes, was another popular way of improving the shining hour.

he discovered the planet, Uranus. Caroline regarded her own discoveries with modesty; she spent the years after her brother's death forming a catalogue of the clusters and nebulae which had occupied him.

Women in professional circles with access to specialist equipment benefited little, then, by the contiguity, deterred by notions of feminine modesty from professional drudgery, or being too busy with drudgery on their father's or brother's behalf. Still, without a male relative of scientific or other academic bent, ladies had no opportunity at all to acquaint themselves with the secrets of science. What of the other arts? Music, the gentlewoman frequently took very seriously, and might lavish hours every day on it, be it singing or performing on an instrument. Here the professional father was a positive advantage to the musical lady.

The most illustrious family of English musicians in the mid-eighteenth century were the Linleys of Bath. Thomas Linley, the father, was Master of Ceremonies at monthly concerts he devised, entitled Attic Entertainments. (These concerts did not take place in a garret but in the Bath Assembly-rooms. They were intended to recall the musical feasts of Ancient Athens.) At these concerts, Linley could call upon his friend, the composer William Boyce, to contribute, and on Johann Christian Bach, youngest son of J.S. Bach and

Mrs Sheridan in the character of St Cecilia, after Sir Joshua Reynolds. On marrying Elizabeth Linley, Richard Brinsley Sheridan, then an actor-manager, forbade her to sing in public for money. She did accounts at his theatre instead.

musician to Queen Charlotte from 1763. Public concerts were still, like public exhibitions of contemporary art, in their infancy, and were much frequented.

In the late 1760s, moreover, Linley's assiduous tuition of his growing family bore fruit, as they developed into fine musicians. There was Thomas, junior, friend of Mozart, and Samuel; Linley's daughters also appeared on the advertisements. Mary and Maria Linley were competent singers; their sister, Elizabeth, outshone all with her beauty, and with her remarkable voice. Her repertoire included the upper part of a glee for five voices, "Hark the Bird's Melodious Strain". Her brother, Thomas, leader of the Bath orchestra, solo violinist, composed the song at her request. The fame of the Linley larks grew, and in 1772 George III summoned the girls to give a Royal Command Performance at Buckingham Palace. He told Elizabeth's proud father that he had never heard so fine a voice, "nor one so well-instructed".

Fair Tea-makers

The Bath concerts, so popular, were sadly doomed to lose Elizabeth to matrimony the next year. She eloped to France with the actor-manager, Richard Brinsley Sheridan, son of a teacher of elocution in Bath and later famous as dramatist and politician. After her departure, the Attic Entertainments lost much of their appeal. Sheridan would not permit his wife to sing again in public, thinking it not respectable. He relaxed his rule only once, when Lord North, the Prime Minister, was invested as Chancellor of Oxford University. Elizabeth sang in an oratorio, and North told Sheridan that he ought to be awarded an honorary degree, *uxoris causa*, or, in honour of his wife. When Sheridan and his father-in-law, Linley, went into business together, managing the Drury Lane Theatre, Elizabeth was given charge of the actresses' wardrobes and she also helped her mother with the accounts. The only tangible memento of her singing career is the portrait by Reynolds, "Mrs Elizabeth Sheridan as St Cecilia". Elizabeth sits in profile at the keyboards, with heavenly choristers at her knees representing her children.

The keyboard was traditionally the musical instrument associated with women, and the iconography for St Cecilia, patron of music, seated at the keyboards, extends back to the middle ages. There exist many "social" portraits of gentlewomen at the virginals from the sixteenth century on, while the seventeenth century had seen the costly harpsichord appear in the great country houses. As a matter of prestige, the lady of the great house might be painted seated at it. Her steward's wife might be painted at its country cousin, the spinet, which arrived from France with Charles II's Court in the 1660s, to supplant the virginals as the convenient, domestic instrument.

Spinets were still not cheap, or widely available, and keyboard playing remained the preserve of the rich. With the introduction of the forte piano in 1758, the picture changes. In 1758 some refugees from the Seven Years' War arrived in England from South Germany. They began making, as they had done at home, the small square forte piano, which became immediately popular. By 1785, it had put the harpsichord quite in the shade. From 1729 to 1793 the partners Shudi and Broadwood made 1,200 harpsichords. In the next six years they made only pianos, and by 1799 had made 9,000 of them. Most of these instruments were destined for the domestic home, forerunners of the small "upright", or cottage piano, to be observed in every Victorian middle-class home. As we see from portraits, it is the lady who sits at the keyboards, who learns to play the instrument. Apart from a few composers like Gluck and Haydn, who are shown composing at the keyboards, or children, performers of the forte piano in paintings, as of the harpsichord and the virginals before, are invariably women. (Gentlemen are shown with their flute resting on one crossed knee, or with their violin held at their side.) From the 1760s on, with the piano readily available and cheap – a forte piano cost a twelfth of the price of a harpsichord – music as an accomplishment came to mean piano playing. Music masters proliferated, and did good business. Now they taught "use of the instrument" as well as singing. "Fingering" played a major part in tuition from now on; many

young ladies must have cursed its inventor, J.S. Bach's second son, C.P.E. Bach. Families which had never possessed any musical instrument now put their forte piano proudly in the drawing-room, and subjected their guests to the wearisome business of listening to the daughter of the house perform her party piece. In any gathering, however provincial, now there was always a lady who could play a polka or a minuet for others to dance to. Books of songs entitled *The Ladies Evening Companion*, or *Fancy's Medley* littered every drawing-room.

Some gentlewomen displayed a skill far above that of the average drawing-room performers. The hours available to the lady of leisure for study and practice were invaluable. Today Catherine, Lady Hamilton, could have been a professional pianist. As it was, she made strenuous efforts to perfect her art for art's sake. Catherine seems to have acquired her musical education as if by magic in remote Wales, where she was brought up, plain but rich daughter of a gentleman farmer, Mr Barlow. On marriage to Sir William Hamilton, she removed from her native Wales to London. Here Catherine joined with her husband and five of his friends to pay the musician, Felice Giardini, to give a master class of "Academy of Musick" each week. The next year, Catherine accompanied her diplomat husband to Naples, whose conservatories and opera houses were famous. Catherine continued with her playing – on both harpsichord and forte piano. Her husband kept a "band of musick" in the house – no great luxury in Naples – and she would play with them; she invited the singers, and the musicians and composers like Millico and Piccinni from the San Carlo opera house to perform at her home; she played – very nervously – before the young Mozart in 1774; and she composed a sombre *Funeral March for Hector*. She helped Fanny Burney's father acquire material for his *History of Music* on his visit to Naples in 1770, and she played melancholy duets with the young William Beckford in 1784.

Lady Hamilton was probably the ablest performer on the keyboards of all Englishwomen in the eighteenth century. There were fine teachers at work in London who brought pupils to an agreeable level of proficiency. Thomas Attwood, from 1796 organist at St Paul's, had among his pupils the daughters of the Jewish banker, Abraham Goldsmid. The whole family was intensely musical, and the Misses Goldsmid would perform for their father's royal friends, and other distinguished guests. (Attwood, a coal merchant's son, also acted as music master to the three royal ladies – the Duchess of York, the Duchess of Cumberland, and the Princess of Wales.) The musical inventor, John Joseph Merlin, was an intimate of the Johnson and Burney musical group in the 1770s. On Johnson's advice, Mrs Thrale engaged him to teach her daughter, Hester Maria.

It was considered quite smart to have one or two singers from the Italian Opera at an evening party. As for the ladies of the Opera, Madame Mara, "the Grassini", Mrs Billington – they had their own society, and members of the nobility and gentry who visited them were strictly male. They were certainly not invited to teach delicately nurtured young ladies the rudiments of music. Male music masters, it was thought, could be trusted. Occasionally, however, the undesirable happened. When in 1784 Mrs Thrale married Gabriel Piozzi,

*Jane, Countess of Eglinton,
by Sir Joshua Reynolds. The
Countess touches her harp
against a background
intended to recall the
grandeur of ancient Rome
and of her position. Noble
patrons favoured the
"costume" portraits which
Reynolds and Romney
pioneered.*

tutor of the piano forte – he carried around in his carriage a miniature instrument to advertise his profession – Dr Johnson never spoke to her again.

Any lady of good birth, then, was ready to seat herself at the forte piano with her music, and amuse the company, if called upon. The sketches of John Harden, of Thomas Baxter, of Cassandra Austen, show that, in the circles of the gentry, groupings round the instrument of an evening were common in genteel circles. A gentleman might turn the pages, or hold a candlestick or join the lady at the instruments in a duet. Generally, it was for the ladies to show off their paces, and the installation of the forte piano in the drawing-room made both room and instrument all the more the lady's domain. Jane Austen recorded in

After Tea, *a sketch by Olivia de Ros, 1825. Division of the sexes after dinner began in the eighteenth century when ladies retired to brew tea. They moped till the gentlemen came through; then sprightliness was, as here, general.*

her "Plan of a Novel, according to hints from various quarters" the requirements of the "Heroine": "particularly excelling in Music – her favourite pursuit – & playing equally well on the Piano Forte & Harp – & singing in the first style."

If music was not pleasing to all, one pastime which enjoyed very wide currency in the eighteenth century was gaming. There were gambling "hells" for the gentlemen; great ladies would provide a card room at their ball, for gentlemen who did not wish to dance or walk about in the assembly, or make conversation in the supper room. The ladies gambled themselves as furiously as the men in private and some, like Lady Mornington in 1745, kept public gaming houses. In the late eighteenth century, the Ladies Buckinghamshire and Archer ran a faro bank with all the expertise of a modern croupier in a casino. Gaming was the vice of the age from Queen Anne's reign onward. The essayist Steele commented in 1713: "Hollow eyes, haggard Looks, and pale Complexions, are

Fair Tea-makers

the natural Indications of a Female Gamester." Alexander Pope's *Rape of the Lock* (1714), includes a scene where two ladies and two gentlemen enjoy a card party, following a water-party at Hampton Court. Ombre, a game introduced from Spain, featured in Pope's poem; basset and whist, quadrille, and loo became popular later in the century. Everyone gambled, and in the way of things, most lost fortunes. Georgiana, Duchess of Devonshire and her sister, Harriet, Lady Bessborough, were in constant dread of their husbands' discovering the extent of their debts. In the desk drawer of Abraham Goldsmid, on his death in 1811, were found promissory notes from the Duchess of Devonshire and other ladies; the benevolent banker never requested repayment.

The Card Table, by Rowlandson (c. 1780), showing fashionable ladies indulging in the vice of the age. The dejected lady with her purse hanging empty on the left and a husband to face in the morning was all too common a sight.

Other ladies suffered when their husbands or fathers lost fortunes at cards. Lady Caroline Capel was forced to flee with her husband, and many children, to the continent in 1814, to escape his creditors. In 1804 he had owed £20,000. She had the consolation of being at Brussels to hear first-hand reports of the Battle of Waterloo in 1815. Her brother, the Earl of Uxbridge, commanded the Allied Cavalry brilliantly, despite the loss of a leg. Lady Caroline discovered only after the victory that her husband had continued gaming secretly at Brussels – at an establishment purporting to be a Literary Club, where he was in the habit of going to "read the English newspapers". Philippina, Lady Knight went to live in Italy in 1785, being, like many other naval widows, unable to secure a pension following her admiral husband's death. Lady Knight, friend of Dr Johnson, and her daughter, the bluest of blue-stockings, Ellis Cornelia Knight, lived frugally among the extravagant English community in Rome. They never entertained, and Cornelia made all their clothes, when not writing

lively works like a *Life* of Marcus Flaminius. One principle to which they adhered was, no gaming. The Knights were thought most singular in this. Though gambling in women was deplored, everyone did it, just the same – and ladies filled their diaries with notes that some arch-enemy had been seen, playing "very deep". (Their own losses or winnings for the evening were recorded below.) In the English country vicarage, the total winnings were likely to be a few shillings. As country ladies discovered to their cost, a fashionable card party in London might end with a lady throwing her jewels on to the table. No social pastime ever caused more acute social distress than the "accursed craze for card-playing". As the financial position of women had not changed – their fathers or husbands still had charge of their income – ultimately the father or husband must be told of the losses.

Did any gentlewomen take steps in the eighteenth century to obtain some measure of financial independence? There were very few options available, which could be reasonably considered by a lady, and which would guarantee her an income on which she could live otherwise unsupported. Writing was an uncertain business. The ladies who wrote Gothic novels for the Minerva Press in the 1790s did not all enjoy the staggering success of Mrs Radcliffe. She made £500 from *The Mysteries of Udolpho*. Ladies like Jane Austen who wrote in a more sober vein could expect little pecuniary regard. Jane Austen's forerunner, Fanny Burney, had a £30 advance payment for *Evelina* in 1778. In 1782 a first edition of *Cecilia*, comprising two thousand copies, sold out in three months. However, after a period at Court as Keeper of the Robes, when she was kept too busy to write, she had for income only a royal pension of £100 a year. (On this small support, she and the French General, d'Arblay, married in 1793.) In 1796 *Camilla* sold 3,500 copies by subscription, and she made an estimated £2,000. She celebrated by buying and christening a small cottage Camilla Cottage. It was her last success. *The Wanderer*, published in 1802, was read by nobody.

The gentlewoman in need must either become a governess, or, if of an age, a companion or chaperone. These posts included wages, and board and lodging. A lady must be indigent indeed to consider acting as companion, as the century proceeded. With houses and apartments within the houses decreasing in size, the household of servants decreased also. The great chamber and great room, or large saloon, existed only in the grandest houses. Drawing-rooms and libraries became the norm, and formal attendants like footmen were not needed in these modern reception rooms. Attendant ladies were needed still less.

What was needed in these smaller, elegant apartments was a plentiful supply of housemaids to keep all clean, and a housekeeper to direct them, in place of a major domo. (A butler was kept only in the town houses of the nobility, or in the houses of misogynists.) This was to prove the pattern from now on in the English genteel household. To the housekeeper, moreover, the lady of the house assigned all the responsibilities which she had previously undertaken herself when male servants had predominated. The housekeeper's room was placed next to the still-room, which the lady made over to her. The

Fair Tea-makers

housekeeper made preserves and pickles here, where earlier ladies of the house had made healing ointments which physicians now supplied. Here the house-keeper washed the delicate porcelain which her employer's mother-in-law would have washed herself. The housekeeper and not the lady of the house now used the small charcoal stove in the still-room to supplement luncheons and dinners on special occasions with sweetmeats or some delicate "made" dish. The housekeeper was in her mistress's confidence, if the house was to run smoothly; hers was the comforting ear which the companion or gentlewoman's gentlewoman had provided. The lady of the house now had her dresser or maid, and her housekeeper – neither of them wellborn – for her confidantes. When a family such as the Spencers had a town house and a principal country seat, the housekeeper would remain resident in town or country, while the family came to and fro.

As elegance replaced grandeur, there were fewer formal occasions where the mistress of the house needed the help of another lady, and fewer quiet evenings where the mistress wanted company at her needlework. By the end of the century there was little call in a busy family house for a gentlewoman's gentlewoman. Fortunately, dowager ladies were a breed who generally wished for a lady companion. Accustomed to directing a large household, they found comfort in their dower houses in nagging ceaselessly at an unfortunate and impoverished poor relation. Fanny Price's relations with her aunt at Mansfield Park have all the seeds of such an existence to come – happily avoided by marriage to her worthy cousin, Edmund.

Silhouette family piece, by Francis Torond, of Mr and Mrs Smith of Hailsham and Aunt Everard (c. 1777). Named after Etienne de Silhouette, Louis XV's finance minister, these affordable profile portraits were only supplanted in genteel homes by photography.

113

Chapter Three

Ladies who were so eccentric as not to marry and to set up their own household, to appease propriety generally provided themselves with a duenna or chaperone – again, often a poor relation. Sometimes, the position elevated a woman's status. When Eleanor Butler and Sarah Ponsonby eloped together, and went to live in a cottage at Llangollen in 1778, their families in Ireland were scandalised. The ladies' confidante was Mary Carryll, who had been a housemaid at Sarah Ponsonby's home and came to be more companion than maid. The ladies of Llangollen kept two housemaids, to do the housework while they paid for powder for Mary's hair, and invited their farmer landlord and family to dine with them and with Mary each Christmas.

Diana Sperling, whom we encountered enthusing at Netley Abbey, resided till marriage – at the age of forty-three – at her parents' home, Dynes Hall, on the Essex-Suffolk border. Two charming sketchbooks filled with her watercolours and dating from 1812 to 1823 are preserved. They chronicle the daily life of the "ranks of the substantial gentry", to which the Sperlings belonged – "the sort of well-to-do squires who dominated village affairs and helped fill up the county bench of magistrates". We see Diana, her sister Isabella, and Mrs Van Hagen – the married sister, identifiable by her cap of consequence – making lavender oil, pasting up fresh wallpaper and a border in Mrs Van Hagen's Elizabethan manor in Buckinghamshire, "murdering flies" in the high cornices of

Papering the Saloon at Tickford Park, a watercolour by Diana Sperling (1816). Printed wallpaper was an innovation of the eighteenth century. Here the lady of the house, assisted by her eager sisters, glues the borders on the thick walls of her unfashionable Tudor house.

114

Fair Tea-makers

Dynes Hall. These domestic exertions were not undertaken by ladies in the higher echelons of society – in the ducal and other great houses – but the lady of the house did well to interest herself in the details of the household management.

Dean Swift has left us a merciless satire on slatternly habits rife among servants of the early eighteenth century. His *Directions to Servants* suggests that the chambermaid, in the event of breaking a mirror accidentally with the long end of her broom, should cut the cord by which the mirror hung from the wall, lay the mirror flat on the ground and pretend the cord was faulty – or just say it was lightning. The waiting-maid must be sure to get false keys for the chests where it was now regrettably the fashion to keep the tea and the sugar. For the housemaid, the best tip was to lay "the foul, wet cloth" on the next chair, when she had finished scouring brasses and irons by the fire. Then the lady of the house would know she had not neglected her work. Swift himself lived as chaplain between servants' hall and parlour; he knew the sins on both sides of the baize door, and perhaps his sharpest comment on the domestic scene comes in his satire, *A Description of the Morning*:

> Now Betty from her master's bed has flown
> And softly stole to discompose her own.

Betty was the generic name in this period for that invaluable aid to all ladies of fashion, the lady's maid. She acted as dresser and coiffeur to her mistress; she waited up till her lady returned from a midnight ball, to take and fold her clothes and prepare her for the night. She attended her mistress at all changes of clothes, brought her her chocolate in the morning, and generally was regarded with some respect by the other domestics. While not a gentlewoman by birth – a lady's companion would not have dreamt of becoming a maid – the dresser or lady's maid was still far removed from the life below stairs of the housemaid or kitchenmaid. She absorbed all the fine notions of her mistress, and, at a wage of £8 a year, the rest found, she could afford to indulge herself a little finery – which no doubt attracted her master.

Mistresses often offered to Betty dresses or cloaks or trifling ornaments when they felt in a good mood. As a result, Voltaire could go walking about Greenwich Fair and think the servant maids so elegant, managing their hired horses with such ease, that he mistook them for "persons of fashion". Which, indeed, they were. Their passion for ornament was pronounced, perhaps fed by the long hours they must spend caring for their mistresses' wardrobes. The Sessions courts were crowded with cases of ladies' maids accused of robbing their mistresses' purses, the better to afford costly items of fashion.

The fashions for ladies became quite outrageous in the mid-eighteenth century. Every help the deportment master could offer was needed to manage the side-panniers and hoops with grace. Hair styles and jewellery reflected the taste for extravagance. The late 1780s and 1790s saw reaction, and an interesting

phenomenon – the revival, for the first time in English fashion, of historical costume. A passion for the antique world, stimulated by sightseeing in Italy and by neoclassical painting, led ladies to dress like Greek nymphs. The English weather was not conducive to the wearing of a tunic alone, though some ladies suffered for art. (Famously, Lady Caroline Lamb dampened her muslin dress, to attract Lord Byron at a ball with its clinging folds.) Most wore a chemise or drawstring shift, with a pelisse or over-dress of some warmer material on top.

There were times when this new informal attire was inappropriate. The Queen's Drawing-Rooms continued the demand for full Court dress, of a stiff, boned and feathered shape. Sports also made their particular demands. The riding habit did not alter much throughout the century, but "walking costumes" became sturdier, as ladies began to use their limbs with greater freedom. Archery was a sport which became very popular, after two centuries of neglect, in the 1780s when a Mr Waring made trial with a bow in an attempt to alleviate constriction of the chest due to business oppression. He and Sir Ashton Lever founded the Toxophilite Society at Leicester House in London in 1780, and the Prince of Wales became a keen patron. Societies of Archers burgeoned nationwide, and ladies became among the most ardent bowmen.

The Brockman Family and Friends at Beachborough House, Kent *by Benjamin Hateley (c. 1745). The arrival of an artist to idealise a sojourn at a country house caused great excitement. Ladies chose to fish, sketch, ride in their finest gowns.*

Fair Tea-makers

The Marchioness of Salisbury was a keen bowman as well as huntswoman by 1791 and contributed an article on archery to the first issue of the *Sporting Magazine*. Invitations to Mrs Crespigny's archery breakfasts at Grove House in Camberwell were prized, though bad shots had to pay a fine, which went towards the upkeep of a Sunday School. As the lady patroness, she decided on the serious matter of the costume of the lady archers. Lady patronesses generally incorporated "grass green" into the colour scheme. There was both the costume for the contest to consider, and the dress for the ball which followed. In 1796 the Royal Surrey Archers proposed for the ball dress, a white muslin round gown, with green and buff sash, and a white chip hat with two bows atop a ribboned crown. A magnificent snow-white ostrich plume waved aloft, with a sprig of box "so arranged beneath, as to appear just above the wearer's left eyebrow".

Indoors the gentlewoman had the responsibilities of her household, in particular Nurse and the governess. Nurse generally remained much longer than the governess – though there is the case of Miss Sarah "Selina" Trimmer, who was a devoted and beloved governess to the Devonshire children for ten years. She was the only member of that rackety household in whom the Duchess's mother, Lady Spencer, placed any confidence. Miss Trimmer was one of twelve children; all of the six girls were educated by their mother who published six volumes of Bible stories for children, and was active in the Sunday School movement. Miss Trimmer made valiant efforts to give the Cavendish girls a Christian education and an interest in charity.

There was the academic Miss Elstob, who was employed on Mrs Delany's recommendation, to teach the Duchess of Portland's daughters at Bulstrode Park from 1738 till her death in 1756. With smaller houses, and smaller households, it became a genuine problem to know in what part of the house the governess should have her being. It was not appropriate for her to eat with the upper servants in the housekeeper's room, or in the kitchen; she could not remain fixed in the schoolroom, yet she was not always a welcome addition to a sparkling dinner table. Parents preferred to send their daughters to school, and governesses preferred to teach in schools, in consequence of this social awkwardness. In 1772 Mrs Montagu visited her niece at a school in Chelsea, and found conditions much improved since the 1730s, when she herself had attended a school in Kensington. "I was pleased to find my niece perfectly clean and neat, tho' I called on ye Saturday, which is usually only the eve of cleanliness. I remember at Mrs Robartes', at Kensington, the girls used to be so dirty, sometimes one could not salute them!"

Schools in the eighteenth century might claim to offer a wholesale education. In practice, they taught girls from the country how to behave in Polite Society – and all the emphasis was on dancing and dress and deportment. Generally girls had picked up their scholastic education at home, before going to school, with a governess or by conning their father's libary. Lady Mary Pierrepoint taught herself Latin during a solitary adolescence in Nottingham-shire, from the classical texts in the magnificent library. Her father had taken

her when a child to the famous Kit-Kat Club in London, where the literati had been much impressed by her babbling. Her later education she had to find for herself. The Reverend George Austen had a library of five hundred volumes, which was large for a country parson. This was fortunate for his daughter Jane. The schools to which her parents sent their daughters – at Southampton, Oxford and Reading – were not a success. At Southampton Jane and her sister nearly died of a fever; at the Abbey School, near Reading, they were fed and their clothes kept clean by Mrs Latournelle, but an artificial cork leg was their preceptress's claim to respect. She had been married to a Frenchman, but spoke no French. In 1785 the Austen girls returned home, after only a year of

Tradecard advertising a genteel "Ladies-school". In a 1786 comedy, The Heiress, the character of tutors at such establishments is derided: "a strolling-player for a dancing master, and a deserter from Dunkirk to teach the French grammar".

lackadaisical tuition, to complete their education by reading and conversing.

The proprietors of the schools for young ladies which flourished as the eighteenth century proceeded knew where their duty lay – which was to provide "the first Rudiments of a Polite Education". Lord Chesterfield considered that "the genteelness of a man consisted more in . . . graceful gestures with heads and arms, than in anything else, especially in dancing." He recommended that his son paid careful attention to his dancing master who doubled as teacher of deportment in the eighteenth century. The youth must learn to sit genteely, to loll genteely, to greet inferiors and equals and superiors appropriately. Young ladies were taught the same wearisome details of etiquette and deportment. Matthew Towle, dancing master in Oxford, published *The Young*

Gentleman and Lady's Private Tutor in 1770. A list of proprietors of boarding schools for young ladies gave public approval to the work. "Dancing", stressed the dancing master, "gives a proper Deportment, a genteel Behaviour and an easy Address." He painted a hideous spectacle of those who had not learnt "the Art" – "their Toes will lap one over the other in Walking, their Heads will project forward, even until their Chin touch their Bosoms." They will be "awkward . . . uncouth . . . deficient in Civility, and even Boorish". So dancing "adds greatly to the happiness of Society, for the happiness of Society depends on civility."

Towle enjoined that young ladies should be "dress'd genteel, that is in Silk or linen" for dancing. Their stockings should be silk or cotton, their shoes, leather "Pumps" of "thin, soft and yielding leather, with no Heels". Girls to the age of fourteen might sport a feather, a "pompoon" or "ribband" in their hair. Older pupils must doff their "Hats, tippets & Shawles". Towle taught his pupils how to use a fan, how to curtsey, how to stand and sit, and , finally, how to dance. The steps were less important than the demeanour: "let your Eyes appear lively and Modest, express neither Mirth nor Gravity, but the medium, which will make you agreeable and genteel." For a year's course of dancing

An Elegant Establishment, by Edward Burney (1760-1848). Jane Austen visited such a school in 1813: "If it had not been for some naked Cupids over the mantlepiece, which must be a fine study for the girls, one would never have smelt instruction."

119

lessons, a pupil at Mrs Sneath's school in Great Marlow, or Mrs Perfect's in Streatley, might pay their dancing master four guineas.

Generally included in the main charges, with English and French, was teaching of needlework. In the eighteenth century the custom that a young lady completed her education by working a sampler continued, but excellence in embroidery was now less prized, with the interest in drawing and music. Still, on completion it was often framed and hung for general admiration. The young lady now stitched on a woollen cloth called "tammy", not silk and she composed her work to show numeracy, piety and good taste – and to make a pleasant picture. Letters of the alphabet and numerals in regular lines were succeeded by a verse, such as:

> This I did to let you see,
> What care my parents took of me.

A picture might then fill some space – Adam and Eve, a ship in full sail, a shepherdess with sheep were common subjects. The whole was edged with a narrow border and signed and dated by the conscientious sempstress.

Not through use of the needle and tambour frame but by reading and conversation, ladies made their minds elegant, and could now discuss a wealth of ideas and subjects with their male relations. They could now be companions, rather than housekeepers. A bookseller, James Lackington, commented in 1791: "there are some thousands of women, who frequent my shop, that know as well what books to choose, and are as well acquainted with works of taste and genius, as any gentleman in the kingdom, notwithstanding they sneer against novel readers." In conversation, too, ladies – with confidence newfound, and, perhaps, opinions acquired from their reading – now came into their own. Mrs Elizabeth Vesey hosted meetings of the Literary Club at her home in the 1780s: "Mrs Montagu, Mrs Thrale, and Lord Mulgrave talked all the talk, and talked it so well, no one else had a wish beyond hearing them." Widows had no thought of retiring from the world. At Richmond, Mrs Garrick continued to invite guests to her villa after the death of her husband, the illustrious actor-manager, David Garrick. She belonged to a coterie of "blue-stocking" ladies who insisted on literary conversation and no cards or political discussion at their homes. The company might include young ladies in their twenties, clever Miss Mary Hamilton among them, and they conversed and disputed as hard as any. The old etiquette of respecting the opinions of gentlemen, and of elders, had ceded to a more rational view of social intercourse.

It took time, of course, to adjust to adult life, and for this purpose, the Season was introduced. Most girls spent their childhoods in the country, uneventfully. Some, like Catherine Morland in *Northanger Abbey*, were "noisy and wild", enjoyed "cricket, baseball, riding on horseback", and "loved nothing so well in the world as rolling down the green slope at the back of the house". Others were brought up to have a care for their clothes, to cosset them-

Fair Tea-makers

The Ladies Waldegrave (1781), by Reynolds. Horace Walpole commissioned this portrait of his "three fair nieces . . . embroidering and winding silk". Lady Horatia works on a tambour frame with a hook. Knotting, using a shuttle, was other popular ladies' work.

selves, and exhibit dolls' dresses which they had made themselves, rather than a knowledge of French, with pride. Others were keen to rival their brothers. Henry Fielding's sister, Sarah, persuaded a neighbouring clerygman, Arthur Collier, to teach her Latin. (Henry encouraged his sister in her study of English literature; he became jealeous when she could read Virgil.) But on coming to Town all must exhibit the kind of decorum and elegant deportment which was required to crown a successful Season with marriage.

Free as girls might be in their manners, in the matter of marriage they were expected to follow their parents' wishes. From 1710 to 1714, the last four years of Queen Anne's reign, Lady Mary Pierrepoint agonised whether or not to marry Edward Wortley Montagu. To do so would be to disoblige her papa, the Marquess of Dorchester; he had "broken the treaty", or refused Edward's offer for his daughter's hand already, on a financial quibble. On the other hand, to marry Edward would be to free herself. Lady Mary mused, from the constraints of family life, which seemed to increase as she grew older. And Edward thought of travelling. ". . . it is the thing upon Earth I should most wish . . . I should prefer that manner of living to any other . . ." she wrote eagerly to him. Four years later, Lord Dorchester had found an Irish nobleman as a suitable husband

for Mary. An elopement with Edward seemed the only solution. "I tremble for what we are doing," she wrote. "Are you sure you will love me for ever?" Ruin would naturally follow upon her clandestine marriage. She was philosophical. She looked forward to living abroad, "in an agreeable Country, with a Man that I like, that likes me, and forgetting the rest of the world as much as if there was no other people in the world, and that Naples were the Garden of Eden."

The deed was done, and Lady Mary Wortley Montagu, the intrepid traveller, had begun her first adventure. In 1715, after the accession of George I to promote Whig interests, Edward was appointed Minister Plenipotentiary to the Porte, the Sultan's magnificent court at Constantinople. Lady Mary busied

Lady Mary Wortley Montagu with her son, Edward (c. 1717-18), attributed to J. B. Vanmour. Lady Mary revelled in her husband's appointment as Minister to the Ottoman Porte, sported rose-coloured Turkish pantaloons and received guests on cushions on the floor.

herself finding liveries of blue touched with silver for the Embassy servants, then gathered up her baby son and set off on the Turkish travels which were to bring her such fame. Her object was at last achieved. She was a travelling lady, and she boasted that she and her husband were the first Christians from Europe to journey across the Hungarian plains. Lady Mary was undoubtedly the first Englishwoman to make the trip. Clad in rose-coloured pantaloons and wearing rose-tinted spectacles, she wrote home letters describing her impressions of the Turkish people, of Islam, of the countryside customs. Published some years later – she had kept copies with an eye to publication – the *Turkish Letters of Lady Mary Wortley Montagu* caused a sensation.

Fair Tea-makers

Lady Mary was exceptionally lucky visiting Turkey, and at the King of England's expense. Most English gentlewomen who felt a curiosity to travel had to make the most of a winter's trip to France, or to Italy and the German states. The expense of travel was very great. Not only the chief travellers, the gentleman and his lady, had to be accounted for; there was my lady's maid, and my lord's valet, and a courier and footmen and cooks and running footmen to be hired in each country, and in each city. The cost of transporting an entire family, with children and governesses and tutors, was easily affordable only by the very rich. Travel was thought to lend polish, however, so it became the custom to send young gentlemen, when they reached their majority, to visit the sights of Europe. A deserving prelate generally accompanied the young gentlemen, at the expense of their parents. The good vicar accompanying young Lord Bruce on his Italian tour in 1794 had to break the news to his parents that he had become engaged to a Miss Hill, daughter of Lord Berwick. The Duchess of Argyll received constant complaints from Dr John Moore, her son's pedagogue, in the 1770s. The young Duke was being led astray by other young Englishmen. He was neglecting antiquities and scientific phenomena for the card table, and had bought an expensive carriage. English diplomats abroad dreaded the regular incursions of their young countrymen. The callow youths had constantly to be rescued from "scrapes". Few of them seemed likely to have their "taste" formed by their Continental tour – unless their taste for a pretty girl or for cards or for *grandes battues*. Or so one would imagine from the scathing descriptions their elders sent to their mothers. Nevertheless, when the youths' packing cases were opened, back in England the Continental tours were seen to have had an effect. Statue galleries, collections of Italian paintings, Italianate porticoes, and neo-classical saloons sprang up all over England in the homes of eighteenth-century noblemen. The gentry brought back lesser booty. Their souvenirs of the Grand Tour were watercolours of the Forum, books of engravings of waterfalls in the German States, bronze Renaissance medals. The taste for travel for pleasure and for acquisition was formed; on future trips, further booty would be bought and the treasures of English country houses multiplied.

A lady did not have this vested interest in acquisition to take her to the Continent. As she had no money of her own, would very likely never have the opportunity to furnish a house of her own – this was for her husband to do – thus there was no need for the gentlewoman to acquire an eye for French furniture and Italian painting, let alone Palladian architecture. Interestingly, of the very few gentlewomen who designed and furnished their own house like their male peers, neither Henrietta Howard, nor Elizabeth Montagu, owner of 32 Portman Square, travelled abroad. Mrs Montagu, like Mrs Howard, got her ideas for the house she commissioned from other fashionable houses of the day – and from her own sound intuition that large, airy rooms were necessary to her happiness.

Two distinct types of English travelling lady emerge from the crowds who crossed to France in large numbers from the mid-eighteenth century. There was

the lady who hoped to eke out dwindling finances in some foreign town, currently judged to provide cheap accommodation and entertainment. Friends and relations abroad were pestered for recommendations. Lord Nelson's sister and brother-in-law, Kitty and George Matcham, thought of settling in Schleswig-Holstein. The Hon. Arthur Paget, diplomat in Austria in 1800 recommended Dresden to his debt-ridden brother-in-law and sister, the Capels.

There was not "a cheaper place. . .In the environs, there are, I fancy, country houses to be had at a moderate rate, and as my friend Capel must have Game, he will find it there." In the event the Capels only went abroad in 1814, and then to Brussels. For £100 a year they rented a delightful house with a "beautiful bright blue" drawing-room. Items in "the Glove, shoe & ribbon line" were very cheap, commented the eldest Miss Capel. Her mother was more thankful that the food bills were only £7 odd a week, a good dancing master would teach five of her daughters for under a guinea, and a singing master would give eight lessons for one guinea exactly.

Marianna Starke's *Letters from Italy*, published in 1802, contain an appendix where she lists parts of the country free from revolution and economical for settlers. Lady Knight and her daughter, Cornelia, toured Switzerland before choosing Naples as most suited to their pocket. The *pensiones* in Florence crowded today with earnest English ladies keen to absorb the atmosphere of Italy have their prototypes in the cheaper hotels in Rome and Naples and Leghorn of the eighteenth century, where Cornelia and Lady Knight found several other distressed countrywomen. It was undoubtedly more exciting to live cheaply on macaroni under a warm sun than dine on fish in cold lodgings in London. Even Calais would do at a pinch, when the question of evading "duns" and creditors was urgent. Emma, Lady Hamilton lived for a time in a farmhouse just outside the town with her "adopted" daughter, Horatia Nelson, and found that provisions were agreeably cheap. "We have excellent beef, mutton, and veal at five pence a pound, . . . turbot per pair half a crown, . . . milk from the cows on the common like cream." She had seen enough of grandeur not to regret it, she informed a correspondent. All she wished was "comfort, and what would make Horatia and me myself live like gentlewomen."

The other type who relished Continental life was the lady seeking to escape scandal. Lady Elizabeth Foster was the daughter of Frederick Augustus, the Earl-Bishop of Bristol and Derry. In 1785 she found herself pregnant by her best friend's husband, the Duke of Devonshire. The ladies of Devonshire House enjoyed outraging society by canvassing for parliamentary candidates and kissing butchers to gain votes. Illegitimate children were still not tolerated. Lady Elizabeth had lived under the protection of the Duchess for some years, since she left her clerical husband and two sons to their own devices in Ireland. Now she called on her brother, Lord Hervey, to escort her to Italy, where she declared she wished to see the antiquities. John, Lord Hervey, duly wandered alone round the buildings of Pompeii, admired the murals at Herculaneum, viewed the Sybil's cave at Cumae. His sister, meanwhile, spent the middle

months of her pregnancy in seclusion on the island of Ischia. Gay, pretty Lady Betty was miserable without companions, but the subterfuge worked. Lord Hervey wrote home to their friends describing his solitary archaeological journeys as trips undertaken with his sister. Lady Betty grew steadily larger. When the time came near, Lord Hervey escorted her to a horrible den in Sorrento, up grimy stairs and smelling of cold grease. Here reigned the *Archiprêtre d'Amour*, who was to deliver Betty of her child. A baby girl was duly delivered and deposited in France. Insouciante, Lady Betty returned the next year to Naples, and viewed the island of Ischia and the coastline of Sorrento with apparent equanamity.

The Byres family against St Peter's Rome, attributed to Philip Wickstead. James Byres was chieftain of the courteous Scots in Italy who formed the English taste for the antique, found important statues for husbands and economical trifles for the ladies.

Lady Betty's best friend, Georgiana Duchess of Devonshire, went still farther in her efforts to avert suspicion when she became pregnant with Lord Grey's child. She persuaded her mother, Lady Spencer, that a family visit to France would benefit her sister, Harriet Bessborough's health. (The Duke of Devonshire fortunately showed no interest in joining the ladies.) Only when the family party was safely in France did the Duchess explain to her mother the purpose of the trip. Lady Spencer was a deeply religious woman. This went too far, but she stayed by her daughter throughout the shameful pregnancy. She needed all her spiritual resourses when, only a few years later, Harriet rose from her perpetual sickbed to conduct a flagrant affair with "G", or Lord Granville

Leveson-Gower, hopeful sprig of the Stafford family at the Foreign Office. Other ladies went abroad not to avoid scandal but to court it. Elizabeth Vassall married Sir Godfrey Webster when she was twenty; on a honeymoon jaunt to Italy, she discovered that young Lord Holland made a more agreeable companion than Webster. She travelled back to England with Holland, bore him a son, and, after an acrimonious divorce from Webster, married her paramour to become queen of the Whig citadel, Holland House.

Interestingly, for all the jaunting abroad, Englishwomen tended to marry their own kind. A winter in Geneva or in Vienna might offer to a determined matron six or seven eligible English peers sojourning there. Lady Berwick

Georgiana Duchess of Devonshire with her child by Reynolds. A warm-hearted beauty, who openly and unusually adored and cuddled her children in public, and later dressed herself in simple white chemises, modelled on children's "frocks". She set fashions in both directions.

"caught" Lord Bruce for her daughter, Miss Hill, in Rome. (Lady Dunmore went too far, however, when in 1794 she connived at the secret marriage of her daughter Lady Augusta Murray, to HRH Prince Augustus, the Duke of Sussex in the same city.) Naval captains were pursued relentlessly on their rare moments on shore during the Napoleonic Wars. Cornelia Knight sighed in Sicily in 1799 for Captain David Gould – without success.

Miss Betsey Wynne was more fortunate with Captain Thomas Fremantle three years earlier. Richard Wynne sold estates in 1786 in Lincolnshire so as to travel on the continent with his five daughters. A rag-taggle and bob-tail of tutors, drawing masters, music masters, maids and secretaries accompanied the family but only compounded their troubles when they were at Florence in 1796, and news came that the French were within a few miles. Betsey and Eugenia had both kept full diaries since they were ten and nine. Their reaction to danger was,

Fair Tea-makers

as, usual, intense excitement; they wanted to stay and see the festivities for St John in Florence, and the chariot races in the Piazza of Santa Maria Novella. Fortunately, a gallant captain who had been with Lord Nelson at the Battle of the Nile, Captain Thomas Fremantle, came to the party's aid, and shipped them down to Naples in a frigate ship, *L'Inconstant*. Betsey began a ship-board romance with her saviour, and after some hesitation – "he would and he would not; she would, and would gladly" – the captain duly offered for her hand.

Few English ladies settled abroad for good in this period. The call of the homeland was still strong, dull though country life might be. It is only with the later nineteenth century that we see English ladies like Elizabeth Barrett Browning and Violet Paget abandoning the restrictions of English life for good. In the eighteenth and early nineteenth century, the English gentlewoman lived for a few years, perhaps, abroad, but always in "the English style", characterised by "painful constraint". Harriet Capel might be forced by her father's addiction to "the tables" to live in Brussels. Nevertheless, she informed her grandmother, the Dowager Countess of Uxbridge: "We shall not return foreignized, you would be sure of it too, could you . . . see the . . . abhorrence with which we reject every innovation even of the most trifling nature that in the slightest degree swerves from English dress, manners, or sentiments."

Fretful ladies like Claire Clairmont, lady friend of Lord Byron, who pursued him to Italy in 1816, bore his illegitimate daughter, Allegra, went off to Moscow as a governess on the child's death and retired from there to Switzerland could hardly be called gentlewomen. Claire's most gentlewomanly trait – and one she shared with all Byron's ladies – was her tendency to succumb to "the vapours". The *Ladies' Dispensatory*, 1770, recommended as cure for this popular ailment: "it is proper to apply Vinegar . . . Hartshorn . . . Assa Foetida . . . to the nose. Also brown Paper, or Feathers set on fire, and held fuming under the Nose." Lord Byron was more rough and ready in his medicine. He slapped or douched his ladies back to sensibility, if not sense.

Portrait of a young woman, wearing a black riding habit, by Sir Francis Grant (1803-78). The Victorian gentlewoman wore quantities of embroidered petticoats, or even trousers beneath her habit, lest she should fall from her mount indecorously.

CHAPTER FOUR

The Angel in the House

1815-1870

THE YEARS FOLLOWING WATERLOO WERE CONFUSED FOR THE English gentlewoman by a lack of moral direction from secular heights, and by a welter of advice from religious bodies – Anglican and nonconformist.

Royal circles provided no lead. As Prince of Wales, George IV had made his view of filial duty and family ties plain when he hosted a lavish ball at Carlton House in 1811 to celebrate the deterioration of his father's health, and his own appointment as Regent. In 1816 *The Times* attacked his introduction of "the indecent foreign dance called the Waltz" at his Regency Court as a "novelty deserving of severe reprobation". It was quite sufficient, commented the indignant newspaper, to observe "the voluptuous intertwining of the limbs, and close compressure on the bodies . . . to see that it is . . . far removed from the

The Waltz, by E. F. Burney. The Times *learnt "with pain" of the introduction of this "indecent foreign dance" at court in 1816 and warned "every parent against exposing his daughter to so fatal a contagion".*

modest reserve which has hitherto been considered distinctive of English females . . . We pay due deference to our superiors in rank, but we owe a higher duty to morality.''

The Regent's wife, Caroline, Princess of Wales, furnished no better model of propriety than her husband. She lived apart from her husband from the early days of their marriage, and made rare appearances at Court. From 1814 to 1820 the Princess of Wales jaunted about the Mediterranean in a series of feluccas and yachts, alighting occasionally, like a plump Mandarin duck – she had orange hair and a fondness for bright colours – to outrage English inhabitants of Continental towns. Her finest exploit was to enter Jerusalem on a donkey; it was for

Cartoon of Caroline and Pergami (1821). In 1820 Society was convulsed by the cross-examination in the House of Lords of Continental chambermaids and valets on this delicate point – had, or had not, George IV's wife committed adultery with her travel courier?

adultery with Bartolomeo Pergami, her travel courier and "a Low Man", that she was put on trial in the House of Lords in 1820, at her husband's command. George IV, newly the monarch, wanted to end his farce of a marriage to Caroline, and marry again; all London was fascinated by the intimate details of the Queen of England's sexual habits, to which a stream of Italian and French chambermaids and valets, summoned from the Continent, bore witness.

If royal manners and morals were revealed at their lowest ebb during the trial, royal scandal was everywhere. When the infant daughter of the Duke of Kent was christened in Kensington Palace in 1819, her uncle, the Prince Regent, was invited to stand godfather. The Regent was not sober, and took exception

The Angel in the House

to the names, Georgiana Charlotte Augusta, which the child was destined to bear; on his loud insistence, his niece was christened instead Alexandrina Victoria. The future Queen Victoria's other royal uncles were no less wayward, and were characterised by a taste for vulgar company. Frederick, Duke of York, William, Duke of Clarence, Augustus, Duke of Sussex, and Adolphus, Duke of Cambridge, supported mistresses and streams of illegitimate children and married in defiance of the Royal Marriages Act. At the Court balls, there was "cornering" and "squeezing and hugging" in state rooms "crowded to such an excess as to . . . render the quadrille a scene of pressure and confusion." Strait-laced Queen Charlotte had bred in her sons a bunch of bonhomous, indolent thugs.

Not till George IV's death in 1830 and the accession of stately, stout Queen Adelaide as Queen of his brother, William IV, did manners and morals begin slowly to improve. The movement towards decorum was mirrored in the world of fashion where the light and flimsy muslins, delicate with neo-classical embroidery, had been popular for thirty-odd years. Now thicker skirts, heavy with braid and elaborate with frills and tucking, made their appearance in sombre crimsons and strong blues and purple; the use of heavy satin and plush, bobbles and tassels, and the immense popularity of the fringed shawl in combination with tiered crinolines was to make the gentlewoman of the mid-century look as if she had visited an upholsterer's by mistake for the milliner's. Concealment of charms was the ideal.

There was good reason for the excess of "Victorian prudery", at which it is now the habit to scoff. The degree of rusticity into which manners had lapsed during the Regency required drastic remedy. The High Church movement in the Anglican Church, and the Evangelical Church were thought by the Reverend Charles Kingsley in 1862 to have been equally responsible with the "virtuous, humane and beneficent" Court of Victoria and Albert in sweeping the stench of the Regency stables from the land. "There is no aristocracy in the world," commented Kingsley approvingly, "which has so honourably repented . . . which has so cheerfully asked what its duty was, that it might do it."

There were inevitably hiccups before the graver tone became established. Members of the older generation, like Lord Melbourne, Victoria's first Prime Minister, could not be persuaded to adopt the new fashion for churchgoing. Melbourne said quaintly in 1838 that he was afraid to go to church for fear of "hearing something very extraordinary". "People didn't use to go so much formerly," he reflected, "it wasn't the fashion, but it is a right thing to do." The young Queen Victoria was worried that her fiancé, Prince Albert, was so very religious. Melbourne reassured her that "strong Protestant feeling" was a good thing, when not breeding intolerance. Albert was a lynch pin in the moral reform of the country, which spread from churchgoing to dancing. He persuaded Victoria, who loved dancing, to leave the ballroom for supper at eleven, and quit the ball for bed on the stroke of midnight.

For those who did not wish to repent altogether, there were hostesses with

Splendid engravings from The Belle of the Season *(1840), and from* Gems of Beauty, *illustrating* The Passions *(1838), in this case* Envy. *Lady Blessington, author of the verses which accompany these illustrations, maintained a handsome home with these "glamour" publications.*

the manners and mores of the Regency who lingered on into the 1840s and 1850s, like Lady Blessington at Gore House. She charmed literary lions of the day into contributing to the Books of Beauty, which she edited to support her entertaining. Ladies, however, did not attend Lady Blessington's salon. If her rackety history before marriage to the 1st Earl of Blessington were not stigma enough (she had been passed, in return for cash sums, from one gentleman to another), her life after her husband died in 1822 left still more to be desired. She insisted that her stepdaughter marry the Count d'Orsay, close companion of herself and her husband. When her stepdaughter fled the *ménage*, Lady Blessington continued to live with d'Orsay. In 1849, to the relief of much of Society, debt compelled the Countess and her Count to flee abroad.

Lady Blessington was a last survivor of the Regency spirit. In 1840 Prince Albert hoped that his baby son, the future Edward VII, would grow up as unlike his unruly great-uncles as possible. This pious wish reflected the great change in the moral climate of England which was being effected; painstaking and serious-minded were the families of Victorian England. It was a time of confidence. Whatever the defects of the Industrial Revolution, it provided opportunities for men of enthusiasm and vision to realise schemes to improve society on a grand scale. Industry, and glory in industry, became a characteristic of the Victorian gentleman and respect for industry made of professional men, like doctors and lawyers, respectable gentlemen. The middle-class manufacturers and professional men worked long hours in pursuit of the capital which would enable them to live pleasantly as gentlemen of leisure. Meanwhile, the gentry and nobility whom they sought to emulate spent hours every day in

The Angel in the House

the public arena and out of the home, serving on any of thousands of public committees or acting as magistrates of doing Parliamentary business in the expanded Houses or Parliament.

Oh what industry, and what grave responsibility! At the end of the day, how thankful our careworn heroes were to return home, "the shelter", as Ruskin put it, "not only from all injury, but from all terror, doubt and division". In 1837 or 1838, Charles Darwin, bachelor, set out for himself reasons to marry, and not to marry, in two columns. "A nice soft wife on a sofa with a good fire and books and music perhaps – compare this vision with the dingy reality of Grt Marlboro' St.", his lodgings, he wrote. "Marry Marry Marry", was his conclusion. "Home, and someone to take care of house", and "constant companion (friend in old age) who will feel interested in one, object to be beloved and played with – better than a dog anyhow", were other material considerations disposing him in favour of marriage. Visits from relations, "the expense and anxiety of children," and the terrible "loss of time" were against it. He succumbed, and married Emma Wedgwood, his cousin, in 1840, to their mutual happiness. Emma, thirty years old and energetic, was well pleased with the match. "We shall live in London, where he is fully occupied with being Secretary to the Geological Society and conducting a publication upon the animals of Australia. I am so glad he is a busy man . . ."

All day the Victorian gentlemen nurtured fancies about the home they had left that morning, fancies which had not troubled their fathers who had lived and worked among the familial surroundings. The fancies were of the demanding order that a traveller homeward-bound after months away might indulge in: the gentleman thought of a warm welcome from wife and from children, all in a flutter of excitement to see him; he thought of a cosy fire to warm himself at, and a neat, plain dinner with soup and a joint and two or three removes to accompany it; he thought of order and quiet, above all. The Victorian gentleman demanded this high standard of welcome every evening of his life. Domestic cares of the household must be hidden from him, offered to him at some later date, for fear of spoiling his ease; on his return home, the breadwinner, the *pater familias* must find his wife, the core of the household, performing as exact an imitation of *The Angel in the House* as possible. Coventry Patmore's popular poem of this name poignantly describes the virtues of his wife, Emily, who died of tuberculosis in 1862 after ten years of marriage in which she bore six children.

To the Victorian gentleman, his wife was perfect when she combined, as did Emily Patmore, "a strange beauty with extreme innocence of manner". Patmore wrote of the purity of a bride's blush, "When she says, I will, unto she knows not what." Sexual innocence was not hard to come by. The Potter sisters, emancipated daughters of a railway entrepreneur, would tell the youngest sibling, Rosie, nothing of their marital experiences while she remained unmarried. When the middle-aged painter, George Watts, made advances to the young Ellen Terry and kissed her "differently – not much differently but a

little", she told nobody for a fortnight, then confided in her mother. "I told her *I must* be married to him *now* because I was going to have a baby!!! and she believed me!! I was *sure*, THAT kiss meant giving me a baby."

It was part of the High Gothic revival that ladies were revered as chaste objects of chivalry. Gentlemen went to the counting house to do battle for the favours of the lady they left in the tower, or villa on the outskirts of Town. In 1839 Lord Eglinton gave most tangible expression to his High Gothic spirit, when he hosted a medieval tournament costing £40,000 on his estates in Scotland. Queen Victoria and Prince Albert appeared in equally medieval but more stately fashion at a ball of 1844 as Queen Philippa of Hainault and King Edward III. The Duke of Wellington's sons clanked about in hired armour and Richard Monckton Milnes came as Chaucer.

When passion was sanctified and crystallised in this pallid style, sensuality was inappropriate. Yet the fact was that a woman and her body were her husband's to dispose of as he pleased. Mrs George Norton experienced the roughest of lovemaking from her husband, younger brother of Lord Grantley. She made no protests, only noted in her novel, *Stuart of Dunleath*, of a harsh hero modelled on Norton: "Of course, he would be glad to inspire her with affection if he could, but if not, still let her be his. Hope, tenderness, courtship, delay, were as little present to his thoughts as in the hawk that drops through the air. There are women who think it sublime to be loved with this sort of passion."

Without benefit of motherly, sisterly or published advice on the sexual norm, ladies accepted the wooing they were offered. Queen Victoria enjoyed kissing Albert's hand when they sat "so nicely side by side on that little blue sofa . . . We kissed each other so often and I leant on that dear soft cheek, fresh and pink like a rose . . ." On the third day after their marriage in 1840 she confided to her Journal: "My dearest Albert put on my stockings for me. I went in and saw him shave; a great delight for me." The same year the spinster essayist, Caroline Meysey Wigley, sallied forth with Waldron, her maid, from Olton, the Solihull house where she lived quite alone and in great comfort, with several bad-tempered dogs for her protection, on a visit to the Continent. She was thirty-nine, lame and ugly, some would have said an old maid set in her ways. Not at all. She was joined on her Continental jaunt by the handsome Rector of Solihull, the Reverend Archer Clive. Bachelor and spinster trundled about the Rhine country together, aloof to any scandal they might generate. Archer kissed Caroline once, at Antwerp, "on my mouth . . . when I never thought, never hoped, would not think and would not hope, to be more than what he once called me, his sister." On their return to England Archer noted his proposal and acceptance in his diary thus: "I dine at Olton.? Yes."

The Victorian wife usually responded with gratitude to her husband's love-making and other demands of her. Mrs Sarah Ellis wrote in *The Women of England* (1842) that her lady reader should recognise "the superiority of your husband simply as a man . . . In the character of a noble, enlightened and truly good man, there is a power and sublimity . . . nearly approaching what we

Morning Prayer. *The Victorian fondness for church going and church building had its domestic counterpart in this grim daily ritual, in which the head of the house led both family and servants. If congregation was reluctant, he felt duly important.*

believe to be the nature and capacity of angels . . ." *Two* angels in the house, then! "To be admitted to his heart to share his counsels, and to be the chosen companion of his joys and sorrows; it is difficult to say whether humility or gratitude should preponderate."

The only difficulty was that pressure of business so often called the Victorian gentleman from his "chosen companion's" side. Beatrice Webb, daughter of the railway entrepreneur, Richard Potter, recollected of her childhood: "The restless spirit of big enterprise dominated our home life." Her mother, Laurencina, attempted to follow, with their nine daughters and staff, where Richard Potter's varied interests led him, and the family lived in a succession of rented houses. When Richard crossed the Atlantic, however, to take a hand in the development of the Grand Trunk Railway in 1874, thirty years of resentment boiled over. A daughter, Maggie, had accompanied her father to Montreal and replied to her mother's complaints: "Of course we all feel how disagreeable it must be to you to be so much alone at home. Papa feels it very

Chapter Four

Many Happy Returns, *by W. P. Frith (1819-1909). Children's party clothes afforded an opportunity for display of wealth. Mothers remorselessly imposed kilts, tartan dresses, and velvet suits with Vandyke collars on their embarrassed children, to whom sailor suits alone were acceptable.*

keenly . . . But . . . the sudden breaking of all intercourse with the railway life . . . and retiring entirely to private life with no career left, would be dangerous to his health and spirit and very unsatisfactory to you in the end . . ."

It was often as much the emotional as the physical withdrawal consequent on a gentleman's entrance into a public life which left the wife so lonely. Mrs Gaskell entirely approved of her Unitarian husband's work as tutor at a succession of classes, and then colleges, in Manchester for working men. She worried, however, about his workload. He also had committees, and "the plaguing *Unitarian Herald*" to edit. These commitments meant that his wife and his daughters saw him "only . . . at mealtimes". In 1860 Mrs Gaskell discussed briefly in her novel, *Sylvia's Lovers*, the limitations of man as husband. ". . . Even in the most tender and stable masculine natures, at the supremest seasons of their lives, there is room for other thoughts and passions than such as are connected with love. Even with the most domestic and affectionate men, their emotions seem to be kept in a cell, distinct and away from their actual lives."

In gentle compliment to their wives' supposed knowledge of the science of domestic economy, the typical Victorian gentleman made it a point never to interefere in her arrangements; he demonstrated his perfect trust in her skills by becoming as helpless and unable to make shift for himself at home, as she was outside the home. David Copperfield thought silly, childish Dora with her

The Angel in the House

pretty pouting ways adorable as a bride; poor though they would be, her dog, Jip, would have his mutton chop each day at twelve, he promised her. Confusion ensued when Dora did not develop into a good manager, but played with Jip when she should have been learning, from a weighty tome, the mysteries of household accounting. The house of David Copperfield could never prosper, for all the child wife's charms. It was the paramount duty of the Victorian gentlewoman to provide on whatever income was set aside for the purpose, an atmosphere of respectable affluence from which the head of the house might issue out each morning, charged with the wish to maintain this prosperity.

Emily Tennyson, the Poet Laureate's aristocratic wife, was the perfect mate, thought Coventry Patmore. She was "neither brilliant nor literary at all. She seems to understand Tennyson thoroughly, and waits upon him and attends to him as she ought to do." In short, Lady Tennyson echoed the behaviour of Patmore's own Emily:

> Man must be pleased; but him to please
> Is woman's pleasure.

Geraldine Jewsbury, unmarried confidante of Jane Carlyle, wrote in about 1849: "I believe we are touching on better days, when women will have a genuine, normal life of their own to lead. There, perhaps, will not be so many marriages, and women will be taught not to feel their destiny *manqué* if they remain single . . ." She regarded herself as a "mere faint indication, a rudiment of the idea, of certain higher qualities . . . that lie in women." Few felt with Miss Jewsbury. Most women were content to nurture their husbands' "higher qualities" in return for status, respectability, security. The author, Harriet Martineau, was exceptional in relishing her Unitarian father's financial collapse as providing her with an escape from the demands of gentility, giving her the impulse to work and write to support herself. Most women were happy to be supported by husbands, to have their husbands take their property and income on marriage, to have no legal existence of their own.

Agitation for political enfranchisement did not become widespread till the Household Franchise Bill of 1866 proposed widening the franchise to include householders who paid £10 rental and upwards. Women were not specifically excluded from the enfranchisement. In Manchester 3,924 out of 4,215 women householders claimed the vote on this ground and took their claim to court where they were defeated. This strength of feeling about the vote developed late. A few women – and they were all of the upper class – did challenge law and tradition earlier on specific injustices in the domestic sphere. Centuries of weighty Church and secular training in submission, obedience and self-effacement were against the Hon. Mrs George Norton when she protested in a publicly printed letter in 1855, addressed to Queen Victoria, about Lord Chancellor Cranworth's Marriage and Divorce Bill. Caroline Norton knew the force of public protest: in 1836 her husband had accused her of adultery with the Prime Minister, Lord Melbourne, and had obtained custody of their three

children, despite her acquittal. "If my children are kept from me, all else is trivial and indifferent," she stormed. "I will sign nothing, do nothing, listen to nothing which has reference to any other subject . . ." she wrote, and told Norton bitterly, "You always speak as if the refusal of my boys was like a refusal of tickets for Almacks." Caroline's protests led to the first Custody of Infants Act in 1849, which gave mothers limited access to their children. Despite their estrangement, George Norton still enjoyed Caroline's earnings from her writings. He even took her earnings from her pamphlets protesting at his behaviour! When their eldest son died while in Norton's care. Caroline was not informed in time to arrive for the funeral.

The Honourable Mrs George Norton (1832), by George Hayter. Fathers invariably got custody of children following a separation or divorce. When Caroline Norton was denied access to her children following a separation, she bravely petitioned the Government to amend the law.

"Women must submit, those who don't are bad women, depend upon it; all bad women," wrote Mrs Norton. She had no money with which to provide for her children when she did have access to them. Surely divorced and separated women should be allowed use of their own earnings? She was successful in her protests about the proposed divorce bill and, in the Matrimonial Causes Act of 1857, many of her suggestions were adopted. Divorce, which had required an individual and costly Act of Parliament for each instance, was now to be granted in civil courts to be specially set up. The daring and novelty of Caroline's foray into legislation must not be underestimated; she was a most effective campaigner, while it was no hindrance that she was the granddaughter of the

The Angel in the House

politician, Sheridan, and highly connected; one of her sisters became Marchioness of Dufferin; the other, Duchess of Somerset. Once she had won her object, however, Mrs Norton relapsed into quietude. She was a petitioner, not a suffragist. "I never pretended to the wild and ridiculous notion of equality," she wrote.

Caroline's efforts to establish married women's rights were preceded by those of a very successful artist, Barbara Leigh Smith Bodichon. Barbara equally had a political background: her father was a radical MP and she had £300 a year of her own, in addition to profits from sales of her marine and coastal paintings. In 1853 Barbara published *A Brief Summary in Plain Language of the Most Important Laws Concerning Women*: "her existence is entirely absorbed in that of her husband," she noted, of married women. "She lives under his protection or cover, and her condition is called coverture . . . A woman's body belongs to her husband . . . and he may enforce his right by a writ of *habeas corpus*. What was her personal property before marriage . . . becomes absolutely her husband's, and he may assign or dispose of them at his pleasure whether he and his wife live together or not . . ." Inflamed by these injustices, Barbara led a committee to organise support for the first Married Women's Property Rights Bill in 1856. The bill failed to pass, though Barbara's petition supporting it was signed by an impressive collection of women who had an income to gain by its passing. Mrs Gaskell signed, though she shed doubts on the efficacy of the measure proposed. She thought husbands could always extract what property or income they wished from their wives by beating or wheedling. Mrs Gaskell was, of course, fortunate in a husband who merely held her literary earnings in his bank account on her behalf, and never dreamt of spending them himself. Barbara Bodichon's husband was similarly honourable and encouraged his wife's artistic career. Barbara continued to wade into political dispute in other areas of women's rights, and helped to found Girton College. She was a natural, disinterested reformer.

Other gentlewomen put one foot into radical waters where they saw injustice being done, but did not remove their other foot from where it was planted firm in the compact sand of respectable womanhood. Young Emmeline Goulden in Manchester was taken by her mother in 1872 to hear Lydia Becker, fiery Editor of the *Women's Suffrage Journal*, speak. The *Journal* came each month to Mrs Goulden, and she read Harriet Beecher Stowe's classic, *Uncle Tom's Cabin*, to her daughter in the 1860s and took her to bazaars to raise money for newly emancipated negro slaves. Yet Emmeline, later famous as the suffrage leader, Mrs Pankhurst, was sent to a school where the chief aim seemed to be to learn the art of "making home attractive". The education of Emmeline's brother was a source of anxiety to both her parents; it was enough for them where their daughter's education was concerned that "the headmistress was a gentlewoman". Young Emmeline was very puzzled about "making home attractive". For whom? Her brother? He showed no signs of wishing to make it attractive to *her*.

Who would be a girl by choice in Victorian society? Up till the age of nine or ten, admittedly, nursery life made little distinction between boy and girl. Both wore uncomfortable clothes. The rage for Highland dress, promoted first by Scott's novels, then by Queen Victoria's and Prince Albert's love affair with Scotland in the 1850s, produced some particularly uncomfortable outfits. At the Great Exhibition of 1851 the young Prince of Wales appeared in full Highland rig. A horror for one eleven-year-old girl was "a Douglas plaid – tight waist, tight sleeves, a most waxlike fit", with, built into it, "a pair of stays with bones which cause infinite trouble and dismay to the whole household". Young boys were not better off, as their parents dressed them as often as possible in silken fancy dress, a form of "vicarious consumption". Miniature soldiers, and sailors and cavaliers and tin Highlanders, however, could look forward to the age of nine or ten when they could properly eschew plumes and buckles for sensible "skeleton" jacket and trousers. Their sisters had no such luck. There was no simplified dress for young ladies till late into the century, when the sailor suit became daily wear for boys and girls.

Their clothes, of course, made it difficult for girls to play any sort of vigorous games. That was, if not the intention, at least not an unwelcome consequence, to their parents, for Society now decreed that a gentlewoman must, above all, be careful of her deportment. Boards to straighten backs were common in the schoolroom. "Drilling with heavy books on the head, and sitting upright for hours . . . on backless chairs with aching spines and singing heads," were other postural remedies. Even when a girl acted in the amateur theatricals which were an elaborate and popular pastime in this period, she must exhibit a straight back; dramatic skill and expression were secondary. One manual giving advice in recitation boasted a supplement, where a "system of gesture" might be found. In its 23rd edition by 1866, the manual taught to generations of young ladies recitation accompanied by gestures of the head and "the lower limbs" only. The more extreme mannerisms of eighteenth-century deportment were now not taught; "mere outward polish" was frowned upon, as betokening an empty soul.

"Dignity of manner . . . next to modesty" was now the highest ornament of the female character". So the *Young Ladies' Book*, reprinted ceaselessly from 1829 on, assured its readers. Deportment became less a matter of technique, more a matter of behaviour, and dancing masters taught their pupils how to dance, not how to sit and how to stand, nor even how to curtsey. At the beginning and end of dances ladies just inclined their bodies; their knees remained unbent. On meeting and parting, they shook hands instead of curtseying. In fact, the curtsey became obsolete, except on formal occasions and for those fortunate enough to encounter royalty, when "it is scarcely possible . . . to bend too low." Mannerisms, airs and graces, like cosmetics, were abjured in the frank and forthright age of Victoria; however, dignity must prevade all activities. There was no relaxation; on marriage, decreed the *Young Ladies' Book*, a gentlewoman's bearing should display only "greater quietness and dignity".

The Angel in the House

The Star Parlour, The Vyne, *by Martha Wiggett Chute (1868). On inheriting the Vyne, Martha's husband built on to, refloored and improved the house; Martha made a loving inventory of the principal rooms in a series of charming watercolours.*

There was only a small range of activities which could be enjoyed under these conditions. A publication entitled *Every Girl's Book* (1860) gives a dismal picture of permitted entertainments. Part One gives a list of indoor games, like spillikins, which would depress the liveliest maidens. Part Two treats of "ladies' work", or fancy work. Under this heading come the embroidering of stove-aprons, the manufacture of silk and of wax flowers . . . Again it does not make the heart leap. If a girl had no taste for reading or for painting, or for some variety of needlework, she was doomed to a tedious adolescence. "Oh, weary days – Oh, evenings that seem never to end – for how many years have I watched that drawing-room clock and thought it never would reach the ten!" wrote Florence Nightingale, of her family life at Embley Park in Hampshire.

When Florence wrote this, she was a woman of thirty-one but, unless she married, a gentlewoman was treated as a species of child all her life. "Some women the family dooms to a life of silent misery, others to one of incurable infancy," she wrote elsewhere. At least by this age she had put away from her such very childish things as the sampler which every Victorian girl stitched. Gone were the pictorial samplers on silk and in a variety of stitches of earlier centuries. Now, reflecting the sobriety and Godfearing nature of the period, in black silk on coarse tammy cloth, girls sewed in laborious cross or tentstitches, long verses from the Psalms. These efforts were framed and hung, as the Brontë sisters' work still hangs at the Haworth Parsonage, as a record of assiduity, if not imagination and enthusiasm.

141

Panel of Berlin wool-work (1840-50). No skill was needed for this needlework-by-numbers, canvas was swiftly covered with the thick, bright wools and lack of imagination was supplied by pleasing, ready coloured patterns of royalty, animals and flowers.

In the 1830s the introduction of Berlin wool-work heralded the death of the sampler, and an increased vogue for the embroidered figure subject worked from a pattern in lurid and three-dimensional colour. Patterns published in Berlin were imported and sold by Wilks' Warehouse, Regent Street from 1831, and later by other shops. The great attraction of Berlin wool-work was that the wool was so thick that bellpulls, cushion covers, footstools, smoking caps, fire-screens and mantel-lambrequins were finished in no time. Beads and silk thread were sometimes introduced into the embroidery; later beading of cushion covers and evening bags became popular on its own account. The most popular images to work were floral designs, and figures connected with royalty. Por-traits by Winterhalter of Queen Victoria and her family were very favoured; gentlemen rested their feet on footstools embroidered with the Prince of Wales's face. Cats and dogs were also liked, with the Queen's King Charles spaniel dog, Dash, painted by Edwin Landseer, naturally a best-selling pattern.

The choice of patterns became vast; by 1840 there were over 14,000 to choose from. Needlework was no longer a skill, with these ready-to-sew pat-terns; it was now a "parlour occupation". The only interesting advance came when that man of foresight, Sam Beeton, introduced the needier gentlewoman to the hobby of dressmaking. He stuck into individual copies of some of the many magazines he founded, paper dress patterns devised from Paris fashion plates. Beeton imported, by arrangement with the Editor of *Le Moniteur des Modes*, copies of the French magazine. His wife, Isabella, studied the plates,

translated the descriptions and devised instructions to accompany the patterns which another assistant made from them. Even during the 1871 Siege of Paris, amateur dressmakers received their patterns. Sam had the fashion plates flown out of the embattled city by balloon.

Besides needlework, music and art continued as traditional solace for the gentlewoman. In music, the piano dominated, and, from 1800 onwards, the small upright or cottage piano became the popular instrument. Firms like Broadwood and Clementi improved on the tone and introduced the "soft pedal", and other accoutrements; families eagerly shed the old to acquire the new and a flourishing trade in secondhand instruments developed. Every inn-keeper's daughter had her cottage piano; the suburban Pooters, with genteel distaste for the secondhand, purchased their piano from Bond Street on the three-year purchase agreement. The ladies of the upper classes could only counterattack by forcing their daughters to practise their scales and fingering for longer and longer hours.

In addition to the showy pieces of piano music which young ladies all over Europe learnt, the English lady developed a passion for the Ballad. The lively Irish and Scotch airs of the turn of the century gave way to English songs expressive of Christian domesticity. *Home Sweet Home*, from Sir Henry Bishop's opera, *Clari*, is perhaps the most famous. Dykes's *Abide with me*, and *Nearer, my God, to thee*, were hymns also popular. With this passion for ballads, singing masters were widely employed: Queen Victoria enjoyed lessons from Lablache; Mrs Gaskell used the income from her writing to pro-

Victorian sheet music copies, Let Me Teach Thee How to Play, *and* Fairie Voices. *This simplified music for piano and voice complemented the large-scale manufacture of upright pianos from 1800, and satisfied prosperous families' taste for home entertainment.*

143

The Artist in her Painting Room, York *(1838), by Mary Ellen Best. The foundation of the Society of Female (later Lady) Artists in 1861 recognised the need of enthusiastic amateurs like Best for an exhibition space of their own.*

vide lessons for her daughter, Marianne. For a land with few composers of note, early Victorian England was full of song. It imported, besides, all the best composers, musicians and singers of Europe to form the musical taste of its inhabitants. Mendelssohn became a frequent visitor, Berlioz visited, Jenny Lind was an English institution. The musical gentlewoman was spoilt for choice. If she did not, as yet, take to the concert platform, she admired the performers she heard and emulated them in her private musical study.

In art, the gentlewoman made similar bounds towards professionalism. Watercolour continued to be her natural medium, but bolder now, she exhibited at the shows of the Society of Lady Artists founded in 1861 and studied, like Elizabeth Thompson, later Lady Butler, at the school attached to it, or at the South Kensington School of Art. Till he saw Lady Butler's *Quatre Bras* exhibited at the Royal Academy in 1875, Ruskin held that "no woman could paint". Nevertheless in the 1850s he had taught Mrs Gaskell's daughter, Meta, drawing and encouraged her to see for herself in Italy the elements which ought to infuse her drawings. No one could paint who had not seen Venice, he declared. Mrs Gaskell took Meta to Florence in 1862, to see the Old Masters, and reported her as "gobbling down pictures all day". Florence Nightingale's cousin, Hilary Bonham-Carter, had some lessons at an atelier in Paris in 1843. Unfortunately, she was needed at home to care for putative cases of measles in her sisters' families, and to do the flowers. She was allowed to attend a "ladies' atelier" in London, "when social engagements permitted".

The Angel in the House

English ladies like Mary Ann Evans at Geneva in 1849, confirmed European opinion of the species' oddity by taking long, solitary walks, and playing difficult music on a hired piano in her pension room. The desire to inform the eye and mind became obsessive with some ladies who regretted the narrow confines of their earlier scholastic education. Michael Faraday lectured on electricity to audiences of ladies who listened with as much enthusiasm as to sermons by fashionable preachers. In the eighteenth century, Dr Erasmus Darwin, in his "Plan for the Conduct of Female Education in Boarding Schools", had recommended Bewick's woodcuts and tales of "quadrupeds" to supplement pupils' interest in natural history; they should be taken to see travelling exhibitions of foreign animals. In the same way, ladies read Ruskin's volumes on the history of art, and then travelled themselves to see the paintings he described. In the pursuit of science, Darwin had recommended visits to potteries, ironworks, foundries; in the mid-nineteenth century, ladies found a visit to Paxton's Crystal Palace, re-erected in Sydenham after the Great Exhibition of 1851, an equally pleasing trip, and its collection of sculpted dinosaurs a more entertaining vision of prehistory than Dr Darwin's grandson's *Origin of the Species* (1859).

In the "retiring rooms" of the Crystal Palace, for the first time in England, public conveniences were made available to visitors, male and female. George Jennings, who was responsible for installing the "wash-down" water closets, overcame considerable opposition. Visitors had not come "merely to wash", it was grumbled. Public conveniences were instituted, but multiplied only slowly. In the 1870s as more suburbs were built, together with railway stations to connect them to Town, Jennings' firm won more contracts. In the 1870s ladies from the North London district of Canonbury still had to retire home after half a morning's shopping as there were no public conveniences in the West End.

Ladies interested in floriculture had, from the 1830s onwards, opportunity to visit exhibitions of "florists' flowers" at the Piccadilly Egyptian Hall, and at the Horticultural Society's Hall in Chiswick. These exhibitions supplemented the gardening magazines and the gardening manuals of Jane and of J. C. Loudon which became popular at the same date. Where there was curiosity, there was, inevitably in the Victorian period, some entrepreneur providing an exhibition to assuage it, with Prince Albert and his Great Exhibition of 1851 an example to all. The profits from this imaginative venture were ploughed into purchasing land between Knightsbridge and Kensington where museums, colleges and premises for learned societies were established to further whet the public appetite for information.

The Great International Exhibition of 1862 was held on the site at once of Lady Blessington's old home, Gore House, and of the future Albert Hall. Here, for the first time in two centuries, the porcelain, textiles and paintings of Japan were displayed to the great excitement of artists and discerning visitors. A craze for the Oriental swept England, promoted by Whistler and by a young shopkeeper, Arthur Liberty. Liberty persuaded his employers at

145

Farmer and Rogers' Great Shawl Emporium to buy all the Japanese exhibits when the Exhibition closed. The Oriental Bazaar department which he established swiftly became popular with customers fascinated by the delicate silks and blue and white china. The famous Shawl Emporium itself closed in 1880, its shawls as defunct as the crinolines they had once adorned; Liberty opened his own store in 1875 to drape thousands of Aesthetic ladies with his famous silks. For this fashion change the Great International Exhibition of 1862 was directly responsible.

Exhibitions, museums, lecture halls, all provided an Open Sesame to a wider world. This was fortunate for the gentlewoman, as her schooling had

Advertisement for Farmer & Rogers' India Shawl Emporium. This famous Regent Street showroom was crowded with Royal and commoner customers for twenty years from 1850 to 1870, when the crinoline dictated fashion, and the shawl was its natural companion.

done little to arouse or satisfy the most ordinary curiosity about the outside world. "Nurse" gave way to nursery governess, who taught the "three Rs" and plain sewing; then might come the "finishing governess", to administer accomplishments. Alternatively, at about fourteen, she might be sent to a "select seminary", run by some gentlewoman who had a capacious town house and need of extra income. Anne Cobbett, author of *The English Housekeeper* (1824), and daughter of the radical MP, William Cobbett, thought the habit of sending girls to expensive schools had much to answer for: they came home with heads muzzy with scraps of information about Scipio and George Washington, but no certainty as to which had been President of America.

Responsible for this confusion were the question and answer manuals which had become the approved textbooks at the turn of the century; a schoolmistress from near Wakefield, Miss Richmal Mangnall, compiled *Historical and Miscellaneous Questions for the Use of Young People* in 1800. Mangnall's *Questions* brought its authoress £130,000 (though she had sold the copyright to Messrs. Longman for 100 guineas) and was the deficient governess's Bible till at least 1880. Later came *Eve's Questions*, a popular manual in the 1850s. These teaching aids encouraged disconnected snippets of information to float loose in a thousand feminine minds, and echoed earlier "swarms of Abridgements, Beauties and Compendiums", which the educationalist Hannah More had

Noses to the North!

THE SCHOLASTIC HEN AND HER CHICKENS.

Miss Thimblebee loquitur.—*"Turn your heads the other way my dears, for here are two horridly handsome Officers coming."*

The Scholastic Hen and her Chickens, *by George Cruikshank. "Crocodiles" of young ladies issuing out from select seminaries with a governess were a common sight in Brighton and other fashionable endroits. Pupils recited verbs on these "dismal diurnal walks".*

condemned in her "Strictures on the Modern System of Female Education", (1799), as "an infallible receipt for making a superficial mind". The question and answer system was prevalent in all girls' schools in the midcentury, even those supposedly superior.

Miss Cobbett's strictures on boarding schools for young ladies are fierce: history and geography . . . are learnt by rote, a page of Greece on Monday, a page of Rome on Tuesday, a page of Universal Biography on Wednesday . . . and application being made to maps, globe charts, &c ., to fill up the time which is not devoted to the fine arts (for it all goes on at once) . . ." Her complaints are borne out, not only in Thackeray's inimitable description of Amelia Seddon's

147

and Becky Sharp's education in Brighton, but by the Ango-Irish journalist, Frances Power Cobbe, in her autobiography. Educated at home near Dublin by her mother and then by governesses, Frances was unprepared for life at the Brighton seminary which she attended in 1836, when she was fourteen.

The seminary, she thought, was typical of the hundred-odd such establishments then open in Brighton. Her school was superior in tone, boasting mostly the daughters of "men of some standing, mostly country gentlemen, members of Parliament, and offshoots of the peerage", but it was run on the same lines as all the others. The fees were a staggering £500 a year, not counting the many extras which were *de rigeur*. (Charles Dickens earned £250 as a superior Parliamentary reporter at this date.) Frances was one of twenty-five pupils who spent their days in large double classrooms, equipped with four pianos. Lessons in French and Italian were given simultaneously in different parts of the same classroom, over the sweet music of scales and practising at the piano. Music was considered supremely important by both mistresses and parents; drawing was less important, because less "voyant" or showy. Besides the piano and the harp, the "new instruments", the concertina and the accordian, were also taught. Dancing came second in importance. Every national dance ever performed in Europe from the bolero to the Italian tarantella was taught to Frances and her friends. The only relaxation from this exhausting programme of "higher education" came in the afternoon; the girls paraded up and down the esplanades and terraces of Brighton for an hour under the eye of a mistress, who heard their verbs as they trotted along.

A girl emerging from a few years of such schooling acquired a liking for tittle-tattle and finery, but she had had no opportunity to learn habits of industry. As Miss Cobbett complained, boarding school education was no preparation, with the false notions of accomplishments and consequence it inspired, for the humdrum regular habits she would need in her housekeeping on marriage. Pupils emerged, fine ladies, who thought it beneath them to be able to make a pudding, merely because they could execute a sonata with taste. In 1852 Sam Beeton, the newspaper editor, attacked "The Boarding School Miss" in similar terms: "the young lady's peculiar talents consisted in dress and fancy-work, with some interludes of novel-reading and playing fantasias on the piano (in company) and . . . in a great faculty of talking and laughing about nothing."

Curiously enough, in the very year Beeton wrote, his future wife, who would do so much to make the ladies emerging from boarding schools to marriage competent to cook a pudding, was herself attending a boarding school in Islington. Isabella Beeton, *née* Mayson, had been brought up with a herd of brothers and sisters, and stepbrothers and sisters, in a most haphazard way by her grandmother in the Committee and Refreshment Rooms which lay under the grandstand on Epsom Racecourse. Her stepfather was Clerk of the Course, and there was not room in the Clerk's house for all the children he and Isabella's mother had accumulated in their first marriages. Perhaps the lavish hampers from Fortnum and Masons's, stuffed with lobster mayonnaise and champagne,

The Angel in the House

with which the Derby Day racegoers arrived, stimulated Isabella's interest in catering. At any rate, when she went to a school in Heidelberg after Islington to learn French and German, she also took patisserie lessons, and, on her return, took a further course of lessons at a pastry-cook's in Epsom. Still, she had no practical experience of cookery till she married Sam in 1856, and set up house in one of the new villas at Pinner. Till then, she studied music in London with Sir Julius Benedict, who composed *The Lily of Killarney* and acted as accompanist to the celebrated Jenny Lind.

Isabella's sisters, less enterprising, remained at Epsom. She described them: "dragging out a miserable existence, doing plenty of embroidery and going out for gigantic walks and coming home covered with mud," in 1855. In common with other girls of their class, they certainly had not learnt how to make a pudding. Maids and household manuals on marriage must be their instructors in such arts. On the other hand, they had not acquired any scholastic education, either.

The Governess (1844), by Richard Redgrave, a study in loneliness. In 1841 a clergyman founded the Governesses' Benevolent Institution, to provide aid and educational lectures for indigent gentlewomen like this, who became governesses for want of a respectable alternative.

Chapter Four

The problem lay partly in the poor standard of education of the seminaries' instructresses. Teaching was the only profession deemed suitable for a gentlewoman; in the 1830s and 1840s there was nothing to say that she must be suitable for it. What a nuisance governesses were, exclaimed Blanche Ingram in *Jane Eyre* and in front of Jane, governess to Mr Rochester's ward, Adèle: "half of them detestable and the rest ridiculous, and all incubi." One Madame Joubert she recalled with especial pleasure. How enraged the poor woman became when the young Ingrams "spilt our tea, crumbled our bread and butter, tossed our books up to the ceiling, and played a charivari with the ruler, the desk, the fender and fireirons." Accomplished Miss Ingram – she still played, sang, "talked French apart to her mamma", and in a discourse on botany, "ran over its vocabulary with an air". She had been more fortunate in her preceptress than some. Governesses from the Continent were often a credit to their stricter educational establishments; Charlotte Brontë herself went to Brussels as an economical location where she would widen her education.

Steps were taken in the 1840s to promote some degree of education in governesses. Under the aegis of the Governesses' Benevolent Institution, founded in 1841, F. D. Maurice established Queen's College in 1848 where lecturers from King's College, London University, addressed governesses on subjects which would increase their stock as employees. In Reading and in Salisbury in 1841, diocesan training colleges had been established with the same end in view, although the emphasis was as much on religious education for the aspirant governesses as scholastic. They were intended to act as missionaries of the Anglican faith to pupils attracted by worldly varieties.

Two graduates of Queen's College, in particular, profited by their improved education. Miss Buss founded the North London Collegiate School for Ladies in 1850. Miss Beale became the first headmistress of Cheltenham Ladies' College in 1858. Both ladies were firm believers in the benefit to girls of physical exercise, and fought battles with parents and governors to promote both sports and suitable, unrestricting dress. Miss Buss did not allow dresses below the ankle, and disapproved of corsets; Miss Beale recommended "various harmless substitutes for stays", and for high-heeled, pointed shoes. They modelled their schools on boys' public schools, and introduced, with the large number of pupils, an Assembly Hall and Speech Day and other novelties in girls' schools, such as the idea of public duty.

When Miss Buss was called to give evidence to the Schools Enquiry Commission in 1865, she was asked about the composition of her school. Were they children of what might be called the upper division of the middle class? Miss Buss thought that they would wish to be considered so. Did they learn Latin and French? They did. Arithmetic they also learnt, since the establishment of the Cambridge University External Exams. (In 1840, twenty-year-old Florence Nightingale had wished to study mathematics with her Aunt Mai. Of what use were mathematics to a girl whose destiny it was to marry, asked Florence's mother. She attempted to forbid the enterprise.) And what was the state of the

Left: Miss Dorothea Beale, formidable headmistress of Cheltenham Ladies' College, one of the first "reformed" schools. Right: Elizabeth Garrett Anderson. Josephine Butler found she could "tell" this first British woman doctor "so much more than I ever could or would tell to any man".

girls' education when they arrived at the Collegiate School? "Extremely ignorant." On the question of accomplishments, which had so dominated Frances Power Cobbe's Brighton school thirty years before, Miss Buss was gruff: there was a large demand for accomplishments, "but we try to make the accomplishments as real as possible." Miss Beale and Miss Buss might do their utmost to train rational women from the poor material they received; in the year of the Schools Enquiry Commission another educationalist, Elizabeth Sewell, was obsessed in her book, the *Principles of Education*, by the delicate health of females. She was sure it would break down, were women ever to strive after the educational standards of their brothers. "Not a girl in a hundred would be able to work up the subjects required for an Indian Civil Service examination," for instance. Miss Sewell deplored the "bustling millwheel life of a large school" as having no connection with the quiet home lives girls were to lead on marriage.

Few young gentlewomen had the grit of Elizabeth Garrett, who persevered in her determination to study medicine against considerable opposition. In 1861, after she had attended lectures at the Middlesex Hospital for eleven months, the other – male – students presented a Memorial to the Medical School Committee. (Miss Garrett had brought their resentment of her presence to a head by being alone in the class to answer a difficult question correctly.) The presence of a young female as passive spectator in the operating theatre, felt the male students, was "an outrage to the natural instincts . . . calculated to destroy those sentiments of . . . admiration with which the opposite sex is regarded by all right-minded men." The presence of a female at the Middlesex had exposed

its male students to "taunts". Separate classes for the sexes were normal in other sciences, like the fine arts; "the promiscuous assemblage of the sexes in the same class is a dangerous innovation . . ." Miss Garrett's family attempted to bribe the Medical School Committee with a handsome scholarship for female students of £2,000, but the Committee stood by its male students and refused to allow her to continue her studies. She only won a licence to practise from the Society of Apothecaries, an obscure body, in 1867. In the intervening years London and Edinburgh Universities refused her application to study.

Elizabeth Garrett was fortunate in her family's support. When Florence Nightingale wished to train as a nurse at Salisbury Infirmary in 1845, her

Florence Nightingale (1820-1910). "The accumulation of nervous energy, which has nothing to do during the day, makes them feel every night when they go to bed, as if they were going mad," she wrote – from experience – of young gentlewomen.

mother and sister were her chief opponents: "Mama was terrified" by "things about the surgeons and nurses which you may guess . . ." Florence endured five years of "going mad for want of something to do", before she decided to be ruled by her family no longer in her thirtieth year. Her diary reveals that she was quite literally going mad with a passion for Richard Monckton Milnes whom she had refused to marry in 1849. Only the determination of her friend, Mrs Bracebridge, saved Florence. She and her husband were part of a group interested to reform the insanitary and immoral conditions of nursing and medicine in hospitals with whom Florence consorted, despite her family's misgivings. The Bracebridges deposited Florence at Pastor Fliedner's Kaiserswerth Institu-

tion, not as patient but as visiting inspector. Miss Nightingale had long been anxious to see the nursing methods employed by the German deaconesses.

Progress towards working in a hospital herself was slow. In 1853 an opportunity arose. The Governesses' Benevolent Institution had established in Harley Street an Institution for the Care of Sick Gentlewomen in Distressed Circumstances. It needed a Superintendent to reorganise it. Greatly daring, Florence agreed to assume the position, though the "Committee of Fine Ladies" who sat in judgement upon her application, apart from Lady Canning, were hesitant about one of their own kind taking the post. Florence took rooms in Pall Mall and settled down to apply all the knowledge of statistics on illness and hygiene and nursing which she had acquired during her long years in waiting. She was now thirty-four. In fact, the experience she had acquired at home of storekeeping and counting linen and keeping a tally of glass and plate (one of many unmarried daughters' responsibilities) was of more use to her. The experience of her Superintendence at the Home was useful in the administrative work which the Scutari Hospital in the Crimea would bring; it offered few nursing rewards. Not unkindly, Florence would imitate at the dinner parties which she attended regularly the injured and self-pitying voices of her patients. It was the sick, not the needy, whom she wished to help. As all the world knows, in 1854 her chance came when she was asked to take a force of ladies and nurses to counteract complaints in *The Times* that the British forces were suffering from having no equivalent band of female nurses to the French Soeurs de Charité. When Miss Nightingale returned, exhausted, disillusioned by her contact with jealous Army doctors and incompetent Army administrators, she had given to the Armed Forces a new tradition of efficient female nursing. She had opened to the gentlewoman of England the chance of respectable fulfilment as nurse to the British soldier. She herself sank back into the demanding routine of life with her mother and sister.

Most gentlewomen of course preferred the traditional route to fulfilment as wife and mother. They were likely to become mother of many. Contraception did not become widespread in England until the 1870s, when Annie Besant published with great daring, *Fruits of Philosophy, or the Private Companion of Young Married People*. This instructed the reader in contraceptive techniques. It also gave ladies some much needed information about the facts of life, which the works of Havelock Ellis would only later fully explain. Till then, the population of England was ever increasing. This meant that among the middle class and upper classes, large families were practical, as they were not in America and in France where contraception had been practised since the turn of the century. In England mothers found there was a limitless supply of wet-nurses to be had.

The absence of contraception had two obvious drawbacks. In a large, mixed household the maids might become pregnant, or indeed the governess. More personal a worry for the mistress of the house, was the fear that she, already the mother of six or seven children, might again become pregnant.

Miss Catherine Herrick with her nieces and nephews, the five elder children of the Rev. and Mrs Henry Palmer, in 1827 and The Rev. and Mrs Henry Palmer with their six younger children at Withcote Hall, near Oakham, Leicestershire, in 1838, both by John Ferneley (1782-1860).

There was a limit to resources in every household. It was not only a matter of money: there was a limited number of rooms to consider; there was the tax, the sometimes fatal tax on the mother's health; there was the worry of finding an extra "position" later on, should the baby be a boy, or an extra husband, were it a girl. Henrietta Maria, Lady Stanley of Alderley, was one of many women who decided to force a miscarriage. She had given birth to nine children, now all well-grown, and her husband Edward's reaction to the news that she was pregnant again sums up the problem another child posed. "This your last misfortune is indeed most grievous . . . it comes very opportunely to disturb all your family arrangements & revives the nursey & Williams in full vigour. I only hope it is not the beginning of another flock . . . you must make the best of it . . ." In Victorian times a pregnancy must be a matter for anxiety, with the high infant mortality rate and the frequent deaths of mothers after childbirth from puerperal fever.

Lady Stanley was determined that it was not too late to mend the misfortune. The same day that Edward wrote to her, she sent off an exuberant letter to him: "A hot bath, a tremendous walk & a great dose have succeeded . . ." Edward wrote next day, worried, but thankful for her "violent proceedings . . . if you are none the worse the great result is all the better." Henrietta was triumphant in answer: "I was sure you would feel the same horror as I did at an increase in family but I am reassured for the future by the efficacy of the means".

The public ideal of motherhood as woman's finest aspect and women's private opinion of it were often quite different. That most maternal of women, Queen Victoria, affronted her daughter, Vicky, in 1858 by her frank views on

The Angel in the House

childbearing. Vicky, recently married to the Crown Prince of Prussia, had written delightedly of the liberty afforded to married women. "If you have hereafter," responded her mother, "(as I had constantly for the first 2 years of my marriage) aches and sufferings and miseries and plagues which you must struggle against and enjoyments, etc. to give up – constant precautions to take [during pregnancy] you will feel the yoke of the married woman!"

A very practical person, Queen Victoria accepted the new painkiller, chloroform, during her eighth pregnancy, thus providing an example to thousands of women who dreaded the moment of birth as the supreme evil. Her comments on this moment to Vicky, not yet a mother, were typical of her: "What you say of the pride of giving life to an immortal soul is very fine, dear, but . . . I think much more of our being like a cow or dog at such moments." Victorian women, faced with a dozen or more pregnancies before they could relax, were far less squeamish in their discussion of the subject than one might imagine. Caroline Meysey Wigley, was a newcomer to the experience when she married her Mr Clive at the advanced age of thirty-nine. Discovering that she was pregnant, she canvassed opinion among her acquaintances on questions like quickening. Lady Gordon, she reported, said it felt like a "wind on the stomach"; Mrs Buckley held that it was "like chickens moving in a basket". Another lady supported this, but substituted rabbits for chickens. When Caroline's labour began her husband remained nobly at home when he ought to have been in church, and heard from the dressing-room his wife's groans as she produced his son.

An enormous amount of literature on rearing children appeared from 1820 on; Madame de Saussure's *Progressive Education* was called by Mrs Gaskell the nicest book on the subject. It was succeeded by Samuel Smiles' *Physical Education*, which provided scientific information about infant development. The obstetrician, Dr Chavasse, and Thomas Bull, "physician accoucheur", provided two more widely read baby books, *Advice to Mothers* (1839), and *Maternal Management of Children* (1840). There were, besides, any number of periodicals and magazines intended for anxious parents: *Mothers's Magazine*, *The Family Magazine*, *Parents' Assistant*. Besides all this practical literature, there was Jabez Burns' *Mothers of the Wise and Good* (1846) which inspired the Victorian matron to emulate Thetis, mother of Achilles, and Lady Byron and George Washington's mother. The distance between Victorian mother and child in early years together has been exaggerated; there was a religio-scientific belief that a mother could do much to influence her growing child and was, as the natural, the best influence. It was generally she who taught her children to read and to write, and, when there were seven or eight children in the family, this required some pains. Queen Victoria and Prince Albert's example as enthusiastic advocates of family life was influential.

On the question of family meals, Dr Chavasse quotes Dinah Mulock Craik: "I always prefer having children about me at mealtimes. I think it makes them little gentlewomen and gentlemen in a manner that nothing else will." How far other parents chose to follow Mulock Craik, we cannot know, but

children were now taken with their mother to pay calls, they spent increasing amounts of time in the drawing-room. While the company of their mother was thought positively good, the influence of servants was now thought baneful. An extraordinary proof of this, and of the pride now shown in quite young children, is that the lady of the house wheeled the newfangled perambulator or baby-carriage to the park. The nurse followed behind, if nurse existed.

The perambulator was introduced in the 1850s: "the most influential of all babycare appliances". By 1856 there were five manufacturers with shops in Oxford Street, among them Charles Burton's. The Queen gave royal approval to the device and purchased three vehicles from Burton's: The *Illustrated London News* offered an engraving showing the Princess of Wales walking beside one of them in St James's Park. By 1870 there were thirty manufacturers of prams, and never again need babies want for fresh air or passers-by in the street want for barked shins and crushed corns.

There was little opportunity under these conditions for gentlewomen to realise talents for business, for scholarship, but on the domestic front conditions were excellent for a woman wishing to make her home a temple to thrift and ingenious contrivances and domestic comfort. Queen Victoria had nine children between 1841 and 1857; large families became a sign of grace. The Victorian home and its maintenance came to be a very weighty affair; already heavily encumbered with servants and silver and massive dining-tables, the home became the target of a stream of books of advice on how best to manage the load.

1824 saw the publication of *A New System of Practical Domestic Economy, adapted to Families of Every Description*. It aimed to show that "good old English housewifery is still a good old English virtue"; ladies must not yearn after fancy French dishes and should "unite elegance with economy". Dr William Kitchiner published, in 1829, as supplement to the earlier *Cook's Oracle, The Housekeeper's Oracle ...* containing "A Complete system of Carving". Dr Kitchiner hoped that "inexperienced Housekeepers" and young ladies, in general, might learn from the Oracle the "delectable Arcana of Domestic Affairs in as little time as is usually devoted to the directing of the position of her hands on a Pianoforte, or of her feet in a Quadrille". Then the "Cage of Matrimony" would be as comfortable as "the Net of Courtship" was charming. Kitchiner also hoped to guard young wives against the "impositions" of dishonest servants and tradesmen.

Through the decades, a stream of advice literature continued to assail worried young ladies who undertook their own housekeeping for the first time. Many women transcribed recipes and hints particularly of use in their own households into personal receipt books; Emily, Lady Shaftesbury, found that: "sassafras shavings will prevent bugs", useful when her reformer husband returned from the East End of London. Anne Cobbett's *The English Housekeeper* ran into its third edition in 1842.

Mrs Jane Loudon wrote *The Lady's Country Companion, or How to*

Enjoy a Country Life Rationally, in 1845 for girls condemned upon marriage to exchange the town for their husband's country dwelling. Mrs Loudon's book is written in a series of letters, addressed to Annie, whom she swears is no fiction, but a dear young friend of hers. Poor Annie, the nearest neighbours on whom she feels she can "call", live seven miles away. As the letters progress, we learn from Mrs Loudon that Annie's antipathy to the country and its pastimes is gradually tempered by a faint interest in the parterre and in the poultry yard. It is as good as any novel and better, for it gives us an accurate picture of what the gentlewoman's tastes and occupations were expected to be in the mid-nineteenth century.

The Tea Table, *from Mrs Beeton's* Book of Household Management, *in an edition c. 1907. The late Victorian addition of afternoon tea to the other meals in the day necessitated an additional change of costume in grander ladies' wardrobes – the tea gown.*

Mrs Loudon gave clear directions to Annie for the management of a country larder. Her husband might at any point unexpectedly bring home a friend to dinner. Let there always be a side of ham cured and hanging from the kitchen rafters, or some preserved beef. Of course, a single dish of meat would not make "a nice little dinner", though "quite sufficient as regards mere eating". Her husband would feel quite mortified if the meat were not preceded by a good soup; here the importance of the stockpot ever at the bubble was stressed. With several dishes to accompany the meat, and perhaps an omelette or some Dutch flummery or syllabub or frangipani to follow, the honours of the house might not be felt entirely lacking. Many a young housewife living some miles

from a market town, where the tradesmen made deliveries only once or twice a week, must have spent sleepless nights after reading Mrs Loudon on "The Unexpected Guest", uncomfortably aware that there was no store of preserved meat ready against the morrow.

The townswoman had more comfort from Isabella Beeton's famous compendium of housekeeping information published in 1861, *Mrs Beeton's Book of Household Management*, still widely admired in the 1980s. It became a bestseller immediately, though Isabella died only four years after its publication. The effort of producing her masterpiece may have exhausted her; she was only twenty-four when it came out. "I must frankly own, that if I had known before-

Group of the Boileau family and servants at Ketteringham in 1865, with the fashionable Gothic great hall in the background. Outdoor servants, indoor servants, upper servants and family all "knew their place". The difficulty was, where was the governess's place?

hand that this book would cost me the labour which it has, I should never have been courageous enough to commence it," she wrote in the preface. The important point about Mrs Beeton's book is its emphasis on the large, urban households which were the main targets of her advice. Large families with children living between day and night nursery on the top floor, their parents on the middle floors and the servants in the basement of spacious, modern houses became the norm.

Some of these houses were in the centre of Town; by 1848 the *Morning Herald* had noted the mania for building and purchasing "eligible family residences, desirable villas, and aristocratic cottages, which have nothing in the world of the cottage about them except the name", in the suburbs of large cities. "The villa mania", in particular, was "everywhere most obtrusive". It was cheaper to purchase or rent a villa with "aristocratic" folding-doors, in the suburbs than to buy or rent the equivalent space in Town. Still, there was the question of the daily railway fare to the gentleman's London place of work to be

considered. (Sam Beeton was given a season ticket by the grateful developer from whom he and Isabella purchased their Pinner villa in 1865.) The primary reason for settling in the suburbs was one of health. The cholera outbreaks of 1832, 1849 and 1854 established in the public's mind, quite wrongly, that the cause of most disease was "the miasma", or germs floating about in the air. Bad drains and ventilation, and overcrowding were the real culprits. The suburbs were held to be free from this dreadful miasma; they were also free from the "smoke and deleterious gases" issuing from industrial chimneys, which the Webster Parkes *Encyclopaedia of Domestic Economy* of 1844 noted. By the 1860s fresh air, and spacious gardens where it could be snuffed up, were widely recognised as beneficial even for ladies, and the movement towards the suburbs did not abate.

In her *Household Management*, Mrs Beeton sets out in simple terms a scale of servants suitable to various incomes in a variety of dwellings. Wealthy noblemen would have a full staff with two dozen indoor servants; on an income of a thousand a year a cook, upper and under-housemaid and man servant could be supported. The scale descended to include incomes of two hundred a year, where a maid-of-all-work, or "girl for rough work" might be supported, with a nursemaid optional. This expense could be saved if there was a daughter old enough, good enough and careful enough to mind the younger ones. With later editions, each a period piece, the details of advice alter. The doctrine remains the same: "There is no more fruitful source of family discontent than badly cooked dinners and untidy ways." Mrs Beeton struck a note of warning: "Men are now so well served out of doors at clubs, hotels and restaurants that to compete with the attractions of these places a mistress must be thoroughly acquainted with the theory and practice of cookery."

Mrs Beeton herself was, as we have seen, not remotely well acquainted with the "practice of cookery" on her own marriage. She learnt her craft by experience, and culled recipes for her book and for cookery articles in her husband's magazines from Dr Kitchiner's *Cooks Oracle* and from Eliza Acton's book which reappear in her own work without acknowledgement. Resourceful Mrs Beeton also wrote to the housekeepers of numerous grandees for recipes, of which a "portable soup" from a Duke's household, a soup in a stockcube, is memorable. One of the few receipes in the great work which were not extracted from others by the wily and hardworked Mrs Beeton is the Epsom Grandstand Pigeon Pie. But in her commonsense Mrs Beeton is her own woman: "Daily purchase is daily waste."

As the century proceeded, the indoor staff of a Victorian household included more and more women. Menservants were felt to lack the qualities of subservience and humility, the air of spurious goodness which were so liked in female servants. Besides, an experienced maid could act as a useful supplementary source of household lore to her mistress, even as a confidante. Harriet Martineau, professional author, who lived in Ambleside alone with her maids, felt a warm sympathy for her servants. She baked the wedding cake herself when a treasured maid got married and hosted the nuptial breakfast. This was

particularly good of Harriet, as her view of matrimony was this: "the older I have grown, the more serious and irremediable have seemed to me the evils and disadvantages of married life, as it exists among us at this time . . ." She wrote this when she was nearly fifty, and declared herself "probably the happiest single woman in England". One hopes that her maids at least contributed useful suggestions to the popular manuals she wrote in the late 1830s: *Guides to Service, The Maid of-all-Work, The Housemaid* and *The Lady's Maid*.

A famous instance of the close ties and confidence which could develop between mistress and maid is the friendship between Elizabeth Barrett of Wimpole Street and her maid, Wilson. In the best manner of melodrama, Wilson aided the poet Robert Browning to ascend, unbeknownst to the Barrett parents, to Elizabeth's bedroom on the top floor. When Robert and Elizabeth determined to elope and go and live in Italy, Elizabeth planned, for the sake of economy, to dispense with Wilson's services. Robert would not hear of such a measure; without Wilson, "you – no I will not undertake to speak of *you*: then *I* should be simply, exactly, *INSANE* to move a step." He would rather propose they live on bread and water and sail in the hold of a merchant ship than leave Wilson behind. Wilson duly played her part in the secret departure from England, and, indeed, took to Italian life like a duck to water. She quickly mastered Italian, "with a little licence in the grammar"; she did not dislike the food; and ended, after a brief flirtation with a "Mr Righi of the Ducal Guard" by becoming the contented wife of the Brownings' manservant, Ferdinando.

In the country, ladies began to experiment with games and hobbies to alleviate the long hours of leisure. Archery continued to be popular, battledore and shuttlecock enjoyed a vogue before croquet and golf made their appearance in the 1860s; even fishing was enjoyed by some ladies in a desultory way. Gardening, however, outdid all these in popularity. Mrs Loudon was author of *Instructions in Gardening for Ladies* (1840), so it was only natural that she should devote part of her correspondence with Annie to urging the young bride to take an interest in her outdoor surroundings. In 1829 Dr Kitchiner had been confident in his assertion "Our fair readers' . . . practical gardening seldom extends beyond the parterre or green house." Mrs Loudon's *Instructions* and her *The Ladies' Companion to the Flower Garden*, published the following year, assumed that *her* fair readers would work in their gardens themselves. In 1845 Mrs Loudon, admittedly a keen gardener herself and married to J.C. Loudon, a great populariser of gardening, urged on Annie "digging"! It was a fine healthy occupation, and a lady's spade with an elegant willow handle would make the task lighter. What was Annie to dig? Not the kitchen garden; this walled enclosure was not a lady's province, but should be the joint care of head gardener, master, and cook. The park, too, was beyond her domain. The parterre, or terrace and ornamental garden outside the morning-room, however, was under her direction. Mrs Loudon recommended that Annie plant the cut-out beds with flowers, so that the parterre appeared a Turkey carpet from the windows above. Annie should choose the colours of the flowers on the same

Opposite: The Fair Toxophilites (1872) by W. P. Frith. Archery enjoyed a revival from about 1780 to 1900. It was considered to be a pastime that set off feminine charms admirably, and ladies formed archery societies, held archery breakfasts and dressed in Lincoln green.

principles that she chose the colours of her dresses. Whether the lady of the house or the gardener was to plant the petunias and pansies, was not made clear. Mrs Loudon conceded that, despite her talk of digging and willow spades, a trowel would be Annie's most useful implement. There was a strange mixture of robust and practical direction, and mollycoddling in all she said. This reflected the novelty value of gardening as an occupation for ladies at this date. Let Annie lay down gravel paths round her roseries and trefoil-shaped beds; they would prevent her getting wet feet in damp weather, "though you must not mind going on the grass, if you are to be a real gardener."

Nathan Cole had direction of Kensington Gardens, and his *Royal Parks*

Potting, 1852 photograph. In the 1830s and 1840s gardening became a popular pastime. "Florist's flower" shows, gardening magazines and gardening gurus like J. C. and Jane Loudon encouraged hesitant amateurs. Ladies potted on and pricked out, while the gentlemen pushed the lawn mower.

and Gardens of London (1877) offers sections of his bright, geometrical bedding plans. This massed bedding of flowers was entirely new in the history of gardening, made possible by the immense amounts of annuals which could be raised in greenhouses. Formally surrounded by gravel walks and interspersed with fountains and statues, this kind of garden became the Victorian norm. Where the blaze of reds and yellows is now offensive, then it was thought immensely original. In the eighteenth century, flowers had never occupied more than a tiny and remote area of the country house garden; landscape gardening, displaying the lord of the manor's lands to their best advantage, had been all-important. It is a sign of the taste for domesticity that the lady's flower

The Angel in the House

garden now encroached on traditional parkland. The shrubbery, that most Victorian garden feature, acted as a transition from the "high state of culture in a flower-garden, to the wild nature of the forest trees" in the park; this was also generally made the lady's province. Here she planted first dwarf shrubs, then larger laurustinus, and, by degrees, larger and larger plants and trees, till the rim of the park was reached. The English lady gardeners of Victorian days, the 1850s and 1860s, had not yet acquired the confidence which Jekyll and others were to display sixty years later; still, they had come a long way from the timorous creatures of the 1820s who would allow flowers only in their dressing-room, never in the bedchamber for fear of noxious vapours. (White lilies in particular were held to guarantee apoplexy, if more than two pots were grouped in a room, and the casement window was to be shut firm on the heady fumes of lonicera or jessamine climbing the walls outside.)

The lawn mower, invented by Budding in the 1830s, made expanses of lawns practical for homes and gardeners of all kinds. Previously, lawns had been sheared by scythe or by sheep. The Wardian case was also invented in the 1830s. This glass-sided container provided a soot-free environment important in smoggy Victorian towns where ferns and rockery plants could grow indoors without water or attention. The indoor garden was an immediate success in sub-urban villas, and smaller Victorian homes. The plant cases could assume any shape, and a "Tintern Abbey Case" provided the frontispiece to the second edition of Dr Ward's book, *On the Growth of Plants in Closely Glazed Cases* (1852). Ladies' interest in gardening was also stimulated by the introduction of mass-produced greenhouses, where they could grow tender flowering plants. Greenhouses had, of course, existed in the form of "stoves", or enclosed spaces warmed by burners, since the sixteenth century. The modern greenhouse, or glasshouse, only appeared in the early 1820s, with the improvements in metal construction and glassmaking. Dazzling glass palaces at Syon (1820), at Kew (*c*.1844) were mirrored by simpler structures in lesser homes.

Besides practical gardening, now practical botany came into vogue. The theory of botany had long been taught in classrooms, young ladies were accustomed to the exercise of copying, from botanical drawings and watercolours, the parts of plants and herbs. *Horti Sicci*, or arrangements of pressed flowers, could be seen in every library, a reminder, along with brothers' collections of eggs and insects, of industrious wet afternoons. But the systematic study of the flora growing wild in the park was quite a different affair from such diversions. It would do Annie good to leave the poultry-yard and the immediate environs of the house, Mrs Loudon assured her; let her walk out to wild corners of the park and gather there plants to identify back at home with her husband's help. "It is pleasant to be schooled by the lips of those we love," wrote Mrs Loudon, never dreaming that Annie's husband would not be proficient in botany. One proviso to the plan: let Annie's maid go with her on her walks, and let her carry a campstool, as a precaution against fatigue overcoming her mistress in some distant spinney.

163

The Angel in the House

One hobby which promised the ladies of England an exciting diversion from the 1860s onwards was foxhunting. As we have seen, this sport had gone in and out of fashion for ladies in earlier centuries. The Countess of Salisbury in the late eighteenth century had kept a private pack of hounds till her death in 1812. Charles James Fox had careered across the countryside in 1800 with dashing countesses. Ladies' participation in the sport then lapsed. The hounds became swifter across country, the large brushwood fences, or "bullfinches", might catch ladies' voluminous habits or scratch their faces. Ladies were to be found only in attendance at the meet during the "Golden Age" of foxhunting from 1750 to 1850, with its hazardous and testing conditions, though they still rode for exercise.

Then, in the 1850s, the high, barbarous fences were cut down, the leaping crutch or pommel made jumping with a side-saddle much safer, and ladies took to the field again in numbers. We hear of a few ladies "out" in the mid-1850s, like Mrs Thomas Wilkinson with the Hurworth Hunt. She came back regularly with her habit stiff with mud from falls. A few daughters and wives ventured cautiously out, to be "piloted" by their menfolk over the easier hedges. Then with the appearance of Maria, Lady Yarborough, at the 1859 season of the Brocklesby Hunt in North Lincolnshire, a wind of change blows. Daughter of the Irish peer, Lord Elliston, Maria was accustomed to hunt regularly before marriage. The fact the the Yarborough family had not been out with the hunt for years, she ignored. She borrowed a mount from a neighbour, and, later, one of the new side-saddles with the leaping crutch from the same young girl. The peeress's interest stimulated other ladies, and soon the Brocklesby was crowded with Dianas of the hunt.

Less respectable ladies also adorned the hunting field. Most famous of them was Skittles, or Catherine Walters, who rode in London with her lovers in Rotten Row. She hunted in the 1860s with the Quorn, under Lord Stamford's Mastership. The dashing costumes she wore, and the elegant picture she made, spurred other ladies to follow her example. The Countess of Cardigan had begun like Skittles as a fair equestrian. In a little leopard skin hat perched on very blonde curls, she would come to the meet in a carriage, later in life, and enquire from its comfortable depths, "Has anyone seen my horse?" Of course, none existed. In provincial villages and in the suburbs, ladies could combine town and country amusements. Dinner parties became an extremely popular form of entertainment. *Enquire Within Upon Everything* had sold 146,000 copies and was in its fourteenth edition by 1860. It proffered advice to the socially nervous on all the etiquette surrounding dinners and balls and card parties, some of it perhaps otiose for the quieter inhabitants of suburbia. A "Paris card of invitation" to an evening party usually implied that the guest was invited for the season, noted the bible of etiquette solemnly. For outdoor activity, "carriage exercise", which was no exercise at all, would suffice for the elderly and delicate; promenades in the leafy streets would provide fresh air for more energetic ladies.

Opposite: At the Bazaar, or The Empty Purse *by James Collinson (1825-81). In 1861 the* Cornhill Magazine *noted that at these popular society events, rose buds could be sold at a pound-a-piece, and "cups of tea remain steady at half a sovereign."*

If ladies wanted other occupation, there was always charitable work. It was thought most important that they should not dispense alms in the form of money, for this would discourage the poor from seeking work. Only in illness should financial aid be given, and then sparingly. *Self-help*, Samuel Smiles' 1859 tract, was the most important in the Victorian philanthropist's armoury of advice books.

Schools in the village were a worthy object of care for the local ladies. They might pay for some woman to show the village girls how to sew and to dressmake, and even how to make provisions in the kitchen go further. It was a source of distress to many an economical lady that the lower classes did not

Bird's Eye View of Society no. VI by J. Doyle. Organising bazaars and balls was pleasant charity work. As the Cornhill Magazine *observed, "it surely does not much matter whether a little frivolity and display take part in what results in so much good."*

retain the water in which they had boiled their meat and make a good stock from it. A little instruction given to the village girls might find its way back to their mothers at the fire. Florence Nightingale, typically, went further, and nursed the sick at Lea Hurst, the local village, in 1843, during a fever epidemic, and taught in the Adult School she established there, till her mother's and sister's disapproval proved impossible to ignore.

Full of noble dreams for the improvement of the poor, were the ladies of the countryside. In the town, there was less nobility, for the distress was not to be disguised by curtseys and "Thank you, m'ms", or forgotten after a walk back to the manor through fragrant pastures. Angela Burdett-Coutts helped Dickens

The Angel in the House

to found a Home for Fallen Women in 1846, when she could bear no longer to see the fallen women crouched on her very doorstep. In towns, there could be no belief in traditional values, no comfort from feudal relationships. The debtors' prisons were within feet of fashionable haunts, and the slums were not picturesque cruck cottages, but filthy tenements like Seven Dials in London on the other side of smart Piccadilly. As yet, few ladies ventured out from their comfortable terraced houses to seek personal experience of those slums. There were other prods to their social consciences in the shape of Church teaching and charitable institutions and committees of ladies who "got up" bazaars and sales of fancywork and subscriptions in aid of chimney boys, or Sunday Schools and other pet schemes. Ladies dug deep in their pockets – none so deep as Baroness Burdett-Coutts, who furnished over a million pounds in charitable subscriptions in her lifetime.

Then, the lecture hall vied with the concert hall in the 1860s and 1870s as an evening attraction. Many of the lecturers concerned themselves with social problems, like population and overcrowding, or conditions in the factories. (Lectures on the Great Social Evil, or prostitution, were *not* encouraged.) Ladies were inspired by personable speakers to form local organisations and committees to swell the charitable societies already burgeoning. It was rare, however, despite all the committees and societies and unions which ladies had joined so avidly, to find a woman presiding over the whole. The ancillary role of the Victorian lady, the convention of her dependence on her menfolk died hard. The Ladies' Committee of the RSPCA was only founded in 1870, after grave doubts had been cast on the ladies' efficacy as committee members. Even Florence Nightingale worked "through" gentlemen like Sidney Herbert.

Angela Burdett-Coutts found it convenient to have Charles Dickens and the Duke of Wellington as advisers. (Admittedly, she rarely took their advice.) George Eliot was Editor *de facto* of the *Westminster Review*, during her infatuation for its titular Editor, George Chapman, but preserved her anonymity throughout. Gentlewomen had no more wish to become public figures than their menfolk well-wishers to see them such. When all sought to laud Florence Nightingale as heroine of the Crimean War, she retired to her bed, and took such stringent measures to shelter her continuing work in the field of sanitation from the public gaze that most people assumed she had died within years of the war's end.

The Family would not have liked it otherwise, and in the end the gentlewoman of this period still bowed to the demands of the tyrannical Family. In 1870 she was probably wise to be more concerned about her maid's "followers" and whether hedgehogs really ought to be imported into the house to eat the plague of cockroaches which had been discovered, than about any higher things. She should also, of course, be concerned to keep news of both "followers" and cockroaches from her husband.

CHAPTER FIVE

"The Odd Women"

1870-1914

*I*N 1910 LADY DOROTHY NEVILL LOOKED BACK OVER ARIS-
tocratic life in *Under Five Reigns*: "Society, in the old sense of the
term, may be said, I think, to have come to an end in the eighties of
the last century," was her expert conclusion.

How do we reconcile this with Daisy, Lady Warwick's
account of country house life in the 1890s? "Entertainment among the élite was
undoubtedly an art. The enchantment lay in setting us at ease in a luxury that
was exquisite, without thought of cost. Here, in an atmosphere of beauty, men
and women reposed . . . It can be said that matters of high importance to the
State were constantly decided between Liberals and Conservatives in the
country houses of England." Simply put, Lady Dorothy was a Victorian.
Though a stout Tory, her preferred dinner companion was Gladstone, mighty
exemplar of the nineteenth-century moral and religious revival; she was proud
of her horticultural correspondence with Charles Darwin. She went so far as to
propose visiting the great man at Down House, his Kentish retreat, but was re-
buffed by his wife. Mrs Darwin, ever protective, wrote that she understood that
those who moved much in London Society were accustomed to find their
country-house visits enlivened by all sorts of sports and practical jokes – she
had read that tossing people in blankets had become highly popular . . . "I am
afraid we should hardly be able to offer you anything of that sort."

Poor Lady Dorothy. Mrs Darwin had mistaken her for a member of the
"smart set", later the "Edwardians", who clustered as early as the 1880s around
the Prince of Wales. Daisy, Countess of Warwick, then "Babbling [Lady]
Brooke", was of their number, while Lady Dorothy's adherence was to the old
Queen, who lurked in seclusion at Windsor. The Royal widow's crêpe and
streamers, and Albert's coat spread on her bed were tokens of her continuing,
paralysing grief, long after the Prince Consort's death in 1861.

It was a grief which paralysed all who attended her Court. "A very whis-
pery dinner," wrote one courtier of a depressing evening at Windsor. Victoria
would have nothing changed from how it had been in Albert's day. In consequence, she resisted introducing central heating, bathrooms, gas lighting,
electricity – devices becoming available in the last third of the century, which

Opposite: The Wyndham
Sisters, *by John Singer
Sargent, American-born
society painter. When this
bewitching portrait of
English womanhood went
on show at the Royal
Academy in 1900, it was
dubbed "The Three
Graces" by the Prince of
Wales.*

169

Albert would have loved. Late in her reign, the father of modern plumbing, George Jennings, did win contracts to introduce flushing water-closets at Buckingham Palace and at Windsor; a splendid water-closet in celestial blue and gold was installed in the Queen's railway coach on the North-Western Railway in 1869. These were necessities as complaints of old age harassed the Queen; there was no innovation for the sake of it. The Prince of Wales named Buckingham Palace "The Sepulchre", and within weeks of his accession in 1901 had the palace aglow with electricity, stocked with bathrooms and a telephone switchboard installed. His father's suite of rooms, long preserved, was redecorated, and the Palace began to assume the alert brilliance of Marlborough House, his

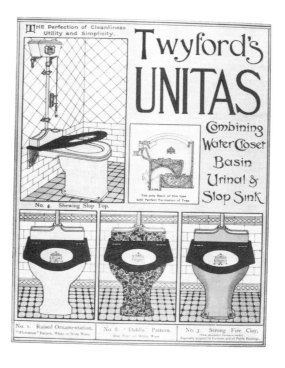

Advertisement for Twyford's famous Unitas water closet, from The Contractor's Compendium, *1890. The 1880s and 1890s saw plain wooden water closets in some country houses being replaced by dazzling examples of the ceramic sculptor's art. The Unitas achieved worldwide popularity.*

previous London home, and of Sandringham, the country house in Norfolk which he bought for the shooting and converted into an opulent mansion. Plumbing innovations were high on Edward VII's list of priorities when he took over the monarch's homes. Following a near escape from death in 1871 owing to bad drains, he had become fascinated by the subject of hygiene and sanitation. "If I had not been a prince, I would have been a plumber," he declared. His example led the less conservative of aristocrats to turn from the absorbing question of public hygiene, and address the sanitary arrangements in their own homes. The long-established wooden Pan water-closets and newer earth closets of the 1860s were replaced in the 1880s and 1890s by some marvel-

lous flights of ceramic fancy, with bowls adorned with poppies and vines, or shaped like dolphins and lions. Ladies still looked askance at such exhibits of Twyford's and Doulton's ingenuity at trade exhibitions, but they were grateful for the Ladies' Lavatory Company which installed public conveniences in the streets in the 1880s – underground but marked above ground by graceful cast-iron pergolas and temples. Delicacy was all. When the British Perforated Paper Company produced the first toilet roll in 1880, ladies requiring such items would say obliquely to the shopkeeper, "I'll take two, please." At Windsor Castle, squares of paper continued to do duty until Edward's accession.

Queen Victoria held her drawing-rooms, where débutantes were presented, in the early afternoon, and refreshment was not offered – though mothers and daughters had to queue in their carriages in the Mall before gaping onlookers for some hours. Edward instituted evening Courts. Moreover, the composition of the list of débutantes was markedly different in 1910 from 1870. Daughters of the aristocracy, of the gentry, of army officers, of selected high officials of State, were now joined by daughters of "merchants, bankers, and members of the Stock Exchange, and persons engaged in commerce on a large scale". As early as the 1870s the careful screening of ladies and their daughters by the Lord Chamberlain's Office for scandal or vulgarity had been found inadequate to accommodate changes in Society. Three American ladies, Jennie Jerome, Mrs Lilian Hammersley and Consuelo Vanderbilt, married into the ducal family of Marlborough in 1874, 1888 and 1895. As Lady Randolph Churchill and as Duchesses of the 8th and 9th Dukes of Marlborough, they

Left: Débutante, vintage 1906, photographed in Court dress with the three ostrich plumes, veil and train prescribed for presentation to the monarch. Right: The camera also recorded, more interestingly, guests at the Duchess of Devonshire's legendary fancy dress ball in 1897. The Duchess of Marlborough came as the French Ambassadress at the Court of Catherine the Great.

could not be denied their place at Court. Other "dollar heiresses" followed and were presented to the Queen, despite their evident lack of English pedigree. There were snubs, of course – Leonie, youngest of the American Jerome sisters, was on a first visit to England. Walking in Hyde Park, she was approached by Sir William Gordon-Cumming. "Over here husband hunting?" he leered. But by 1900 the *Harmsworth Magazine* lamented: "Even trade is not debarred."

Beatrice Potter, later Mrs Sidney Webb, was one daughter of a gentleman in commerce who made her début at Court in about 1876. She had gained a little experience in advance, for she had been permitted to put up her hair – sign of maturity – for a large ball the Potters held in 1874. "The dance; oh! how I did enjoy that," she wrote. "I had two or three partners for each dance." Her exuberance was swiftly followed by self-criticism. "Ah vanity! Vanity! Unfortunately for me my ruling passion." Her sister, Theresa, had less complicated feelings about the Season. She did not enjoy the public charity balls. The air at the Self-Help Ball was "horrible and the dancing so crowded". She enjoyed more a large gathering at some new acquaintances, the Dobrees. "They are immensely wealthy & seem to have a very nice position, not among swells but in our own class, substantial but not fashionable."

Daughters of "substantial but not fashionable" families often felt better able to bear the demands of the London season than shy daughters of "swells", or aristocrats. The Potter sisters widened their acquaintance, and flirted, rode in Rotten Row, and went to concerts and the theatre. Even these undemanding activities were sometimes too much for aristocratic maidens of eighteen, after years of protracted schoolroom life in the remote countryside. Caroline Lyttleton went to her first ball at Devonshire House "with the highest expectation of pleasure . . . and found herself . . . dragged into the first quadrille of 32 she had ever seen and, of course, got quizzed and pitied and does not wish to dance again." Others responded all too enthusiastically to gentlemen's attentions; Lady Adela Child-Villiers eloped to Gretna Green with a scalliwag Hussar.

The "English reserve", which visitors from abroad noted, was strong in many upper-class women of this period (not in Adela) by contrast with American girls' "independence" and middle-class English girls' new "heartiness". This reserve was in part shyness. Aristocrats' daughters did not attend the new large boarding schools, like Cheltenham Ladies' College, or Wycombe Abbey. They were educated at home by a governess, by their mother, by a clergyman upon occasion. They were kept very innocent, for want of worldliness in their preceptors. When Lady Mary Howard, daughter of the Earl of Carlisle, travelled by wagon-lit to the South of France with her governess, a male traveller was allocated a berth in their sleeping compartment. Mary and the governess arrived in tears, sure that his mere presence meant they would give birth forthwith. The corridorless trains of England were regarded with no less suspicion. In 1874 an eccentric Yorkshire baronet, Sir Tatton Sykes, and Miss Jessica Cavendish-Bentinck, granddaughter of the Duke of Portland, travelled together in a compartment from York to King's Cross – whether by design or

"The Odd Women"

by accident, was never established. Jessica's mother, meeting her daughter at the London end, assumed the worst and announced the engagement immediately. (The very next year, Colonel Valentine Baker of the 10th Hussars was cashiered, fined £500 and sentenced to a year's imprisonment for an assault on a lady in a train travelling between Liphook and London. The corridor train made its appearance as a direct result.)

Lady Mary and Miss Cavendish-Bentinck belonged to the world of "the Court representing national tradition and customs", according to the four divisions of London Society in her youth, which Beatrice Webb noted in *My Apprenticeship* (1920). "Persons who habitually entertained or who were

Portrait of Mrs Guinness and child, by Philip de Laszlo. This Hungarian painter succeeded Sargent at the beginning of the twentieth century as elegant recorder of society. He was soon to produce touching portraits of Society in wartime – great ladies proudly wearing Red Cross uniforms.

entertained by the members of any one of these key groups could claim to belong to London Society." The other "key groups" who made up Society were: "The Cabinet, and ex-Cabinet, representing political power; there was a mysterious group of millionaire financiers representing money"; and there was a racing set with its headquarters at Newmarket.

By the 1890s the Prince of Wales's set had widened to embrace, besides American ladies, professional beauties like Lillie Langtry, the Dean's daughter from Jersey whom the Prince established on the stage. Businessmen who had accrued fantastic wealth from the mass production, successful advertising and retailing of such plebeian items as soap, tea, beer and tobacco, also featured. The

173

Chapter Five

wives and daughters of these "millionaire financiers" – the Levers, Liptons, Tennants, Guinnesses, Willses – made their curtsey to the monarch. They plunged into "the brilliancy of society life, in which at-homes, dinners, balls, garden parties, operas and theatres follow each other in a continuous whirl". They were Society now, as much as any descendant of a long train of earls. Sir Charles Tennant and his forebears made a fortune in Glasgow. While his wife could not be persuaded to take an enthusiastic part in London Society, his daughters, Laura, Charty, Margot and Lucy, took London by storm. Laura married Lord Lyttleton, Charty married Lord Ribblesdale, Master of the Queen's Buckhounds, and Margot married H.H. Asquith, the Prime Minister, after due consideration of Mr Balfour's merits. The Prince of Wales was among other guests at the Scottish mansion, Glen, which Sir Charles bought and where he hung a superb collection of paintings.

George du Maurier parodied hostesses like Lady Tennant who fell dismally short of the standard of flippant wit and dashing dress required for Society, in 1880s *Punch* cartoons as Lady Midas, wife to Sir Gorgius Midas, a "succcessful sausage-maker". She was presented as innocent of any intelligence or sophistication – indeed of everything except a vulgar accent and a rampant desire to have as many of the nobility at her dinner table as possible. Nevertheless, wherever Edward was, must be the peak of Society. So if he chose to cruise

The Spider and the Flies, *first of* W. P. Frith's 1880 *series,* The Race for Wealth, *depicting the evil consequences of financial speculation. Here the wicked businessman attracts guileless widow and clergyman, among other poor saps, into investing their all in his risky venture.*

174

on Sir Thomas Lipton's yacht *Erin*, then the grocer's other, less distinguished guests were "in Society". The Tsar of Russia was bewildered by his fellow-guests at the Prince's home, Sandringham in 1894: "Most of them were horse dealers, amongst others a Baron Hirsch!"

Luxury was the keynote of the "smart set's" doings, and finance the meat of its conversation. "Everyone quotes the price of stocks and shares," lamented Sir Algernon West, and "everyone" included the ladies. Financial speculation had once been considered extremely unrespectable; money matters had not been discussed in public, certainly not in front of the ladies. Now the ladies themselves at dinner parties asked their financier friends like Sir Ernest Cassel for a recommendation of "a good thing". They were encouraged by the Prince of Wales who was fascinated by the world of commerce. "In this great business community," said Asquith, "there was no better man of business."

Many gentlewomen – ladies of the landed classes – were attracted by the luxurious life that the *nouveau-riche* financiers and businessmen offered. There was no end to their purses, or to their generosity. In 1897 Alexandra, Princess of Wales, had a charming idea to mark the Queen's Diamond Jubilee Year. 400,000 of the London poor should be invited to a monster banquet. Her call for subscriptions fell on deaf ears; Thomas Lipton thereupon paid for the whole, supplying 700 tons of food and 10,000 waiters. He was made a knight the next

The Race for Wealth III (1880), by Frith. With the silver salver to the family breakfast table comes the morning newspaper, bearing news of dreadful import. The speculation has failed, all the Reverend's capital thrown away. Ruin.

175

year. The full glory of yachts and motor cars, house parties for Royal Ascot, Henley and Cowes Week, and shooting parties in Scotland is only apparent if one considers what went before. A thousand young women had echoed Florence Nightingale's sigh of relief when ten o'clock struck, and they were free to leave the family drawing-room for bed. Married women were not immune from the depressing respectable monotony of family evenings. Consuelo, Duchess of Marlborough found dinner alone with her husband at Blenheim unbearable. The Duke, an adherent of the High Church "Oxford Movement" since undergraduate days, would sit for a quarter of an hour at a time, thinking weightily, while the food grew cold on his plate and his wife grew hot with inner irritation. Then came his formal complaint that the food was cold. In desperation, Consuelo took to bringing her knitting to dinner and the butler read detective stories in the hall.

In the years following 1870, many English families of the landed aristocracy were in financial difficulties. Bad harvests in the late 1870s contributed, with imports of cheap American grain which the Government *laissez-faire* policy permitted, to send income from agricultural land, and agricultural land values, plummeting. Tracts of land, traditionally secure and prime source of English wealth, ceased to be so. By 1910 the industrial income of England was three times its agricultural income. From 1894 there was a new horror for the landed aristocracy to face. Sir William Harcourt introduced death duties in his "Radical Budget". His claim that families would suffer the penalty only "once in a generation" was almost immediately contradicted by the toll of death in the Boer War. Sales of estates became common. Of the families who appeared in the 1863 edition of *Burke's Landed Gentry*, an astonishing 50 per cent had disappeared from the 1914 edition, as having parted from the estates which gave them the right of entry to the august volume.

It was not surprising, really, that the upper classes became poorer. They stuck their aristocratic necks in the sand, emerging every so often to sacrifice an heir to American or plutocratic greed. Then they resumed their petrified stance, and wondered why they felt so poor. Their comfort was to sneer at the new rich, and the luxurious ways which they could not themselves afford. Lady Monkswell "weekended" at Somerhill, Sir Julius Goldsmid's "gigantic" mansion in Kent. She almost fainted with the heat. We find her going again, nevertheless. The alternative, in the homes of older established families, was to put on outdoor wraps when intending to cross the unheated hall from dining-room to drawing-room. Very few landed families could afford to install efficient heating systems in their ancient and draughty castles and homes. They made a virtue out of necessity and prided themselves on their blue-blooded indifference to cold.

This was an age when technical advances were made in every section of industrial science, when sanitation and ventilation were key words in public works. In the last third of the nineteenth century, gas central heating and electric light, superior plumbing and stoves became available – yet the upper classes lagged behind the comparatively poorer middle classes in installing these

176

"The Odd Women"

conveniences, while serving enthusiastically on committees to promote public hygiene. The result was, the upper classes employed armies of servants to achieve the same effect of comfort which progressive families achieved with machines at much less cost. So who was profligate now?

In *The Rainbow Comes and Goes* (1958) Lady Diana Cooper recalled conditions at Belvoir Castle before her grandfather, the 7th Duke of Rutland, died in 1906. "Gas was despised, I forget why. Vulgar, I think," she wrote. Lighting was the province of three lamp and candle men who cleaned blackened glass chimneys, scraped wax off candelabras and cut wicks all day. "Three pairs of candles . . . wax matches, paper spills in pretty little holders, porcelain extinguishers, metal extinguishers" was a Frenchman's description of the materials put by each bed to provide light in the homes of the English rich in the 1870s.

Gas lighting was admittedly horribly smoky, it ruined pictures and curtain pelmets, it hissed. The prejudice against it among the landed classes, however, was one of class – gas lighting was for the middle classes. What of electricity? The Marquess of Salisbury was much taken by the idea of it in 1880, when it was still in a primitive stage. He was unfortunately unaware of the dangers of short-circuiting. Dinner at Hatfield House became an uncertain occasion with guests dazzled by light, or forced to abandon the table when the circuits broke and plunged the Hall in darkness. Faulty wiring caused a fire in the Grand Saloon once, and only by throwing cushions at the ceiling did some resourceful young guests prevent the destruction of exquisite plasterwork.

The Misses Vickers, *by J. S. Sargent (1856-1925). This commission to paint Florence, Mabel and Clara, daughters of a Sheffield engineer, first brought Sargent to England. Distinctly ungrateful, he complained to a friend that he was to paint "three ugly young women at Sheffield, dingy hole".*

177

The Marquess was almost alone in his enthusiasm for domestic technology among the older nobility. At Belvoir Castle there was no heated water above ground level. "Water men" carried enormous buckets on a yoke up to the bedrooms four times a day, and hip baths were taken by the fire whose steel grate a housemaid polished and the coalman replenished daily. This dearth of bathrooms was not peculiar in stately homes before the twentieth century. Bathrooms that existed were not always worth patronising. Lord Ernest Hamilton remembered zinc baths with a promise of *Hot* on a revolving handle. *Hot* came out stone *Cold*, however, rust in colour and with a cargo of beetles to cheer the bather.

Hippolyte Taine summed up the English country house in his translated *Notes on England* (1872): "Their dwellings [are] huge machines, partly Italian or partly Gothic, without distinctive character . . . spacious, comfortable, well kept – nothing more . . . Attention is given to comfort, notably to what relates to the details of sleeping and dressing." At cost of what labour was this comfort achieved! Taine had two dressing-tables in his bedroom, one "provided with a swing looking glass, the other furnished [for shaving] with one large jug, one small one, a medium one for hot water, two porcelain basins, a dish for toothbrushes, two soap-dishes, water bottle with its tumbler, a finger glass with its glass. Napkins are under all the vessels and utensils." He reflected: "it is necessary that washing should be always going on."

At Erdigg Hall in Wales, two thousand napkins were washed each week when the house was occupied. This astonishing figure makes sense when we multiply the napery in Taine's bachelor bedroom by thirty-odd, to reach the complement of the house party. The napery under those shaving vessels was changed each morning, perhaps each time water was brought to the bedroom – in the morning for shaving, before lunch and before tea and at night for ablutions, and before dinner for full splashing use of the hip bath. Besides the ablutions of the guests, there was the nursery wing and the servants, resident and visiting – all requiring further napery. And all this was needed because there was no water above ground level and no bathrooms.

It comes as no surprise to learn that in the 1881 Census of England and Wales, of females above five years of age, one in nine was an indoor servant. The English gentlewoman was employer of an army. However, to her housekeeper she consigned all responsibility for running the house. Mrs Yorke consigned Erdigg to Harriet Rogers – after long years of service as nursery maid, head nurse, personal maid and cook to the family. The author of *A Profession for Gentlewomen* (1916) lamented this abrogation of responsibility, and "the general laxity of the young housekeeper of fifteen to twenty years ago, emancipated young women who demanded freedom from the bondage of children and housekeeping. The result has been that no household stores may now be kept under lock and key, the mistress of the house . . . has given up the storeroom and taken refuge in weekly orders."

The lady of the house did not touch a duster or broom herself. Gwen

178

Raverat recalled the domestic arrangements at Down, the Darwins' home, in the 1880s and 1890s: "There was no bathroom at Down, nor any hot water, except in the kitchen, but there were plenty of housemaids to run about with the big brown-painted bath-cans. Just as there were plenty of hands to lay and light the fires, scrub the floors, black the grates, polish the silver and the brass, dust the mantlepieces, wash the clothes and mend them, clean the windows, range the china on its shelves, wax the woodwork, carry the dishes filled or empty . . ." The ladies of the house were leisured as never before. Mary Curzon, on a visit from India to England in 1910, commented: "Everyone is doing the same old thing – just flirting and dining and dawdling."

Florence Lady Nunbumhalm's pheasant shoot at Warter Priory, December 1912. Grandees and plutocrats indulge an appetite for grandes battues and gargantuan meals. Edward VII was chieftain of the consumer race, and regularly ate the "cold bird" placed at his bedside.

Families deriving their income from trade rather than land prospered and could afford to buy and support country mansions and vast sporting estates in Scotland. In 1909 a junior minister in Asquith's first Government wrote in *The Condition of England*: "We have called into existence a whole new industry in motor cars and quick travelling . . . We have converted half the Highlands to deer forests for our sport, and the amount annually spent on shooting, racing, golf . . . exceeds the total revenue of many a European principality." "Ugly white hotels . . . uninspired dramatic entertainments . . . elaborate banquets . . ." all consumed fortunes. "Yet we cannot build a cathedral." At the end of her reign, Queen Victoria expressed similar dissatisfaction with the materialist tendency of her heir's circle. She asked that he and the Princess of Wales should "deny themselves amusements", so as to preserve "that tone which used to be the Pride of England". The Queen had heard from many that "at no time for the last sixty or seventy years was frivolity, the love of pleasure, self-indulgence,

and idleness (producing ignorance) carried to such excess as now in the Higher Classes . . . those who do not live in the gay circle of fashion, and who view it calmly, are greatly, seriously ALARMED!" The Prince went on as he had always done, and so did "the gay circle of fashion".

The "smart set's" house parties for Royal Ascot were gay, when all the talk at home was of retrenchment. American girls marrying into the aristocracy found the old-fashioned values of their new English families especially trying. The lovely Mary Curzon had led "a sort of official, almost civic existence" as a beauty and an heiress in America. On marriage to ambitious George Curzon, son of Lord Scarsdale, she found: "G's work deflects every form of amuse-

Royal Ascot in 1909. Edward VII and lovely, deaf Queen Alexandra, as Prince and Princess of Wales revived the royal carriage procession down the sacred Turf, and became regular attendants. The June race meeting became the most "exclusive" event of the season.

ment." "I am not going to Ascot this year," she wrote longingly in 1896. To add to her mortification, Consuelo Vanderbilt was newly Duchess of Marlborough and the hit of the season, and would undoubtedly shine at the event.

The Prince of Wales' enthusiasm for the excellent racing at this summer race meeting, his re-introduction of the royal carriage procession down the sacred Turf, his presence, had made these four June days at Ascot the most important event in fashionable ladies' social calendar and certainly the most exclusive. Husbands drank and gambled; the Royal Enclosure was their wives' showcase, where they outdid each other with enormous hats and leg-of-mutton sleeves. As with the Drawing-rooms, the Lord Chamberlain had the power to

withhold vouchers for the Enclosure. Edward arranged that *all* his ladies had vouchers.

A few ladies in the 1880s had horses in training themselves and were firmly in the masterful, horse-faced tradition of English gentlewomen. Caroline, Duchess of Montrose, inherited a stud at Newmarket from her second husband in 1883 and took a keen interest in it, though she had to bow to the convention that ladies might not own horses; her horses raced under the colours of "Mr Manton". The world of racing seems to have stimulated sexual activity. Some ladies formed liaisons with the jockeys who raced in their husband's colours. Fred Archer was the leading jockey from 1874 to 1886. His name was coupled with, among others, that of Daisy Warwick and the Duchess of Montrose, whose husbands paid him a retainer to ride their horses. As the Turf was the theatre of much upper-class social life, so the jockeys, the chief actors in the drama, acquired great glamour. Their humble pedigrees and stable language titillated rather than repelled their employers' fine ladies, as Lady Hastings frankly admitted, when describing Archer's fabled powers of attraction. Other ladies preferred to enjoy liaisons with gentlemen of their own class. When the King himself took his mistress, Mrs Keppel, to racing house parties in the 1890s, his subjects were not slow to mistake ladies' bedrooms in the watches of the night for their own. Plates of sandwiches placed outside the lady's room indicated her availability, under the rules of "corridor creeping" at Lady Warwick's home. When the stable clock struck six, the gentlemen had to return to their own rooms.

The racing world had the lure of sophistication under the Prince and Princess of Wales' patronage. The sums bet on races were recounted with vicarious excitement – the Prince of Wales bet £600 on one race. Everything about the Turf was calculated to offend the ladies and gentlemen true to the values of Victorian England: the ostentation – and expense – of the costumes required; the gambling, and the unrestrained conduct of winning and losing "punters"; the contiguity of the lower orders in the Silver Ring next door to the Members' Enclosure. "Fast" behaviour seemed indivisible from the "smart" life, in the eyes of non-racegoers. Lady Dorothy Nevill sniffed: "The adjective 'smart' . . . was not in former days, I think, much heard outside the servants' hall." To great ladies "of other days", it would "convey the idea of some kitchen maid dressed up in her Sunday best". In short, there were two very different branches of Society in the thirty-odd years before the First World War. Edwardians began long before the King's accession; Victorians continued undaunted by the death of their Queen long into the new century. The one group was distinguished by the cultivation of awesome wealth; the other, of respectability and ancient blood.

Hunting, unlike racing, was approved increasingly by the conservative aristocracy as a sport suitable for ladies. In 1876 it received a royal warrant of approval, when Elizabeth, Empress of Austria, rented magnificent Easton Neston in Northamptonshire as a hunting box. She went out with the Pytchley

181

Hunt, under the aegis of Captain George Myddelton, nicknamed "Bay". Bay was a typical gentleman rider of the age. Without money or title or property, he was welcome everywhere. At first reluctant to "pilot" the Empress, he became enamoured, like so many, of her charms. His fiancée, daughter of the Master, languished, while he accompanied the equestrian Empress. She did not mind falls, she announced, but she would not have her face scratched. Lady Grey de Wilton was enthused by her father-in-law to become a keen hunting woman. When, periodically, she suffered an attack of eczema during the season, she wore two veils, one grey and one white, bound round her head.

Lady Geraldine Somerset, lady-in-waiting to the Duchess of Cambridge from 1858 to 1889, always wore "white embroidery-trimmed petticoats under . . . full and sweeping habit skirts" with button boots and trousers. Mrs Powlett Somerset, daughter of the legendary MFH Jack Mytton, was one of "the hardest women to hounds in her day". "A large brown straw hat with drooping ostrich feather and flowing veil" was her customary headgear, as she flew across the Beaufort country. When gentlewomen ventured into the traditional spheres of their menfolk, at the cost of safety and comfort, they emphasised their femininity in order to lessen the insult.

When she mounted in the stableyard, the groom who held her horse's bridle was told to avert his eyes as a gentleman threw her into the saddle. When the lady fell in the field, her gentleman escort might not be at her side to oblige again, and some strange cavalier might enjoy the shocking sight of her ankles and petticoats. Still less modestly, the habit skirts frequently left ladies hanging upside down from their pommels. In the 1860s and 1870s they took to wearing detachable skirts and breeches. They still felt rather daring to be out in the hunting field at all; by the 1880s they felt confident enough to stride about in boots and wear breeches and divided skirts to ride astride.

The bravery of setting horses over high fences in a crowded field should not be minimised. The side-saddle's discomfort was graphically described in the 1920s, when ladies had won their battle to ride astride, by Monica Sheriffe: "Goodness it was hell! Riding a mile down a road nearly broke one's back." A few women showed outstanding courage, and rode (sidesaddle, necessarily) in point-to-points. Constance Gore-Booth, later the Countess Markievicz of Yeatsian fame, spent a pleasant Irish childhood, riding her pony, Storeen, up the forty steep embankment steps which led to the stables. In the 1880s, with her hunter, Max, she was one of the foremost riders with the Sligo Hunt – "she was not only fearless, but attracted by danger." Even after she had begun studies in London at the Slade School of Art, she would happily go out with the Sligo whenever she returned home. In 1895 she became the first woman in Ireland to ride in a point-to-point, and she became a vigorous collector of cups, a "pot-hunter".

Not all ladies hunted, of course, and the non-combatants – from the cold repose of their drawing-rooms – regarded ladies who took to the field with the deepest suspicion. Lady Sibell Wyndham took "the most melancholy view" of

Countess Spencer on Goldfinch and John, 5th Earl Spencer, on Misrule with the Pytchley Hunt, by John Charlton (c. 1849). The Countess's inclusion in the group may be a conceit to show off Goldfinch's points.

her husband, Percy's, hunting forays to Leicestershire. "To her", chuckled her father-in-law, "Melton is the haunt of men-eating Delilahs." Not all gentlemen condoned the sport of fox-hunting for womenfolk either. As late as the 1880s, spirited Daisy, Lady Brooke, had to creep from the breakfast table to set off for her day's hunting. Her father-in-law deeply disapproved. So there were some wives and daughters who must wait while the gentlemen of the house-party disappeared, and occupy themselves with worsted work till the Nimrods returned.

Fortunately, from the late 1870s on, with the continued enthusiasm for outdoor activities and fresh air, a sport as exhilarating as hunting but more domesticated was sanctioned for ladies of the upper classes. Lawn tennis was developed by Major Walter Wingfield in the mid-1870s. The game became instantly wildly popular, and was played by ladies from the beginning – in private. The flagging All England Croquet Club at Wimbledon added tennis courts in 1874 to help its finances. In 1877 the first All England Lawn Tennis Club championship was instituted with men's singles. By 1884 ladies' singles were included, and from 1913 mixed, as well as ladies' doubles were introduced.

Mixed doubles had been played in private from the beginning; the prospect of a charming partner of the opposite sex at the lawn tennis parties which punctuated the summer from 1880 on, prompted many ladies to practise their "game" with assiduity. The advice on costume given by the editors of the Victoria Library *Gentlewoman's Book of Sports*, in 1892, recognised the importance of the tennis court as a mating ground. "White shoes should be avoided, as they make the feet look large." "The cleanest and prettiest of white underskirts" should be worn under a dark blue serge skirt and flannel shirt. Though gentlemen were in honour bound never to serve with strength at lady

Chapter Five

The Tennis Party *(1900), by C. M. Gere (1869-1957). Lawn tennis, first known as "sphairistike", was developed in the 1870s. It swiftly became a favourite sport of ladies and gentlemen, tired of the gentler charms of croquet. The matchmaking opportunities were immense.*

opponents, and always to try and return balls at any distance from their lady partners, still, upon occasion a lady might run – and fall . . . Decorum at all times. The *Book of Sports* recommended a sailor hat clamped to the head throughout play. For the ritual of afternoon tea on the lawn which was so much part of the tennis party, this could be exchanged for larger decorated headgear, which would show to advantage in the regulatory photograph. American-born Lady Jebb, wife of the Master of Peterhouse College in Cambridge, enthused about the social advantages of the tennis party: it was "a cheap way of seeing one's friends . . . much pleasanter than set dinner parties. I have a cake, a plate of thin bread and butter, and tea all set out on a table in Peterhouse Garden, and Kate in her pretty cap and apron to wait upon everybody."

Maurice Baring recalls in *The Nineties*, that "suddenly in the summer of 1894, I think, it began to be the thing and people bicycled just for the fun of bicycling anywhere, even indoors if they could not bicycle out of doors, and there were bicycling breakfast parties in Battersea Park; and people went to France to bicycle, and discussed the makes of their bicycles . . ." Before this date, nobody "among the leisured" dared ride the bicycle, "not from physical fear, but because it was not the thing." Ladies, in particular, met with strong

opposition in the 1880s if they ventured out on a tricycle, or on the safety bicycle with india rubber wheels. The question of modesty, with the astride pose, was at the root of men's distaste for lady bicyclists. Max Beerbohm thought the lady bicyclist, unlike other sporting women, always looked ungraceful, whether wearing skirts or, worse, breeches. In 1882 the Cyclists' Touring Club decreed that ladies when "out" should wear a sober grey serge costume similar to that worn by the wives of doctors and parsons.

Lilia, in *Where Angels Fear to Tread* (1905) learnt to bicycle "for the purpose of waking the place up". She caused satisfactory outrage when she "coasted down the High Street on Sunday evening, falling off at the turn by the church ... if she had not been a relation, it could have been entertaining." Lucia, queen of E. F. Benson's novels about Rye, hired a bicycle to practise on lonely roads before she appeared in public, determined to avoid such disaster. Lawn tennis was conceived of as an outdoor parlour game played in the privacy of the lady's home, of extreme convenience for chaperones; it was almost impossible to chaperone a lady on a bicycle and, inevitably, she was tempted to penetrate beyond the park gates. Of course, the daring possibilities of the bicycle were exactly what attracted ladies to it.

Dress was something of an obsession with gentlewomen essaying new sports. One gentlewoman competed in sailing races in a seaman's oilskin jacket, sou'wester, and waterproof skirt. "After a rough race, of course, I go on board my steam launch or my husband's steamer and change costumes" – for afternoon tea. One lady in the *Gentlewomen's Book of Sports* tells a sad and timeless tale of a mischievous bathing costume which she purchased and wore at Trouville, the popular French resort. Clad in her most ravishing "get-up" of pure white serge, handsomely braided, with "a large white washing silk sash, and . . . white silk stockings and sandals", the lady was rowed out to sea. She took a header and swam strongly back to shore. She was the cynosure of "a hundred pairs of eyes" as she emerged. The costume had been intended for *"les belles Parisiennes"* who swam not, neither did they dive, but only tripped along the seashore. It was completely transparent when wet. Mrs Sanuda purchased next day a plain black serge bathing dress.

Skating was popular from the 1870s on, and could be an exotic entertainment. The curate, Francis Kilvert, had "the honour" of being knocked over by Lord Royston, who was skating on a Wiltshire pond with "a distinguished company", including his wife, Lady Dangan, and Harriet Awdry "who skated beautifully and jumped over a half-sunken punt". A quadrille band played as Chinese lanterns were lit round the pond's edge, and the skaters carried flaring torches on their peregrinations round the ice. Fur muffs and frogging made Russians of the ladies, as they traced delicate figures on the ice. (There was a machine like an iron cage at Queen's Club in London with whose support they could take those awkward first totters. Grace in public was essential.)

Many ladies took to arduous and masculine sport at home and abroad. In Lady Violet Greville's *Ladies in the Field, or Sketches of Sport* (1894) Mrs C. Martelli contributed a chapter entitled, "Tigers I have Shot", Diana Chasseresse wrote on "Deer-stalking and Deer-driving", and Miss Leale on "Rifle-shooting". Mrs Jenkins bears off the prize with her account of "A Kangaroo Hunt".

Sports could not fill up all a lady's day. Gardening was an activity in which more and more gentlewomen took an active part. They created hundreds of herbaceous borders, a gardening feature promoted as early as the 1830s by J. C. Loudon, and containing perennial plants graded in colour and height to make an informal whole. The herbaceous border taxed neither the amateur lady's knowledge of plants, nor, owing to its perennial nature, her back. "Be not persuaded into buying little toy sets of 'ladies tools'," advised the authoress of the *Gentlewomen's Book of Gardening*. Still, a trowel and a small border fork would probably be most useful. Not till Miss Jekyll, at Munstead Wood in Surrey, "reformed" the border and made it subtle with gradation of tone and of species in the 1900s, did the gentlewoman feel compelled to exert much intelligence about her planting scheme, as long as it was "a riot of colour". *The Wild Garden*, the popular 1883 treatise by William Robinson, encouraged ladies to enjoy colour above form. The colour and form of her gardening dress was as important a consideration. Beige reseda was the material recommended for

summer gardening, nothing could beat serge for winter. A coloured apron would enliven the former, the latter would benefit by a crimson flannel blouse. For serious gardeners, a pair of detachable sleeves and gloves were sensibly suggested.

For every lady who worked in the garden herself or knowledgeably directed a team of gardeners, there were many who: "do not care for working in the garden, yet like to cut flowers themselves for the filling of their bowls and vases." The mistress of "an artistic drawing-room must have plants, ferns, lilies in pots, etc. to carry out the desired effect." Ladies were often drawn or painted holding a watering can in the conservatories where these plants were nurtured. Sometimes, admitted the *Gentlewomen's Book of Gardening*, this liking for interior floral decoration was carried to absurd lengths. At one grand ball, there were so many arrangements of plants on the tables that there was no room to lay down a fan; the head of the stairs was made impassable by banks of flowers – and, when a lady put out a hand to the banister to steady herself on the staircase, she discovered the rail had been replaced by a rope of flowers!

A very important feature of ladies' lives in the late Victorian and Edwardian period was philanthropy. The needlework they did now was not to beautify their homes, but to clothe the poor. Lady Wolverton began the Needlework Guild in the early 1880s. Her friend, Princess Mary Adelaide, the Duchess of Teck, promoted the cause enthusiastically, from the mid 1880s, and organised the London and Surrey branches herself with her daughter, Princess May, later Queen Mary. White Lodge, the Tecks' home (in Richmond Park) in the 1880s, was turned into "a drapers' shop, or a kind of Harvey and Nicholl's storeroom" wrote the Duchess, when the ladies of the branches sent in annually the articles they had made. "May knelt so long just at first over the huge parcels and bundles, that she very nearly gave herself a *housemaid's knee*!" When ladies were not doing "Guild work", as the activity became known, they established schools of needlework in their local villages where the poor might learn techniques of lacemaking, for instance. Daisy, Lady Warwick developed a social conscience in the 1890s, after her years as the Prince of Wales' paramour. She founded a needlework school at Easton for local girls in 1890, then opened a shop in Bond Street, no less – "Lady Brooke's Depot for the Easton School of Needlework" – to sell the beautiful embroidery produced.

Ladies were eager to mother the poor and needy, in village welfare schemes, dispensing food parcels at asylums, subscribing to church charities for "our black brothers" in Africa. They were less anxious to mother their own children, as they found satisfaction in the wider world. Ladies' sharp and general reluctance during these years to play a maternal role at the cost of their own interests manifests itself in the renewed swing against breast feeding, the emergence of the baby bottles, the segregation where possible of the nursery quarters and the rise of the British nanny as a substitute mother for children ignored by their true mother. (The Sitwell children, for instance, adored their nurse, Mrs Davies, who bought them paper bags of shrimps for tea at the sea-

side. Winston Churchill, son of Jennie, hated leaving Everest his nurse, not his mother, when he went to school.) To this period belong all those hurt, childish memories of mother as a sensory collection of swishing skirts, bending bosoms, wafts of tuberose or hothouse scents, and goodnight kisses. Children of the 1890s had a hard time of it if their appointed nurse was not well disposed towards them. Eleanor Farjeon, in *A Nursery in the Nineties*, recalled that her nurse trained her to tell her mother she loved her nurse, by threats of beating with a hairbrush. Nina Hamnett accepted severe beating round the legs from her father as a normal part of a Nineties' childhood. Children sent home from the Colonies and Dominions were worst off. Rudyard Kipling never forgot his

Nanny and charges, perambulator and pets, watching riders go down Rotten Row in Hyde Park, in the Spring of 1911. The umbrella-holder hooked to the pram, and the children's buttoned leggings (generally much hated by wearers) are charming "period" touches.

years with Aunt Rosa in a sandy seaside suburb. In *The Light That Failed*, a small girl enquires of a small boy what punishment he thinks a certain crime would elicit from the guardian with whom they live. "Beat me, lock you up in your bedroom," comes the reply. H. H. Munro, who wrote as "Saki" in the 1900s, was left with two aunts at Barnstaple while his father served in Burma. Saki's *Sredni Vashtar* (1911) tells of a small boy's hideous vengeance on his guardian cousin for continuous cruelty. Mrs De Ropp "would never in her honestest moment, have confessed to herself that she disliked Conradin, though she might have been dimly aware that chastising him for his good was a duty which she did not find particularly irksome."

To counteract any possible guilt mothers of the upper classes felt about leaving their children to the care of others, they could purchase marvellous nursery wallpapers, nursery furniture, and nursery tableware. From the 1880s on, this was a growth industry, as was the publishing of children's picture books. Kate Greenaway and Randolph Caldecott images were imprinted on friezes and

dados and cereal bowls and curtains. In the late 1870s, in the night nursery of Lord Revelstoke's children on the third floor of his Charles Street house, hung coloured pictures of St Petersburg. In the nursery next door, there were Landseer pictures in gilt frames. A big white press or cupboard painted white and a table was all the furniture in the Lytteltons' 1860s nursery. By 1881, the author of *Decoration and Furniture of Town Houses* suggested papering the walls of the nursery with illustrations cut from "the Christmas books ... which ... Miss Kate Greenaway and Mr Walter Crane have so ... enthusiastically illustrated." By the 1890s, nursery pictures, like "The Cat's Half Holiday", were being specifically commissioned. How nice it all looked, when the mother

On a Country Walk, or, Primroses *(1894), by Kate Greenaway. In the pantheon of artists whose book illustrations, friezes, pictures – and even china – decked nurseries in the 1890s Miss Greenaway joined Randolph Caldecott and Walter Crane.*

looked in for tea, and found her children sweetly subdued, having used up all their tears and laughter earlier in the day in battles royal and games with Nurse. Happily, mother reads children a story from one of Andrew Lang's innovatory books about fairies, or shows to the babies a bright picture book – and goes away without any more idea of her children than that they seem better or worse behaved tonight than last night.

The rage these devoted mothers felt when noble lords selected an American or, indeed, a British-born "nobody" instead of their daughters to grace their households may be imagined. The daughters generally bore the brunt of this rage, for failing to attract the desired noble sprig, and had to endure hideous prophecies of the life as an "old maid" which would now surely be theirs. There was warning enough, if young ladies looked around them, of the horrors of spinsterhood. The daughters of the upper classes were expected, if they did not marry, to continue to live with their families. Their status prevented them taking up work of any kind. When Lord Stanley of Alderley died,

his widow moved reluctantly to the dower house, Holmwood, accompanied by her two unmarried daughters. She made their lives quite miserable because she was bored by the small establishment. "The aunts . . . were both so scolded today," wrote a granddaughter of the Dowager, "that Aunt Louisa went into hysterics, and Aunt Rainette had palpitations."

Constance Maynard was another of many daughters who lived on with their mothers when no suitor offered. She described herself and her sisters, also unmarried, as "like eagles in a henhouse". Such women remained "*jeunes filles*", or assistants to their mothers, till death severed the bond. Mrs Maynard, from the sick bed at which she held her daughters in thrall, was expert at "pat, pat, patting down" all their aspirations to a wider life. Mary Kingsley was another daughter held in thrall to her mother's sick bed, and Florence Nightingale abandoned her work in hospital administration and nursing reform to tend her mother. Around the second Mrs Compton-Burnett's room revolved eight anxious daughters. On the demise of these powerful invalids, their daughters acquired an astonishing new lease of life. Constance Maynard attended Girton at Cambridge, and went on to found Westfield College in 1882. Mary Kingsley left Cambridge for the rapids and mountains of West Africa, about which she had read in her father's anthropological library; Florence Nightingale had a burst of energy, and became an expert and unofficial consultant to the Colonial Department on Indian sanitation; Ivy Compton-Burnett and her sisters moved from stifling Hove to London where they "set up" in separate dwellings.

Some other gentlewomen of the upper and middle classes in this period who did not marry resigned themselves to an ancillary role in the family. When their mother died, there might be younger brothers and sisters to care for, as there were for Ethel May in Charlotte M. Yonge's *The Daisy Chain*. "The unmarried woman must not seek undivided return of affection . . . but must be ready to cease . . . to be the first with any . . . Someone there must be to be loved and helped, and the poor for certain." *The Daisy Chain* was written in 1856, but the resigned view it expressed of spinsterhood as an inferior state persisted.

In the closing decades of the nineteenth century the pioneering work of gentlewomen in the fields of education, social welfare and nursing – areas where married ladies were disbarred – saw the emergence of a more cheerful view of spinsterhood. "There must needs be a purpose for the lives of single women in the sexual order of Providence," wrote Frances Power Cobbe. "The 'old maid' thinks to die, if without having given or shared some of the highest joys of human nature, yet at least without having caused one fellow-being to regret she was born to tempt to sin and shame." (This was a dig at the self-indulgent, sexually lax bachelors of the day.) Cobbe's view of spinsterhood is much less bleak than that of Dinah Mulock Craig, who wrote in 1858 that a spinster's death came as the end of a "finished life. At its end it may be somewhat lonely . . . still, such a life is not to be pitied for it is a completed life." By 1911 Rebecca West was preaching that spinsterhood was all in the mind. All who confined

A group of lady authors gathered beneath the banner Writers, in the Women's Coronation Procession, on 17 June, 1911. Over forty thousand women marched in support of the NUWSS (National Union of Women's Suffrage Societies) and WSPU (Women's Social and Political Union) demands for votes for women.

themselves to intercourse with their own sex and had a distorted, exaggerated respect for the opposite sex were spinsters. Walter Pater was a spinster, asserted Miss West. Single women who, like Portia in *The Merchant of Venice*, who met men on equal terms in the workplace, need feel no stigma of spinsterhood.

The "reformed" boarding schools were strong in support of the idea that single women were not redundant. Many gentlewomen made their entire lives within the new schools, as a result. Teaching remained the largest employer of educated women till after the First World War. However, the teacher emerging in the 1870s and decades which followed, was a very different creature from the genteel widows and spinsters, who had reigned so long - and so woefully – over female education in their cramped town houses.

The fashion was now for large boarding schools, with two hundred or more pupils resident, or for equally large day schools. The pioneers, Miss Buss at the North London Collegiate and Miss Beale at Cheltenham Ladies' College had many imitators. In 1877 (Dame) Louisa Lumsden founded St Leonards. She commented in her memoirs: "Dress may seem a trifling thing, but even from childish days it had worried me. I wanted to be free to run, jump and climb trees." Dame Louisa, while headmistress of St Leonard's from 1877 to 1882, introduced the straw "boater" or sailor hat as part of schoolgirl uniform, initiating as well a "games uniform" for girls, consisting of a short tunic worn over knickerbockers.

The Lawrence sisters established Roedean in 1885; Jane Frances Dove founded Wycombe Abbey in 1896. The first generation of headmistresses copied the buildings and curriculum of boys' public schools, and the ethos of team spirit. They intended to prepare their pupils for a life of public service. Miss Beale had a liking for the Gothic, and Cheltenham Ladies' College boasted a collection of towers and spires. Miss Buss made her school formidable with polished wood. The only note of colour was an illuminated text, headed: "Lost, one golden hour." The physical appearance of the new "reformed" schools was felt to be very important by the first headmistresses; they were no amateurs eking a living by taking in boarders. Even small schools like Sarah Compton-

Form 1B, Cheltenham Ladies' College, with Miss Counsell, 1913. The Gothic decoration of Miss Beale's school illustrates the unbridled rein headmistresses of the "reformed" schools gave to their imaginations when building and administering their large establishments.

Burnett's Howard College in Bedford boasted school buildings specially built in 1878. Physical education and the sports field were an important part of the new education offered. Again, even small schools like Addiscombe College in Hove, established in the 1890s, felt compelled to purchase a ground some minutes' walk from the school. Hockey was played in winter, tennis and cricket in summer. (The Misses Cadwallader of Addiscombe College derived some pride from the fact that they had an annual cricket match with Roedean, a school with social prestige from its beginning.)

The centre of each school was its hall, or great hall. Here each morning the headmistress surveyed her pupils from a dais. Here she fired them with

enthusiasm for the school spirit; daily she renewed her spell over them, she dispensed praise and blame, and, annually, she prevailed on a distinguished visitor to present prizes. When the Duchess of Teck came to the North London Collegiate in 1883 in this capacity, the prize-winners were made to practise their curtsey for a fortnight in advance. Molly Thomas, a pupil of the day, wrote, "To Miss Buss, the great assembly hall represented all her glorious aspirations, and she had thought out every possible means of investing it with dignity . . . Everything of importance had been 'presented' – the throne on the high platform, the great organ, the gallery with a medallion of the Princess of Wales who opened it." The headmistresses were well aware of the cachet a visit from royalty lent the school - and of the bad repute pupils' misbehaviour would bring. It is remarkable how well they succeeded in building up in a few years traditions and family loyalties which had been established at boys' schools only over centuries. "Something has been built up for them and given in trust by their predecessors – and they may add to or lessen the good tone which they find there by words or acts," wrote the Principal of Somerville, the women's college at Oxford, seven years after its establishment in 1881. The headmistresses of the new schools felt as strongly about the schools they had created.

The architects of the women's colleges at university and of girls' schools in the last third of the nineteenth century recognised their dependence on each other. The first university colleges for women, Queen's College and Bedford College in London, had grown out of teacher training colleges. Miss Beale at

Chemistry laboratory at Bedford College, 1890s. Bedford College was founded by "the ladies of Langham Place", a group of philanthropists, then absorbed to become the first women's college of London University. The sciences, hitherto a masculine preserve, were taught enthusiastically.

Cheltenham Ladies' College began a teacher training college annexe at her school in the 1870s, to ensure an adequate supply of trained teachers for the school. Apart from her school and a few others, there were few founts of educated women to teach in the new schools before the women's colleges established themselves at London and Oxford and Cambridge. By the 1890s it was virtually impossible to obtain a good teaching position unless the applicant had attended a university college. Correlatively there were very few posts outside teaching which a female university graduate could obtain. In 1903 almost 70 per cent of female graduates became teachers. The philanthropist Sir Thomas Holloway founded Royal Holloway College at Egham in 1886 for the higher

Cocoa party at Royal Holloway College, Egham. These regular events had all the conspiratorial cosiness of children's midnight feasts. They provided young ladies bewildered by the size and scholastic demands of the College with a much needed "family" of friends.

education of women. The gigantic red-brick institution, designed to resemble a French château, could house 250 students. The students formed cosy "College Families" within the vast, heated building, and expressed their independent spirit with cocoa parties. Photographs of cocoa parties here in the 1880s, and at Addiscombe College in the 1890s, show how very similar school and university life was at this date. Sir Thomas specifically enjoined that his college should not serve as a teacher training college; nevertheless, out of 137 students in 1902, most joined the teaching profession.

There were very few other careers available to women, however highly educated. But the 1890s saw a decline in the status of the professional school-

"The Odd Women"

teacher, and in her career opportunities. Earlier women who were good teachers had become headmistresses quite young, owing to the paucity of qualified competitors. There were few headships available in the 1890s, as these young headmistresses grew old but stuck doggedly to their posts. Moreover, in the 1880s, even in the 1890s, parents and pupils were in awe of teachers who had been to university, and respected them for it. A university education became less rare in the 1900s, and less respected. The early pioneering spirit, the sacred bond as between Mother Superior and novice, faded. Pupils felt contemptuous of their teachers' dedication to the "school spirit", their ignorance of the wider world, even of the celibacy which was every teacher's lot. For where within the restricting school walls would they find a husband? Mothers jibbed at head-mistresses' autocratic ways in the 1900s, where before the turn of the century they had been content to hand over all responsibility for their daughters to formidable headmistresses. One misguided Mayor wrote to Miss Dove, asking that his daughter might return to school a day late, so that she could attend a civic function. "Now or never," wired back the obdurate headmistress. When a pupil at the North London Collegiate handed Miss Buss a note from her mother, enclosed in an envelope, Miss Buss's uncertain temper flared. Was she supposed to have nothing better to do with her time, than open envelopes? What would become of her morning if every note came so packaged? How many minutes a week, a year . . .? The 1900s saw mothers fighting to win back their daughters from the strange world of the girls' boarding school, which corresponded to nothing very much in the real world, with its exaggerated notions of honour and loyalty and team spirit. Still, they continued to send their daughters off – to win games girdles, and study mathematics, take the competitive Senior Oxford and Cambridge Local Board examinations, and have "raves" or passions for older girls or for a sympathetic mistress. Boarding school, as the English gentle-women's natural adolescent home, was established.

A strong Christian ethic continued to underlie all work that gentlewomen undertook. Miss Louisa Hubbard is interesting in that, like Florence Night-ingale before her, she turned her back on a life of ladylike indolence which was prescribed for one of her social position. She was brought up in St Petersburg, daughter of a wealthy British trader. On her return to England in the 1860s, she became interested in the Primitive Order of Deaconesses who trained as nurses and teachers to assist the Church of England clergy in slum parishes. Miss Hub-bard bade her Society friends open their purses at several "assistance meetings", for the deaconesses' cause; following the 1870 Education Act, she prevailed on rich friends to help her found Otter College at Chichester, a training college for "lady" schoolteachers. So enormous was the flood of applications from single women, Miss Hubbard founded in 1875 an annual Handbook for Women's Work, giving details of careers and training establishments. She also founded in this year the journal *Woman's Gazette*, later *Work and Leisure*.

Florence Nightingale collaborated on a series of articles in the first year, "Nursing as a Profession for Educated Women". Following the enthusiasm of

the post-Crimean period, hospital nursing had fallen into the doldrums as a vocation for ladies. Although Miss Nightingale had founded the Nightingale School of Nursing under Sarah Wardroper, the admirable Matron at St Thomas's Hospital in 1860, educated women still hung back. The few ladies who did enter the profession, as a result, became matrons and superintendents very young, commanded large salaries, and behaved in the most autocratic way to the nurses under them. Miss Nightingale pleaded for more educated recruits, but not till the Boer War did patriotism inspire large numbers of romantically minded gentlewomen to take to a nursing career. Lady Sykes – she whose married life had begun with the railway compartment fracas - was one of several ladies who went out in 1899 to serve for a few months as a voluntary worker. The army hospital authorities did not like the ladies' interference, but the men were grateful for the "condensed milk, tobacco, chocolate and jelly" with which the ladies supplemented the Government provisions. Mary Kingsley went with characteristic enthusiasm: "All this work here, the stench, the washing, the enemas, the bed pans, the blood is my world." She died, sadly, from the typhus which raged among the insanitary conditions in the Cape hospital which she described. Queen Alexandra personally sent out twelve nurses, and other ladies joined Queen Alexandra's Imperial Nursing Service, which she founded in 1902. Gentlewomen trained in the hospitals as "lady probationers", ate at separate tables from "regular pros", and were prescribed an extra few inches of hem to their uniform, so that patients would not see their ankles when they knelt at the bedside.

Zepherina Veitch, later Mrs Smith, was one of the early batch of gentlewomen nurses. Daughter of a clergyman, she trained at University College Hospital, by 1869 was Superintendent of Nurses at St George's Hospital, in 1870 nursed at Sedan in the Franco-Prussian War, and became Sister-in-charge at Charing Cross Hospital on her return. Concern with the conditions of childbirth care led her to qualify as a midwife at the British Lying-in Hospital in 1873. She was only the tenth person to obtain the London Obstetrical Society's diploma. Out into the slums of Seven Dials she went, and on her first visit to a mother and infant found that "there was nothing . . . larger than an Australian meat tin in which the baby could have its first wash . . . Miss Veitch, who had lived in Palestine . . . speedily solved the difficulty by making a bath in her own lap out of the big waterproof apron she wore." Despite all her experience, when Miss Veitch married the surgeon, Professor Henry Smith, in 1876, she was obliged to give up her career.

Midwives of the nineteenth century well deserved their reputation for drunkenness and lewdness, and their caricature in Sarah Gamp. The struggle to establish a trained body of professional midwives lasted from 1876 till 1903, when the Central Midwives' Board was established. Miss Veitch began the assault on apathy. In 1876, the year of her retirement from the profession, she wrote an article urging improved standards of midwifery in *Work and Leisure*. Out of Miss Veitch's forceful article came, with Miss Hubbard's

encouragement, in 1881, a Matron's Aid Society, or Trained Midwives' Registration Society. At first, meetings were held at Miss Hubbard's house, or at Zepherina Smith's house. The Society achieved little for some years, till the advent of Miss Rosalind Paget in 1886. The word "midwife" was calculated to raise a blush in Miss Hubbard's circle; the whole subject of midwifery was thought indelicate, and there were forceful objections to the choice of midwifery as a career for a gentlewoman. Babies might come at any time of day; she might have to go out *unchaperoned* at dead of night. Miss Hubbard could only do so much, as a result of these constrictions. She could not train as a midwife herself; she found it difficult to attract influential friends to meetings. Then, Mrs Henry Smith had to consider her husband and his position. Controversy of any kind was fatal to a doctor's reputation and practice.

Nursing offered this comfort to parents who hated to see their daughters single and employed; there were opportunities, in a curious way, for marriage. The grateful sick might – and did – offer marriage. As we have seen with Zepherina Veitch, doctors and surgeons within the hospitals were also eligible husbands. There was a convenient phantasm then, about the rigorous profession of nursing – it was an occupation only to fill time till marriage, not a vocation for a lifetime.

A woman who followed Elizabeth Garrett's 1869 example and trained as a doctor could offer no such dissembling explanation to her critics. The hostility felt by male medics to women doctors continued to be vicious. When Sophia

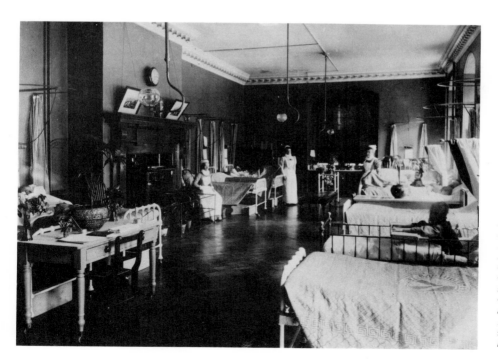

Darker Ward with nurses, St Bartholomew's Hospital, London, 1880s. Florence Nightingale still despaired of interesting educated women in training as nurses in 1880. Hospital nurses were notoriously drunken and promiscuous. By the 1890s it had become a respectable employment for ladies.

Jex-Blake and three other ladies enrolled to take a medical degree at Edinburgh University, students sent a sheep in to the lecture room after them to express their disapproval. To his credit, the lecturer commanded that the animal and not the ladies be removed from the hall. Sophia Jex-Blake went on, undeterred, to found the London School of Medicine in 1874. Of all the hospitals in London, only the Royal Free Hospital would admit the LSM's women students to the operating theatre, to gain the clinical experience they needed for their degree.

Molly Thomas, pupil at the North London Collegiate School in the 1870s, remembered one girl who trained for a most unusual profession, as a result of a clash with her headmistress. She would rather become a dentist than a teacher, declared the pupil. Miss Buss told her not to be ridiculous, women couldn't be dentists. The pupil, out of sheer perversity, discovered that Edinburgh would admit her as a student of dentistry, and she came out top of the class list. It would be interesting to know if she practised and if she had many male clients.

Gentlewomen who left school for university and then wished to pursue a career outside academe were also able, after 1870, to enter the Civil Service and pursue a career as an Inspector of factories, of schools, of hospitals. The Inspectorate was the highest level to which women in pursuit of a career in the Civil Service could aspire – and, if they married, they must abandon their career, as Millicent Garrett Fawcett, sister of Dr Elizabeth, had to. They could become Superintendents in the Post Office, which employed vast numbers of semi-skilled women workers. By and large, however, it was not till after the First World War that women were given the opportunity to burgeon within the Civil Service. The work they did was always assigned a lower grade than that of their male colleagues doing the same tasks.

Less ambitious gentlewomen settled for a few weeks' training at one of the commercial colleges, instituted by the new County Councils, and learnt clerical skills. Lady clerks are unknown in the books of Dickens of the 1860s, but then so are the large business offices of the 1870s and later, with their different departments. The development of the typewriter in 1874 provided work for thousands of lady clerks. It was, from the first, felt to be a feminine instrument – the keyboard was reminiscent, it was held, of keyboards on musical instruments like the piano. Women played the piano; then they must perform on the typewriter. Isaac Pitman's system of shorthand was also felt to be well adapted for women and gentlewomen did correspondence courses with enthusiasm.

Jessie Boucherett and the philanthropist ladies of Langham Place had begun by training unskilled ladies needing employment as governesses. From 1872, they offered lessons in secretarial skills. Gentlewomen, thus armed, became Secretaries of educational societies, Treasurers of charitable bodies, private secretaries, literary assistants. In 1901 Henry James was employing a Miss Mary Weld as his secretary. She crocheted while James paused in mid-dictation for some minutes to frame in his mind his complex sentences. On Miss Weld's marriage in 1904, James employed Miss Theodora Bosanquet, who remained his amanuensis till his death in 1916. She looks serious, capable, and

"The Odd Women"

dedicated, in a photograph taken during her employment at Lamb House in Rye. Her hair is short, her shirt is mannish, and her gaze is firm. This was the New Woman, confident and devoid of sexual charm in her shirt and tie. She had a future.

The surplus of single respectable women – christened *The Odd Women* in George Gissing's novel of 1894 – had two causes. Single middle-class women from the 1870s on were visible and vocal outside the home. They worked, and they complained of the conditions. Married women remained inside the home, and complained only privately. So, in one sense, the glut only appeared to exist. There was a real problem, however. The administrators of an ever-enlarging Empire were drawn from the middle classes. The Indian Civil Service, the British Army, the Chinese Customs Service absorbed large numbers of prospective husbands every year and ejected them only at retirement age. Architects, surveyors, engineers, doctors, lawyers, professional men of every description were needed in the service of Empire. On return to England, they turned for wives to share their accrued wealth to fresh-faced girls, not to the companions of their youth, now past child-bearing age.

To compound the problems of anxious spinsters in England, disease, flood, native uprisings carried off annually large numbers of Englishmen serving under the midday sun. "Indian orphans" were, sadly, not at all an uncommon sight on the boats which went between India and the London docks, carrying ladies' linen and lace for washing, and children for schooling, in England. "An English child in India is an exotic," wrote the author of *Morning Hours in India*, late in the century. Consequently, like any creature of exotic habit, it must be indulged and cosseted. Spoilt and revered by ayahs and bearers, children were invariably despatched home, rosy-cheeked, to England to attend school and grow up in a healthy climate. It seems to have been their parents, and in particular their fathers, who were most at risk from the unsanitary conditions in India.

Many women did find husbands, and occupied themselves with the time-hallowed occupations of the gentlewoman. They consulted recipe books, or Cook; they read Mrs Haweis's useful work on decorating the home, and adorned their mantelpieces with lambrequins or shawls, and the corners of their drawing-rooms with hanging brackets. The over-stuffed rooms of the late Victorian period owe as much to the lady's inventive use of hours of leisure, as to any liking for shell boxes and arrangements of birds' eggs, or feathers or inadequately lacquered tables.

The diaries of a Miss Maud Berkeley, daughter of a schoolmaster and living at home on the Isle of Wight at the age of twenty-eight in 1888, are informative about the lives of young women who had, as yet, neither married nor fled the nest. Maud was one of a group of young women who lived at home with their parents, and had neither function nor responsibility nor occupation beyond what they devised for themselves. They were all daughters of professional men, yet none of them seems to have thought of training to earn a living;

they had little money, yet they did no work to supplement it. One would never guess that pioneers like Elizabeth and Millicent Garrett existed, from Maud's diaries. They did some haphazard charity work with the Coal and Clothing Club; they went for "cold, wet stamps on the sea wall"; they went to a choice of sociable churches twice on Sundays – and they were at the beck and call of their fathers and mothers, and married siblings. Maud read to, or played chess with, her father; she played her guitar for her mother; she washed up dishes when the maid was ill. All this one expects. What is perhaps unexpected is the childishness of Maud's and her friends' pleasures when not on duty. They would "frisk round the drawing-room furniture" to enliven a wet afternoon – this meant re-hanging all the pictures in their parents' drawing-room. They "got up" amateur theatricals, and Bachelor Balls, with a regularity, during the summer, which became monotonous even to them. They darted about on the Island's railway network, visiting friends for tea or blackberrying or going to Redfern's Sales. Almost every day, in Maud's diaries, there is discussion of some new and home-made entertainment, designed to stave off boredom.

The authoress Margaret Oliphant worked because she had to, and sacrificed literary ambition to the duty she felt to maintain her family. Her hus-

Ladies' Pic-nic Wednesday. 29th Mars.

Page from the diary kept by Maud Berkeley, later a Colonel's second wife, when a spinster on the Isle of Wight. While waiting for marriage Maud kept up her spirits with lively illustrations of a passing dull existence.

"The Odd Women"

band, Frank, an artist, died in Rome in 1859, leaving Margaret, aged thirty-one, with two sons and a baby on the way. He also left her £1,000 in debts. An authoress of ten years' standing, Mrs Oliphant now wrote two books a year, to support her family. She managed to send her sons to Eton as day boys on the proceeds of *The Chronicles of Carlingford* in the 1860s. As the years passed, her family came to include a lady cousin, three nephews and her middle-aged brother, William. He enjoyed a quiet existence, going for a daily walk, then settling to read the newspaper in an easy chair, while Margaret worked. She had courageously decided to "give up what hopes I might have had of doing now my very best, and to set myself steadily to make as much money as I could, and do the best I could for the three boys." She reckoned that with interruptions from William, from his sons, from another nephew whom she supported, and from her own children – as well as servants – she never had more than two hours' uninterrupted writing time. As she wrote more and more furiously to support her brood, Margaret consoled herself: "Perhaps, for once in a way, Mammon, which meant the money which fed my flock, was in a kind of poor way God." Mrs Oliphant was in the tradition of that medieval tumbler or acrobat who tumbled and cartwheeled daily before the altar of the Virgin in the monastery, "*ad majorem Dei gloriam*", as the truest expression of his faith, till he died, worn out by his humble exertions.

Mrs Oliphant knew the worries of a mother without economic support from a male protector. Spinster ladies who had to work for a living became increasingly common, especially older ladies whom the professions of teaching and nursing ejected without pension in their mid-fifties as too old to be useful. Their families could not help, struggling themselves in the years of economic distress and resentful that the ladies had not remained at home as useful nurses and companions in the first place. "Distressed gentlewomen" also included ladies who had just waited for a marriage which never happened. In 1892, the newspapers were "full of the distressed gentlewomen". (The Distressed Gentlefolks' Aid Association was founded by a mother and daughter who pitied the distress of a spinster neighbour in Hammersmith in 1897.) Art needlework and decorative painting appeared to be her chief money-making resources. The author of the Victoria Library *Gentlewomen's Book of Gardening* suggested that her readers turn instead to gardening as a profession. A Ladies' Branch had opened at the Horticultural College in Swanley, Kent, in 1891. For fees of £70 or £80, a gentlewoman might study botany, chemistry, zoology, physics and book-keeping at this "bright and comfortable home". Daisy, Lady Warwick, established in the later 1890s a series of colleges where women could train in lighter branches of agriculture, including beekeeping. With these skills and a little capital, a lady might establish herself as a retail grower of choice flowers for private sale, or, more daringly, as a market gardener for Covent Garden.

It became possible to "train" in a variety of ladylike fields in the 1890s. In 1895 Margaret Fairclough caused great excitement at her School of Cookery in the Gloucester Road, when she demonstrated cooking with electricity or

"trained lightning". A journalist present laid his gloves upon the electric cooking stove surround, and they remained quite cool! The *Dictionary of Employment* suggested that ladies could open Cyclists' Rests in country villages. Till the advent of bicycles and motor cars and the new sport of "rambling", there were no refreshment rooms in the country except hotels and public houses, and *The Dictionary* suggested the ideal Cyclists' Rest should incorporate "a large shady garden, where tea, etc. can be served in summer," besides two or more bedrooms, "where lady cyclists can rest or be accommodated for the night." On a small capital of between £150 and £300, *The Dictionary* thought the enterprise should prosper.

Five O'Clock Tea at The Club, from The Woman's World *(1888). Strong-minded women held discussions, and provincial ladies rested between tiring appointments in these cosier imitations of the male institution.*

In town, ladies could make an income by opening a tea-shop, where the new breed of lady office worker might like to take luncheon. Astonishingly, till the opening of the first ABC, or Aerated Bread Company's tea-shop, and of the first Lyons in London in 1894, there was nowhere except a hotel or restaurant where ladies could eat lunch. Debenham and Freebody's was the first of the department stores to offer luncheons in 1907. The rise of the ladies' clubs like the Lyceum and the Alexandra Club in the 1890s owed much to the dearth of cheap refreshment rooms where ladies could respectably and pleasantly relax when out without gentlemen. Harrods, in Knightsbridge, made it plain in 1908 which services it considered its members would value, with a magnificent "Ladies' Club" in medieval style, with stained glass, marble and onyx panels and walnut and marquetry doors to the cubicles. Any lady would feel refreshed,

"The Odd Women"

and ready to tackle committee business, or the shopping in the large department stores, or the dinner party at the Savoy Hotel which had brought her to Town, on emerging from such *grande luxe*.

Ladies like Lady Jebb came from as far as Cambridge to London for the day to shop. Vast department stores were a feature of this period; they reflected the increased wages of the middle classes, and also recognised the heady enjoyment the sport of shopping afforded ladies. Most of the departments were for ladies, and the heads of the departments were women picked for their immense air of ladylike respectability. They presided imperturbably over a new excitement the department store offered to the ladies of England with leisure hours to

Fashion plates of the mid-1890s. In 1881 the tailored walking suit appeared, first in a series of costumes of practical, mannish cut. Other costumes like these, suitable for the New Woman's active life, developed – the shirt and tie being favoured by many.

fill – the seasonal sale. The customers would dive into bales of gingham and cotton, while the assistants stood by graciously like duchesses at a bazaar. The "Drapery and Millinery Establishment" of John Barker & Co., Kensington High Street, wrote to G. K. Chesterton's mother in 1880 in the most refined terms, promising her: "a Bonnet of the latest Parisian taste, of which we have a large assortment . . . Our assistant will wait upon you at any time you may appoint, unless you would prefer to pay a visit to our Millinery department yourself." The bonnet was to be a present from Mrs Chesterton's husband, who "informs us that as soon as you have made your selection, he will hand us a cheque for the amount. We are given to understand that Mr Chesterton proposes this transaction as a remembrance of the anniversary of what, he instructs us to say, he regards as a happy and auspicious event. We have accordingly

entered it in our books in that aspect." The letter ended with hopes that the millinery department would "during many years to come . . . be permitted to supply you with goods of the best description for cash, on the principle of the lowest prices consistent with excellence of quality and workmanship."

When buying furniture everyone went to Maples, the long-established store in Tottenham Court Road. In 1882, for instance, Maples had the custom of 21,000 families, including British and foreign royalty. In 1875 Francis, Duke of Teck, ordered a "new black cabinet . . . for my Christmas", wrote his wife, to further cram a blue morning-room at White Lodge, already heavy with corner sofas and what-nots and chaise-longues. "Highbrows" and followers of the

Corporation Street, Birmingham, March 1914 from the civic fresco commissioned from Joseph Southall. Gentlewomen in the provincial towns were as ardently artistic as their London cousins. Here Southall has depicted Arts and Crafts enthusiasts, with (centre) Mrs Arthur Gaskin, designer of jewellery.

CORPORATION STREET BIRMINGHAM
IN MARCH 1914

Aesthetic movement patronised Arthur Liberty's Regent Street store instead; he profited daily by their love of his Umritza cashmere jersey in "tints that call to mind French and English mustards . . . greens that look like curry, and greens that are remarkable on lichencoloured walls . . ." The Aesthetic movement of the late nineteenth century proved a useful stepping-stone to gentility and fashion for those whose pedigree was not impeccable. The stigma of trade remained very real in gentlemanly England, despite the incursions of the plutocrats into the Prince of Wales's "set". Miss Beale, the pioneering headmistress of Cheltenham Ladies' College, permitted no daughters of persons "in trade" to attend her school in the 1890s. Once the "trade" was sold, however, and a

country estate purchased – then a man could hold up his head as a gentleman – and his daughters could be sent off to attend any school they liked.

Dearman Birchall was one who distanced himself from the family textile business in Leeds in the 1860s by cultivating advanced tastes. He collected Nanking porcelain, and he bought stuccoed Bowden Hall, with a clear view of Gloucester Cathedral, in 1869. He ceased to worry about trade fairs and samples for Germany, and took his place in rural Gloucestershire as a JP and a keen countryman. Emily, his second wife, was a second cousin from Leeds. She, too, adapted easily to life on the land, and encouraged Dearman in his garden improvements. Dearman employed Mr Marnock, curator of Regent's Park Horticultural Gardens, to lay out the grounds; he encouraged William Keen, his head gardener "who is . . . up to all the novelties introduced of late years" – carpet bedding, topiary, Japanese effects – to visit other gardens like Bowood, and the annual Royal Horticultural Show at Chelsea. Emily Birchall was perfectly at home at Bowden Hall. Equally, she was interested by new developments in art in London. Dearman in 1880 reports her wearing "a terracotta aesthetic dress" at their garden party – and, astonishingly, looking well in it! Evidently she did not take the Aesthetic movement *too* seriously, as they went to Gilbert and Sullivan's opera, *Patience*, on the same visit which mocked Oscar Wilde and other "greenery-yallery" young men associated with the movement.

Emily and Dearman had left far behind any taint of "trade", though Dearman only officially withdrew from the Leeds business in the late 1870s. Emily showed herself a thoroughly modern woman and mother, when in 1879 she gave birth two months early to a daughter. She and Dearman were on a cruise to Gibraltar and North Africa at the time. Emily calmly handed over the infant to a wet-nurse who was instructed to carry *"le petit pacquet'* home to Gloucestershire, while the parents continued their travels. After frantic letters from Dearman's mother – a mother of an older generation – Emily added a courier to the homeward-bound party. Six weeks later, she and Dearman reluctantly turned for home themselves.

The Birchalls enjoyed and put to good use the income from the Birchall textile works in their purchases of paintings and furniture and books. Some unfortunates lived in a pitiable state of petrification, following their abandonment of trade for the leisured life of the gentleman. Beatrix Potter's parents had both inherited fortunes from cotton mill-owner parents in Lancashire. They moved to London, to a large house in Bolton Gardens, Earls Court, in 1865. Here they sat in the drawing-room; here Beatrix Potter was brought up in a nursery on the top floor; here she remained, with annual family forays to the Lake District the one diversion, till she began writing her children's tales in 1900. At the age of forty-odd in 1913, she insisted on marrying a solicitor in Cumberland. Beatrix's parents attempted to veto the match. She stood firm though, over-dutiful daughter, she recognised the force of their objections to her country lawyer: "we belong to Bar and Bench." Ten years before, Mr and Mrs Potter had vetoed another suitor – Norman Warne, of Frederick Warne &

Co., the publishers who had the wit to publish *Peter Rabbit*, and *A Tailor of Gloucester*, and the rest. Beatrix's parents' objection to personable Norman was that publishing was trade, and therefore not respectable. How much worse for Miss Potter to become Mrs William Heeles in 1913, and fry bacon and potatoes in a Lakeland farmhouse! The wedding present which she most valued was Mrs Beeton's *Household Management*.

Manifold was the English gentlewoman in the opening decades of the twentieth century: she was rich and she was poor; she stayed at home, she went into the work market; she gloried in her husband and her children, she prized her celibacy as a mark of grace. Astonishingly, however, of all the gentlewomen

Smiling scene with suffragists at a Knightsbridge sale held, probably in 1909, in support of the Pankhurst ladies' organization, the NWSPU. The campaign of violence – destroying Henry James's portrait, smashing department shop windows – and the martyrdoms were still a few years off.

to whom we have nodded, few ceased to be preoccupied by the notion of retaining their status as gentlewomen. The ladies of the suffrage movement wore large picture hats, from the very West End department stores whose windows they attacked with hammers in 1913. That daring explorer, Mary Kingsley, expostulated when she heard that she was rumoured to lecture on African subjects in a billycock hat and native costume – "honour bright I'd got my best frock on." Mary Kingsley subscribed to the theory of "separate spheres" for men and women; she was happy to work "through" men, as had been Florence Nightingale, as were many early suffragists. "I did not do anything [in Africa] without the assistance of the superior sex," she wrote, defending herself against a

"The Odd Women"

charge of being a New Woman in 1895. Feminine diffidence was a powerful tool with which to disarm opposition, as many women realised. Indeed, of those who quarrelled with the militant suffragists, many were anxious that their sisters were openly displaying the iron fist which it suited them to confine in a lace mitten. Mrs Humphrey Ward, best-selling novelist, became president of the Anti-Suffrage League in the belief that suffragettes were wasting valuable energy on violence, which they should be using in women's education, social work, and local politics. The wilder shores of gentlewoman apart, it suited most to remain gentlewomen as a tactic to divert obtuse masculine eyes from observing these same ladies' encroachment. It was as if a giant game of Grandmother's Footsteps were being played out before the First World War, with the gentleman turning occasionally and unexpectedly to detect and forbid the ladies busy advancing at his back towards outrageous goals.

Few gentlewomen acknowledged that their goals were outrageous; over most of their activities still hung a Christian and subservient smoke screen. In the 1900s, Lady Constance Lytton, aristocratic suffragette, felt "the rhythm of the world's soul calling us women to uncramp our powers from the thraldom of long disuse," and threw stones at Lloyd George's car and led delegations to Parliament, and went to jail to be forcibly fed eight times. Till she heard this call to action in her late thirties, she had been a dutiful daughter to her mother and only energetic at home "in love's highest expression – which is Service".

Gentlewomen sought always to serve. On behalf of the poor, not to free themselves from social restraints, they joined settlement houses like Toynbee Hall and walked the streets of the East End cheerfully unchaperoned. When they petitioned Government it was on behalf of prostitutes, or factory workers or shop assistants; they were modest about their growing efficacy as organisers and speakers. The cause, not they, was important. There was ever a cause for gentlewomen to serve in their new life outside the home; they brought all the wiles of their domestic existence to bear on their objectives. Yet until they ceased to be bound by the traditions of subservience and decorum and self-deprecation which characterised the English gentlewoman – until they ceased to be gentlewomen – they must lag behind their male peers. The gentlewoman was poised for flight from the ancillary tradition which bound her at the outbreak of the First World War. Had the War not come, to force upon herself and others appreciation of her worth and capabilities, the gentlewoman might have teetered on for much longer – being helpful.

207

Gentlewomen in Distress

1914-

HEN THE FIRST WORLD WAR CAME UPON THE NATION and swept idolised sons and brothers and husbands off to the trenches in France, the gentlewomen of England were left without moorings. Their experience in the public sphere of late years, fortunately, had not left them wholly helpless. Edith Somerville maintained her brother's pack of hounds with income from her books and acted as MFH while he served at the Front. Other ladies administered their husbands' estates. Gentlewomen of all types discovered that they had capacities for hard work undreamt of. Lady Denman became Chairman of Smokes for Wounded Soldiers and of the Poultry Association. She went on to become in 1917 first Chairman of the Women's Institutes.

Edith Sitwell worked in the Pensions Office and lived in a flat in Bayswater. Her brother, Osbert, home on leave, brought Mrs Patrick Campbell to tea one day. The actress demanded to know *why* her teaspoon was not silver. Edith said calmly, "Because I'm poor and can't afford it." Mrs Pat did very well out of a play in 1917 and sent her twelve spoons of the best silver.

All the sacrifices which gentlewomen made in the War, they made with the thought ever-present that at the Front their menfolk were paying a still greater price to defend what Lord Ribblesdale's idealistic son, Charles Lister, called "that intangible essence unseen save at rare moments, like the Holy Grail – the nation's honour". From her war work as a VAD, Vera Brittain was called by news in December 1915 that her fiancé had got leave, and was on his way home. Her relief was enormous, and on Christmas Eve she had her hair washed at a "pleasant little shop" near Victoria Station. She knew that the boat-train from Folkestone arrived late the next day, so she would see Roland on Boxing Day. She went, uncharacteristically, to the hospital chapel on Christmas Day to pray for him, hoping all the time for news that he had arrived. On the 27th there was a telephone message for Vera. "I sprang up joyfully, thinking to hear in a moment the dear dreamed-of tones of the beloved voice." It was in fact a message that Roland had never left France. A telegram had just reached his mother; "Regret to inform you that Lieut. R. A. Leighton 7th Worcesters died of wounds December 23rd. Lord Kitchener sends his sympathy."

Opposite: The Duchess of York (right) "fishing" for champagne at a garden party in aid of the Princess Elizabeth Hospital for Children in 1933. English gentlewomen raised huge sums for suitable charities by such entertaining antics.

Epilogue

The officer casualties in the War outnumbered the figures for the ordinary soldiers' deaths – appalling enough in themselves – by three to one. Many women never recovered from the fact of their idols' deaths. Mothers and sisters had had almost loverlike relations with their sons and brothers, in all innocence, before the War. Ivy Compton-Burnett said many times later in life of her brothers' deaths: "Them both dying like that quite smashed my life up." The violence of the phrase was most uncharacteristic, but she never varied it. Vera Brittain's "mind groped in a dark, foggy confusion, uncertain of what had happened to it or what was going to happen." Lady Desborough sat down and wrote a detailed memoir of her sons. "Nobody ever wore mourning for Julian and Billy [Grenfell]." Wives and fiancées, mothers and sisters all had to make a new life after the War, in an England which seemed very different.

What the bereaved gentlewomen had not reckoned for was that their own work in the War had brought them both a new confidence in themselves, and the habit of command which had been hitherto reserved for their menfolk. If any good had come out of the dirty, bloody massacre, women had earned the respect of all in England, for the way they had "knuckled down" to hard work in the auxiliary services. They had earned their right to the vote, a right which became theirs in 1919. Earlier the most furious of the battles to correct the inequity of women's position under the law, now the vote was given to women without a murmur of protest.

Women over the age of thirty only had the vote, but Nancy, Viscountess Astor, and the Duchess of Atholl became Members of Parliament. Other ladies became vocal in local and national politics. At the 1924 Conservative Party Conference, lady delegates stood up and declared that they were thwarted in their vigorous campaign to "Buy British" by the absence of indication of origin on merchandise. A Merchandise Marks Bill was duly passed. Women might be subjected to pressure to remain in the home; they were not going to "lie down" under shopkeepers any more. The Conservative journal, *The Popular View*, mourned in 1921 the resentment with which ladies returned to home life and housekeeping. "A highly specialised profession was now looked upon as 'ignoble and menial'." The sanctity of the home, the quietude of English home life had been ruptured by the women's work in the War. As early as 1916, there had been fears that women would be reluctant to abandon salaries and Government benefits like crèches for their children and union rights for the unpaid labour of household management. *A Profession for Gentlewomen, Being Some Reflections on the Philosophy of Housekeeping* (1916) was the first of several books which urged ladies to see the domestic sphere as their natural and glorious element. The author, Mrs F. S. Carey , suggested a radical and exciting project for the gentlewoman who heeded her advice. They should study architecture, "a profession for some years open to women", and design the houses they tended themselves. "Only the housekeeping woman can understand the sufferings and needs of the housewife, and can find the right remedies for complaints. The judicious modification of our houses will be the

Gentlewomen in Distress

first step towards the real emancipation of women." Coercion followed at Government level, when the Restoration of Pre-War Practices Act of 1918 withdrew from women all the employment rights which had been granted them during the War.

Political ladies like Lady Londonderry fumed, but, by and large, the gentlewomen of England did withdraw into their homes again, and cede their jobs to "the gentlemen". Following the War losses, the multiple death duties, the Depression, the homes were run on different lines. The lady of the house was much busier, despite all the vacuum cleaners and other labour-saving gadgets becoming available. Now it was *her* labour they were saving; her body of servants had been reduced from the rows of starched and uniformed bottoms which Vera Cook remembered at prayer in the dining-room before the First World War. The Home for Unemployed Governesses in Harley Street, founded in 1839, moved in 1923 to Cavendish Street. Designed as a temporary shelter between jobs for working governesses, by degrees it became a permanent home for governesses who could find no work. Fewer families had space and income to feed another mouth. In 1930, the Home closed, as it was too expensive to maintain the many petitioners for its services.

Still, the Employment Department of the Governesses' Benevolent Institution registered 365 posts in 1938, and placed 177 governesses. In the country, in particular, where there was space for retainers, a governess was a useful adjunct to a household, if she would "help out" with household concerns, not strictly in the educational department. In the 1930s, Diana Athill ran through seven preceptresses, starting with nursery governesses, progressing to "better qualified women" shared with cousins or neighbours' daughters. There was a "sucker" with a "kind horse face", a Mademoiselle, to whom Diana and her brother were as cruel as they knew how, and "Ursula" with a "broad, red face", and "thin, cottony hair" who did not like "tiring young intelligences". In E. M. Delafield's *The Diary of a Provincial Lady*, the master and mistress of the house are maddened by their children's awkward Mam'selle in the late 1930s and 1940s, who becomes very Gallic and gloomy when asked to accompany the children to the seaside. She becomes still more gloomy, however, when informed that her charge, Vicky, is going to school and that she is no longer required. She refused to eat, wrote "a phenomenal number of letters, all in purple ink, which runs all over the page when she cries", and decided that half-mourning – a black dress with "fragments of mauve tulle wound round head and neck" – was appropriate to the crisis.

Governesses proved increasingly awkward retainers, as the decades wore on. In *The Gentlewomen*, Laura Talbot described Miss Bolby, governess, who lived at Hillstone House, a boarding house in Birmingham, between engagements – fictional equivalent of Rebecca West's "spinster, looking out on the world through the drawn curtains of the boarding-school or the equally celibate boarding-house." She resented an employer's, Lady Rushford's, assumption that she was Birmingham bred. "My room in Birmingham is just my *pied-à-*

211

terre. I don't belong there; I was born in India, Lady Rushford." Miss Bolby expected much more than the Rushfords could offer in the way of grandeur – Lady Rushford did not dress for dinner – and corrected her charges laboriously and incorrectly on matters of social etiquette, while she taught them little.

Laura Talbot's Miss Bolby lived with the Rushfords during the Second World War, years when the Governesses' Benevolent Institution had a working party of retired and unemployed governesses meet every Wednesday. By 1945 they had knitted 1,426 woollen garments. Six ladies continued to meet for nine months after the war, unravelling unsuitable garments which misguided patriots had produced and transforming them into bedsocks and fancy mats. There was little other industry available to them. After the Second World War, the demise of the GBI as an employment agency continued, as more and more girls went to school. In 1945 there were only 57 posts registered, 10 filled, and, of the applicants only one was under forty-five. "The working governess undoubtedly still exists, though in smaller numbers, but she does not now seek the GBI until she can no longer work or is in difficulties." This was the conclusion of the GBI in 1961 when it decided not to reapply for its licence as an employment agency to the London County Council. The gentlewoman's traditional profession had ceased to exist.

Schoolteachers could, of course, exhibit all the gentlewomenly traits which the governess used as her defence against a world where her social status was not appreciated. In Elizabeth Taylor's *Miss A and Miss M*, Miss Alliot is one of those faintly exotic schoolmistresses for whom the narrator, a child, forms a passion. Miss Alliot, in silk pyjamas, is always faintly amused by her companions in the cheap hotel where she holidays. Each year she goes to the Townsends for a short visit; by the standards of the Townsends she judges her daily life for the rest of the year. And yet her reception at the Townsends, it is clear, is never quite satisfactory. She continues to go. How could she bear her life without her annual brush with the great and the grand?

This was not mere snobbery, though Miss A certainly enjoyed slipping references to the Townsends into the most unaccommodating conversations. Enforced abstinence from cultured comforts, long exposure to tasteless, drab surroundings never shook a gentlewoman's conviction that the former conditions represented her natural milieu; other people's washing in the bathroom, and raised provincial voices heard through the thin bedroom partition wall were a purgatory which might not last for ever. It was important not only never to forget one was a lady but also to renew contact with more fortunate ladies and gentlemen whenever possible. How dreadful if one forgot how to behave through lack of practice.

The novelist, Barbara Pym, took a humorous view of the limitations of her life in the 1950s when she worked at the International African Institute and shared a flat with her sister. Hers was a life "bounded by English literature and the Anglican church and small pleasures like sewing and choosing dress material for this uncertain summer". In March 1953, she was "cross with D F [her boss]

Gentlewomen in Distress

and rebellious but I just have a poached egg at the Kardomah (but a chocolate biscuit with my stewed apple), then go to Bourne & Hollingsworth and Dolcis and don't hurry back, yet I am back again by 2.20."

Not all gentlewomen suffered degrees of economic privation, of course. Following the First World War, many beaux and belles of the upper classes threw themselves into a life of relentless gaiety, to compensate for the war years' sobriety. The 1919 Royal Ascot meeting was satisfactorily similar to those of prewar days. In 1925 George V was not approving of English youth's busy and persistent pursuit of frivolity: "I see David [later, Edward VIII, after Duke of Windsor] continues to dance every night, and most of the night too." 1926 saw the General Strike when Bright Young Things played at driving fire engines. The miners' strike was more serious for the nation's pockets; the 1929 collapse of the American Stock Market punished families who depended on investments yielding a fixed income. By 1933, there were three million unemployed. The Distressed Gentlefolks Aid Association, or the DGAA, previously confined to the Home Counties, formed Committees nationwide to help sufferers, but, from about 1935 till the outbreak of war, London especially enjoyed a period of glamour and style not seen since that illusory "Edwardian summer". This was to be the last blooming of a crop of English gentlewomen who asked no more than to follow the programme of the London Season correctly dressed and in the right company.

What began it all? Sir Thomas Beecham had made the Opera, long in the doldrums, fashionable on his arrival at Covent Garden in 1934. The gentlewoman now rarely played an instrument herself; she "appreciated" the music Toscanini and Richard Tauber, among other celebrities, offered in the London concert halls. Ladies of an artistic turn – or anyone who received an invitation – hurried to the Royal Academy to be received by a beadle, imposing in red robes at the head of the stairs leading to the Summer Show. The Royal Horse Show, the Aldershot Tattoo, Wimbledon – and the Derby, and Ascot, and Goodwood . . . The Season had its unchanging pattern, though there were novelties, too. In *A Handful of Dust* (1934), Evelyn Waugh created Mrs Beaver, mirroring the new group of Society women who maintained a fashionable existence by running an interior decoration business. She found and furnished a flat for Brenda Last, a country gentleman's wife who liked to come up to London on a Wednesday half-price excursion ticket for "a day's shopping, hair cutting or bone setting". Brenda had to persuade her husband that the flat would not be the expense he envisaged: "*You* mean by a flat a lift and a man in uniform, and a big front door with knobs, and an entrance hall and doors opening in all directions." Tony admitted it. "Now I mean just a bedroom and a bath and telephone," replied Brenda triumphantly.

A young designer called Norman Hartnell with a workroom in Bruton Street satisfied ladies' patriotic wishes for French fashion cut by an English hand from English cloth. Constance Spry – much more than a florist – arranged artichokes and cabbage roses and even cabbages, and district messengers in pill-

box hats flew around London in taxis to deliver these offerings. The heady whirl never stopped. Young ladies presented at Court with the statutory three ostrich feathers, train and veil, would proceed to the photographer's studio to have the moment captured for stiff eternity. Then off to Quaglino's they went to dine and dance, leaving the emblems of their Court life with the cloakroom lady.

Munich came, the London parks were dug up for trenches, gas masks in cardboard boxes were issued and ladies began their war work. After this war, they did not retreat back into the home. By 1951 43 per cent of employed women were married, and by 1961 the figure stood at 50 per cent. Not all, but many of the gentlewomen who would once have confined their attention to home and family were working as well as, or instead of, running a home. Exhortations in 1954 that "cooking is fun again", after fourteen years of rationing, and remarks about "the satisfaction of knowing that housekeeping is a skilled job once again", fell on deaf ears. So both traditional career of the gentlewoman as leisured wife and mother, and traditional employment, as teacher, were vanishing.

She could still do a little philanthropy, though this became unusual. Meg Eliot, in Angus Wilson's *The Middle Age of Mrs Eliot* (1958), was on the Committee of Aid to the Elderly, "for all its occasional government grants . . . an old-fashioned voluntary body of a now dying kind". As a representative of "the younger hostess type, you know", Meg was an oddity on the Committee and was held in some respect by her more dowdy colleagues.

Since the 1950s, the area where gentlewomen might be thought still to flourish – in the stately homes of England – has seen great changes. Many interesting and historic houses were pulled down in the 1950s and 1960s. The soaring cost of living has encouraged many families to hand over their homes to bodies like the National Trust – and continue existence in the family home in a species of "granny flat". Other families endeavour to "have and to hold" their home. To this end, they establish charitable trusts which will enable future generations to continue to "have and to hold" the home. The ladies of the family, especially, develop a particularly keen sense of business. They throw open the house or castle to the public and, on advice from public relations companies and fellow-châtelaines, litter buhl cabinets with photographs of their children. They appear themselves before tourists – fleetingly and across a thick red rope – like the ghost of Marie Antoinette, at intervals throughout the financial year. Once or twice a year, a colour supplement to a Sunday newspaper prevails upon these busy ladies to let down their hair from its immaculate loose bun, and reveal the secrets of being the guardian of an historic home. The English gentlewoman has always been adept at devising means to preserve her domain. As the flourishing businesswoman who personally pours the tea for groups of Americans curious to see the ways of Olde England, she is only a variant on the strong mistresses of Tudor palaces who wooed royal favour with lavish hospitality.

In 1914, the august editors of Burke's *Landed Gentry* firmly ruled that those families who had parted from their lands should be expunged from the

new edition of the encyclopedia of gentility. Between 1914 and 1977, a new tolerance developed. Over half the families listed in the 1914 edition had parted from their estates; it was decided that these miscreants should be included, in the 1977 edition, denoted as "formerly" or "late of" . . . (This was an extremely shrewd decision by the prescient editor. Without the lackland gentry, the book would lack both weight, and subscribers.) It is noted in the 1977 edition as cause for congratulation that the occupations followed by the heads of the families noted have increased dramatically in variety since 1914. There are publishers and industrialists and doctors and estate agents today, where they would earlier have been "gentlemen" plain and simple or, perhaps, "gentlemen farmers". The editor's thesis is that the landed gentry are still a discernible and important feature of the English landscape – alive and well in 1977. In fact, we learn from him that, as a class, the landed gentry has become resistant to classification. Is there still such a class of person? The peerage, with its two groups – the hereditary nobility, and life peers – is easier; the title is the salient feature. In the hereditary nobility, its descent may be traced, regardless of disappearing acres. There may even be some interest in a title, to which lands have long ceased to be attached. The present Earl Nelson is a policeman: his father was a publican. With the landed gentry, the salient inheritance being the land, there is less to say when plain John Smith, formerly of Smith Hall, in Smithshire and now of Earl's Court, London, dies. There is no inheritance, except in the matter of genteel origins, for his eldest son, James Smith of Beckenham, any more than there is for his daughter, Jane. Equality of the sexes at last! Should not Burke's abandon commercial instincts and observe common sense? Let the remains of the old gentry of England "come down in the world" in peace; there is no need to chart the decline from manor to villa to numbered street house.

Sightings of English gentlewomen are more satisfying to the observer than real. Where the English gentlewoman today does exist, she has a limited existence – she is the beneficiary of grants made to Section 202 (e), in the 1987 Directory of Grant Making Trusts. Welfare Section 202 (e) is concerned with Gentlefolk, as 202 (b) deals with the Nursing Profession (including Governesses). The Guild of Aid for Gentlepeople, established in 1904, defines its intended beneficiaries as "people of gentle birth or good education in financial distress". In 1985 it had an income of £124,434. Mrs Jolly's Gentlefolk's Association was founded in 1939, and distributed in 1982, of £1,634 income, grants to a value of £1,202; the Eaton Fund for Artists, Nurses, and Gentlewomen, established 1954, converted all its £20,000 income in 1985 into grants. Since then, no benevolent funds have been established with gentlewomen or gentlemen "in reduced circumstances" exclusively in mind, although certain trusts like that of Lavinia Duchess of Norfolk, established for the needy of the Arundel district in 1963, recognise members of Section 202 (e) as suitable candidates for their help.

The most famous of benevolent foundations specially for ladies and gentlemen in reduced circumstances, the Distressed Gentlefolks Aid Association, was founded in 1897 by a widow and daughter living in Hammersmith,

Epilogue

Mrs Elizabeth and Miss Constance Finn. The decay of an elderly friend's investments prompted their concern; the old lady was living, in increasing poor health, on eight shillings a week. The Finn ladies found other friends knew ladies – and gentlemen – in a similar state of distress. The name of the trust they established to alleviate this distress – at a time when there was no State Pension, no National Assistance – was perfectly intelligible. The foundation of the DGAA presaged the death throes of the English gentlewoman. The clear understanding which existed of gentlefolk, and gentlewomen in particular, as a special group suffering special hardship, has now faded; no new gentlewomen are being created. The mould is broken. However, as in all institutions, the death throes of the English gentlewoman have been prolonged and painful.

To the administrators of the DGAA's substantial funds, and the case committees who interview applicants for grants, the concept of the English gentlewoman is real. She is an economic entity, with fixed assets and balance sheets and accounts requiring audit. The range of ladies considered suitable for benevolence has expanded since 1897 – they now include those who have been of service to the country, or are of a professional background. Faithful to the spirit of the original foundation - and to the letter of some later legacies which call for legatees to be "of genteel manner" – the committees must decide whether or not a lady is a gentlewoman – 80 per cent of beneficiaries are female – as well as whether she is "distressed". (One gentleman applied for relief, because he could no longer afford to feed his pets; his "pets" were discovered to be two thousand pheasants on a farm in Hampshire.)

The average age of ladies in DGAA homes is eighty-four or eighty-five. Centagenarian parties, with a telegram from the Queen, are not uncommon. The twilight of the English gentlewoman is not dull. While an extension to one Home in Harrogate will provide additional space for traditional ladylike occupations like tapestry painting, the residents are also clamouring for bingo evenings. The case histories of all beneficiaries of the DGAA are confidential, so we cannot know the former social standing in the world, the former professions of these ladies. It seems that there are no titled persons among them. Some, born a century ago, may have been ladies' maids, others, secretaries, governesses ... All are ladies living on a fixed income from investments which proved inadequate to the rising cost of living. The Council of Management and the various Committees, national and county, who administer the Association's affairs, make up, in the matter of titles and marks of honour, for the lack of them in beneficiaries. They raise funds with an imaginative variety of events – Donkey Derbys, Clay Pigeon Shoots, Gourmet Suppers and Antique Quiz Evenings.

Earlier philanthropists like the Duchess of Teck would approve of the relentless badgering of radio, television and performing personalities to "compère" these events, and chivalrously shore up a little longer the English lady in distress.

Index

220

Acknowledgements

The illustrations appear by kind permission of the following: Her Majesty the Queen 22, Royal Library Windsor Castle 24, 26; Abbot Hall Art Gallery, Kendal 61; Ashmolean Museum, Oxford 34; BBC Hulton Picture Library 171, 178, 180, 188; Birmingham City Art Gallery 204; Blenheim Palace, in the Green Writing Room 85; Bridgeman Art Library 102, 109, 142; British Library 7, 19, 20, 35, 76, 77, 83, 132, 170, 202; British Museum 30, 90; Cameron Books 42, 44, 101; Chatsworth (*photo Courtauld Institute of Art*) 138; Cheltenham Art Gallery (*photos Bridgeman Art Library*) 92, 184/5; Cheltenham Ladies' College 192; Colnaghi's (*photo Bridgeman Art Library*) 129; Viscount De L'Isle V.C. K.G., from his private collection 38; Governors of Dulwich Picture Gallery (*photo Bridgeman Art Library*) 89; Fitzwilliam Museum, Cambridge 106; Brinsley Ford (*photo Courtauld Institute of Art*) 125; Graves Art Gallery, Sheffield 164 (*photo Bridgeman Art Library*), 177; Hardwick Hall (*photos National Trust Photographic Library*) 36, 49; Harrogate Art Gallery 136; Harvard University, The Houghton Library 111; Knole House, Kent (*photo Frank Mancktelow*) 26, (*photo National Trust Photographic Library*) 50; Lady Lever Art Gallery, Port Sunlight (*photos Bridgeman Art Library*) 64, 68;

Philippa Lewis 3, 96, 157, 203; Manor House, Stanton Harcourt (*photos Bridgeman Art Library*) 52, 69; Mansell Collection 37, 55, 126, 135, 146, 147, 151, 152, 158, 162; Mary Evans Picture Library 130, 143, 189; Metropolitan Museum of Art, New York 79, 169; Minneapolis Institute of Arts 47; Museum of London 191, 206; National Galleries of Scotland 120; National Gallery of Victoria 116; National Portrait Gallery, London 16, 22, 25, 57, 78, 99, 122; Neville Ollerenshaw (*from 'Mrs. Hurst Dancing', Victor Gollancz*) 114; Paul Popper 208; Private Collection (*photo The Harris Museum & Art Gallery, Preston*) 2; Royal Albert Memorial Museum, Exeter (*photo Bridgeman Art Library*) 161; Royal Holloway and Bedford New College 193, 194; St. Bartholomew's Hospital, London 197; The Marquess of Salisbury 29, 110; Sotheby & Co. 93; The Earl Spencer, Althorp (*photo Bridgeman Art Library*) 183; Tate Gallery, London 58; The Vyne, Hampshire (*photo National Trust Photographic Library*) 141; Victoria & Albert Museum London 33, 43, 67, 86, 105, 119, 129, 149; Witt Library, Courtauld Institute of Art 173, 174, 175; Weidenfeld Archive 71, 74; Lorraine Wood (*photo Secker & Warburg*) 200; Yale Centre for British Art 56, 94, 154; York City Art Gallery 144.

The illustrations on pp. 1, 5, 217 and 224 are from *The Perfect Hostess* by Rose Henniker Heaton (Methuen, 1931). Silhouette artworks by Philip Hood.
PICTURE RESEARCH: PHILIPPA LEWIS